The Complete Funky Winkerbean

Volume 1 1972–1974

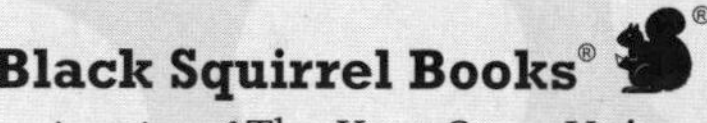
an imprint of The Kent State University Press
Kent, Ohio 44242 www.KentStateUniversityPress.com

THE COMPLETE

VOLUME I 1972–1974

TOM BATIUK

ISBN 978-1-60635-112-3
Manufactured in the United States of America
Designed by Christine Brooks
Cataloging information for this title is available at the Library of Congress.

16 15 14 13 12 5 4 3 2 1

For Cathy

Always

In memory of Jim Mateer—

who always liked the

earlier funny stuff.

Contents

FOREWORD

Antic Authenticity: Funky and the Teenager in Newspaper Comics

R. C. Harvey

Kids have populated the funnies since the very beginning. Teenagers, not so much. The earliest successful newspaper comic strips—the ones that established comics as important circulation builders for newspapers—were kid strips. The Yellow Kid, who started his newspaper run in February 1895 in *Hogan's Alley; The Katzenjammer Kids,* December 1897. Then the Katzies in reverse, *Foxy Grandpa,* wherein the title adult outsmarted mischievous juvenile delinquents, January 1900; but the strip would be nothing without its rapacious little scamps. After that, came such strips as *Buster Brown,* May 1902; *Little Jimmy,* February 1904; *Little Nemo,* October 1905; *Freckles and His Friends,* September 1915—to name a few. Freckles eventually matured into his teens, but he debuted as a ten-year-old.

It wasn't until 1919 that an authentic teenager showed up in the comics section. *The Love Life of Harold Teen* started in the *Chicago Tribune* on May 4 that year.

Harold Teen owes his origin to a novel by Booth Tarkington. His *Seventeen* was published in 1916, and its popularity was of sufficient intensity and duration to make Joseph Patterson, co-publisher of the *Trib,* pause when he saw on his desk a comic strip submission with that title. He was on the cusp of expanding the *Sunday Tribune* comic section from four to eight pages, and this strip looked promising. At the time, there were no strips about teenagers. Never had been. Not surprising, perhaps: the term "teenager" wasn't even around then. It wasn't coined until the late 1930s in America, but "teen" had been around since at least 1673, the year the first use of the term is recorded by the *Oxford English Dictionary.*

Patterson, one of comics' most successful managing maestros, did what he often did when accepting a new strip: he renamed the submission, in this case, emphasizing its protagonist's preoccupation with the opposing gender, and with that, cartoonist Carl Ed's lifetime career was underway: *Harold Teen* lasted until 1974. But shortly after it started, the American social landscape would be overgrown with the talk of "teens."

Ed was soon producing a daily version of his Sunday venture. The strip was slow to generate reader enthusiasm, but once the twenties began to roar, *Harold Teen* became a national pastime, popularizing such expressions as "shebas" (girls), "sheiks" (boys), "cute canary," "dim bulb," "kissable kid," "Yowsah!" "Yeh, man, he's the nertz!" "pantywaist," and "fan mah brow!" Ed's highschoolers congregated at Pop Jenk's Sugar Bowl soda shop to imbibe Pop's "gedunk sundaes"—a confection that so captured the imagination of readers that Ed had to invent a recipe for it.

"Harold came along just in time for the youth movement of the Roaring Twenties," Brian Walker says in *The Comics: The Complete Collection,* "—sporting such fashions as toreador trousers, sloppy socks, and whoopee hats. . . . It provided a sanitized picture of a Jazz Age teenager, suitable for family viewing."

Kid strips continued to flourish into the Jazz Age—among them, *Reg'lar Fellers,* which started in 1917 and became popular enough in the 1920s to inspire nearly overt imitation in *Just Kids,* which started in 1923. And then in 1925, another teen strip began.

Paul Robinson's elegantly rendered *Etta Kett,* as the eponymous heroine's name proclaimed, started as a daily lesson in etiquette for the nation's youth, but "that sententious theme was soon played out," Dennis Wepman writes in Ron Goulart's *Encyclopedia of American Comics,* and the strip rapidly became one of several strips about the flappers of the era, albeit in this case, a well-behaved sheba. Says Wepman: "If Etta stopped representing teen manners, she never exceeded the bounds of middle-class propriety and never troubled her patient parents overmuch. Her life revolved around dances and dates at the Sugar Shack with her amiably simpleminded and eternally ravenous boyfriend."

Little Orphan Annie, whose title character may have aged into her teens by the mid-1930s, began in 1924 when Annie was probably about ten or younger. With her cute mop of curly hair, Annie reminded newspaper readers of the best of Mary Pickford films and was therefore very popular, inspiring several imitations, one of which was 1925's *Ella Cinders,* whose protagonist, a twentieth century incarnation of Cinderella, was arguably a teenager when she first appeared, but soon matured into movie-star material.

But neither *Annie* nor *Ella* were comic strips about being teenagers.

Neither was Milton Caniff's *Terry and the Pirates,* another strip in which the title character was, at first, a teen. Starting in 1934, Terry buckled as many swashes as his guardian, Pat Ryan, but in 1938, we're made aware of Terry's emerging puberty when, for a revelatory week, he displays his adolescent infatuation with the dazzling blonde errant siren, Burma. But Terry went back to doing deeds of daring the next week.

In the 1940s, soon after the word *teenager* was established in the national lexicon, teenagers established themselves in newspaper funnies. *Penny* was among the most visible, infiltrating the funnies in 1943, followed a year later by *Teena* and then *Bobby Sox* and then, in 1946, *Aggie Mack.* All these heroines traded on the popular notion of grown-ups that America's young womanhood was made up almost entirely of silly girls who wanted no more in life than a boyfriend. The comedy ensued entirely from the girls' relationships with boys (all markedly chaste and abstentious: the characters never even kissed) or their preoccupation with clothes, make-up, hair-dos, and whatever the current fad was among the young—except *Penny,* which, without neglecting the foregoing, often regaled us with the difficulty the protagonist's father had in understanding his offspring's world of trivial pursuits.

And the most famous teenager in the American funnies never wandered far from the same trivia. Archie, a refugee from comic books, where he started in late 1941, was the titular figure of the comic strip spin-off that started February 4, 1946. The strip is still running, and so are the comic books, now comprising a flotilla of four-color vessels named for the principal characters—Archie's girlfriends, Betty and Veronica, and his best friend, the cynical Jughead. When *Archie* first hit the newspapers, it told stories that continued from day to day, each day ending with a punchline that usually doubled as a cliffhanger, and the stories were almost all about Archie Andrew's fevered pursuit of the erogenous Veronica Lodge, unaccountably ignoring his next-door neighbor, Betty Cooper, who, although wholesome, was rendered equally voluptuous by cartoonist Bob Montana. In a special 2009-2010 series of comic books set in an alternate universe of the kind comic book writers frequently invent, Archie married both of the girls.

Archie the comic strip eventually abandoned continuity for the joke-a-day formula that took over newspaper comics pages in the 1950s, but Archie was still in perpetual pursuit of Veronica to the everlasting neglect of Betty not to mention textbooks and classrooms; nor was he much engaged in the other of teenagers' extracurricular obsessions, sports or cars.

No notable comic strips about teenagers came along to challenge *Archie* until 1960, when a panel cartoon, *Ponytail,* debuted. But its heroine, too, was concerned mostly with boys and grooming. And then in 1972 came Tom Batiuk's *Funky Winkerbean,* which commences all over again a few pages to the right.

For the first couple of days, it looks as if we might be into the teenage dating game once more. Funky's arrogant approach to a nameless long-haired beauty on the second day is suitably repulsed, and he and Les are thinking about girls while watching a movie on the third day. Girls as datable creatures show up again a couple of times in the second week, but not in the third. Although Livinia appears every now and then during the first weeks, she seems more Funky's buddy than his romantic interest. Otherwise, girls appear, so to speak, in absentia, as desirable but distant beings: mostly as the focus of Les' unrequited desire, they are the off-camera certifiers of his inability to function as a teenage lothario.

Instead of concentrating on teenage adolescent sex life, the first month of the strip saunters through other topics, surprising in their number and variety only by comparison with Archie and his ilk—pollution, unctuous school counselors, acne (unmentionable in teen strips until *Zits* took the slang term for it as a title in 1997), punning and other word play (the April Fool joke and Roland's aspiration to be a poet), sex education, the school newspaper, communing, bullying, loud music, feminism, and ecology, then a week about various tests the ostensible students are taking at school.

Clearly, this is a different kind of teenager comic strip. *Funky Winkerbean* was firmly rooted in the actual concerns and preoccupations of real teenagers, and it remained so for the next twenty years until Batiuk did something nearly unprecedented in the history of comic strips: in 1992, he jumped four years in the lives of his characters, skipping their college years (foregoing the mining of a rich vein of potential comedy) to throw them all into the adult work force. (To the best of my knowledge, only Garry Trudeau had performed a similar feat when he and *Doonesbury* returned from a 18-month Sabbatical in 1984.) With the enviable perversity of a incurable innovator, Batiuk would do the same thing again 15 years later, leaping over a decade in order to focus on his cast members in their maturity. But in the first years of the strip, he was content to explore the teenage life he had observed as a high school teacher (and continued to witness as a regular visitor in the art classes of a friend at his alma mater, Midview High).

Funky Winkerbean's connection to the life teenagers lead in high schools is continuing and pervasive. Scenes are often set in classrooms, with characters seated at desks—regardless of the topics they discuss. The subjects they study are part of the strip's ambiance—and its comedy: Les confesses that when expected in biology lab to determine the sex of a worm, he doesn't know where to look to make the determination.

References to the world outside the school are occasional but they underscore the authenticity of the milieu—the streaking fad, rock festivals, presidential election, the draft, Vietnam, the oil industry, prayer in school vs. big business and government having no morality, President Nixon. In the summer of 1973, the U.S. endured an oil embargo as a result of American support of the Yom Kippur War, and Watergate revelations surfaced, so when Les the nerdish loser visits the White House and exchanges pleasantries with the President, he can commiserate: "I know what you mean," he says, "—my summer has kind of been like that, too."

None of these current event references aspire very high to satire, but they nudge up against it, and Batiuk doesn't overreach: his strip is about teenagers in high school, not about antiwar protesters. Still, it's satisfying to bump up against such sarcastic albeit penetrating cultural commentary as Funky makes when he and Les encounter Christmas decorations on October 9, 1972: "It's hard to believe it's October already."

In the first months of the strip, Batiuk is getting to know his characters a little better. They are all based upon persons he actually knew—friends in college, colleagues from his teaching days or students he had in class—but as comic strip characters they acquired idiosyncratic quirks that further refine their personalities, creating an ensemble cast the actions of which would be character-driven in the best traditions of fiction everywhere.

Les is the exemplar nerd: he can't get a date, and his propensity to take things literally (he once associates "barbarism" with hair cutting) reinforces the sense that he's the stereotypical, completely ineffectual intellectual, not fit for the practicalities of day-to-day life. Bull Bushka is another stereotypical high school habitué—the dumb athlete, whose very presence in a room during an IQ test lowered the scores of everyone in the room. Crazy Harry is a typical teenager gone berserk over loud music: he doesn't just revel in the ear-shattering volume, he blows his mind with it, and he doesn't just play the latest records: he plays frozen pizza (it's round, like a phonograph record—so why not?), relishing, particularly, the "pepperoni section." And then he takes up residence in his locker, which, before long, assumes the dimensions of a loft apartment. In this looney environment, we need Funky to keep our feet on the ground.

Funky is the strip's norm, a teenage everyman, but he soon relinquishes much of the spotlight to his friend Les, who emerges over the months as the strip's central figure, a sort of alter ego, perhaps, for Batiuk. As a teenager, the cartoonist may not have been quite the wistful loser that he gives us in Les, but Batiuk, like most teenage boys with interests somewhat broader than chasing girls or catching footballs, was doubtless insecure enough among his classmates to think of himself as a no-account also ran—like Les. Les is exactly the sort of serious successful student but failing teenager whom teachers and counselors entrust with such jobs as hall monitor. And Batiuk, with his teacher instincts and experience, knows it.

But authenticity isn't enough. For genuine comedy, we need a little more. And so Batiuk pushes realism just over the line into the outlandish but still shy of pure giddy fantasy, when, on March 12, on the cusp of the strip's second year, he arms his stereotypical hall monitor with a machine gun. Arming the hall monitor is a perfectly logical extension of the hall monitor mystique, and Batiuk has been (perhaps unconsciously) setting up for this improvement in school security for some time. On his second day of hall duty (April 28, 1972), Les shifts into a military mode, intoning the sentry's time-honored watchword: "Twelve o'clock and all's well!" And by the end of the year, he won't let firemen into the building unless they have a hall pass. Les is ready for the machine gun when it arrives.

Derek, the resident African American in the strip, shows up the second week of the strip's run, and his arrival is heralded by no fanfare or fuss for racial equality. Mort Walker had introduced an African American, Lieutenant Flap, into the *Beetle Bailey* ensemble just two years earlier—then, a somewhat risky undertaking that Walker announced by defiantly drawing attention to its audaciousness when Flap comes up to Sarge's desk and bellows: "How come there's no Blacks in this honkie outfit?" It was a beautifully achieved balance of comedy and commentary on a sensitive subject.

Two years later, having an African American in a comic strip is apparently not such a big deal anymore. Batiuk's objective is not so much to break the color barrier as it is to reflect realistically the contemporary high school scene where racial diversity prevailed. Still, Batiuk is not content to be realistic without idealistic overtones. Accordingly, he creates a color-blind community: Derek's race is seldom acknowledged and almost never the point of his appearance.

Although the school's faculty is represented at the strip's outset by the counselor Mr. Fairgood, teachers are not a vital part of the comedy until the fall of 1972, when school resumes after the summer vacation. Principal Burch presides on November 20 at a PTA meeting the purpose of which, he says, is to deny everything the parents have heard about the school from their children. But it isn't until the strip's second year that the faculty is in effect a functioning "character" in *Funky Winkerbean,* the interaction among teachers becoming an integral part of the enterprise. They all do their jobs as best they know how, always frustrated by adolescent angst or ignorance. Another dose of reality.

As always, Batiuk injects his realities with healthy doses of idiosyncrasy. "His eye for the ridiculous is especially keen when he turns it on his former colleagues," writes Wepman, "and his shrewdly observed faculty members are memorable: the starry-eyed recent teachers-school graduate," the counselor whose reliance upon official statistics emphasizes his failure to connect with actual students, and the obsessive band director with delusions of grandeur.

Long before the faculty's emergence as a part of the comedy, Batiuk had started exploiting the medium's capacity for humor in set pieces that repeat themselves with slight comedic variation. With an assortment of these motifs, he can compensate for the absence of reader familiarity with the characters that plagues every newly launched strip; in effect, he could telescope the twenty-year setup period he envied Charles Schulz for having in *Peanuts* (as he explains in his autobiographical introduction).

In the strip's first weeks, hippy counter-culturist Roland's encounters with "girls' libber" Wicked Wanda end repeatedly with violent physical "repartee," as predictable as Ignatz's hurling a brick at Krazy Kat in response to some krazy idiocy. Batiuk is courting the feminist sensitivity here, but he would eventually achieve a somewhat more broadly humanistic version of womankind when one of the distaff cast admits that she aspires to be the coach of a major baseball team because it's the only job where it's acceptable to go around patting guys on the fanny. And with the September 1974 introduction of Holly Budd, the band majorette, Batiuk dares to introduce a character whose personality is her sex appeal, another dose of realism in a world of two sexes.

With similar comedic repetition, Les' confrontation with rope climbing prolongs the humor inherent in the teenage horrors of being physically inept. And, later, with "Sayings from I Chong," Funky enacts humorously another aspect of the adolescent mind—its tentative exploration of philosophical interests. And Funky continues this preoccupation when he starts staring thoughtfully into the starry night skies.

But the most insightful of these motifs in the early weeks, and the most poignant, is probably Roland's home life. In Roland's encounters with a wholly unresponsive father, absorbed in television viewing, Batiuk gives us a painfully acute portrait of what many teenagers think of their parents—a stolid image of adults who are always detached from their offsprings' lives and entirely uninterested in their frustrations and pursuits, culminating, in this instance, when Roland's father, as requested by his son, says two words to him: "Beat it." A brilliant conception skillfully presented.

But not always so heartrending: on January 6, 1973, Roland is baffled by his father's sleeping sounds—"ssssss" instead of the usual "zzzzz."

In other playful turns of this kind of medium-consciousness, Batiuk toys with the very nature of the comic strip as an artform. When Les tries to think positively, a plus sign fills his thought balloon. Once Bull takes hold of an exclamation point and hits Les with it. And on another occasion, Batiuk says he can't think of anything "to put here today," so he draws guys oogling a pretty girl with a bare midriff.

The most pervasive of this kind of self-awareness takes place in the last panel of several strips every week. When someone says something particularly lame, the listener turns to us, the reading audience, and glares in mild disgust. Some may call this fracture of the fourth wall a threadbare maneuver, and it's undeniably monotonous in a collection of years' worth of daily strips like this, but when the strips were first published in newspapers, the stare of disgust occurred days apart, its frequency virtually unnoticeable except that it built a relationship with the reader, bringing us into the strip. And Batiuk makes the grimace his chorus.

Much of the wit in *Funky Winkerbean* is essentially verbal. The "counter culture" joke on January 5, 1973, for instance. But also the joke that transpires on August 10, 1972, when Funky wants to know how a black-and-white TV dinner differs from a color TV dinner (although much of the comedy here resides in the very notion of applying the black-and-white and color designations to TV dinners, not television itself); and on December 7, 1972, when Les confesses his embarrassment at being a "total idiot" in conversing with Mary Sue, and Funky reassures him by suggesting that she will admire him for his honesty; or on September 19, 1974, when Funky observes that it's "a funny world" and Derek responds: "So how come nobody's laughing?" And much of the humor, as in the actual world of teenagers, has nothing to do with being teenagers.

But pictures usually contribute substantially to the hilarity—for instance, the repeated image of a hallway being simply a mob in motion, accompanied by a sound effect, "rumble rumble rumble." And with a talking computer and, later, a musing desk-chair, Batiuk exploits the unique capacity of the medium to blend word and picture to create a comedy that neither word nor picture, alone without the other, can convey.

And pictures also create comedy through the simple maneuver of pacing the daily episodes. In every strip, Batiuk proves an expert at timing, the fundamental attribute of comic strip artistry. A couple instances seem exemplary. On August 8, 1972, for instance, after Funky notes that "mental illness will strike one out of every three people," Batiuk postpones the punchline for a panel, creating a sense of passing time—and of pregnant suspense—which, in turn, sets us up for the joke. And a few days later, as Les tries to work up the courage to jump off the diving board, Batiuk divulges the essential elements of the joke on August 16, one ingredient per panel, timing the disclosures to build to the punchline in the last panel.

One of my favorite examples of this aspect of comic strip crafting occurs on April 15, 1972, when Funky and Les are talking about the test they've just taken. All the vital bits of information are carefully disclosed, dribbled out a piece at time, each building upon the knowledge conveyed by the preceding panel, until we arrive, finally, at Les' confession. And it takes a second to realize that he's been cheating, looking at Funky's paper in search of an answer. With that realization comes the laughter.

"Writing," Batiuk once said, "is like breathing to me; drawing is like an asthmatic attack." But you wouldn't know his drawing hand was afflicted from the evidence of the pictures he made.

As a visual storyteller, Batiuk did part of his writing with his pictures. As we've seen, he carefully, deliberately, paced the action with successive pictures, a visual undertaking. And he avoided the static imagery that has so often pervaded comic strips since the arrival of *Doonesbury.* Sometimes the *Funky* gags derive additional impact through a series of nearly unvarying panel compositions. But more often, Batiuk aimed for visual variety by altering his compositions from panel to panel, changing camera angles and distance. From the first, Batiuk's drawing style was simple and relatively uncluttered. His inflexible line gave his renderings a chiseled edge, highlighting the clarity that is essential in storytelling with pictures.

We can see some slight changes in appearance through the three years of the strip at hand. Batiuk's drawings become somewhat crisper as he achieved greater assurance in rendering the wrinkles in clothing, for instance. And over the years, Batiuk would become better and better at depicting his characters and telling their stories. His line would become livelier, and his renderings, looser. Eventually, Batiuk's interest in telling realistic stories would lead him to take up provocative issues in everyday life.

After the first of the two jumps in time, the strip was less and less a joke-a-day and more and more a serialized chronicle recording the lives of its characters, and Batiuk sometimes left the comedy behind to explore such serious aspects of contemporary life in America as teen pregnancy, steroids, teenage suicide, dating violence, dyslexia, gun violence, alcoholism (Funky shakes it), combat in Afghanistan—to name a few, and, with Les's wife Lisa, living and dying with cancer, for which the cartoonist contrived a poetic conclusion that was humane and human, sensitive without being maudlin. Episodes like these earned the cartoonist accolades for openly discussing sensitive matters. For Lisa's story, Batiuk received appreciative recognition from the American Cancer Society for sharing important information about how to deal with a modern scourge.

But those are stories for another time. They all lurk in the strip's future. For the present, we have the past, starting forty years ago, just to the right.

****

Robert C. Harvey is a comics chronicler and author of The Children of the Yellow Kid: The Evolution of the American Comic Strip *and other aesthetic histories of the medium. He has also written biographies of cartoonists Milton Caniff, Gus Arriola, and Murphy Anderson, and he produces a biweekly online magazine,* Rants & Raves, *of comics news and reviews, cartooning history and lore.*

Prologue

On March 27, 1972, *Funky Winkerbean* landed on the American comics page. It took up residence there with *Little Orphan Annie,* which in turn had once run alongside *Gasoline Alley,* which in its time had once run next to *The Grumps* . . . and so on in a long line stretching all the way back to *Hogan's Alley* and the *Yellow Kid.* Nope, no pressure there.

INTRODUCTION

Match to Flame

It was September 1970, and I was a week away from having my bluff called. From the time I'd seen my first comic strip, I'd been telling anyone who'd listen that I was going to have a comic in the newspaper one day. At my high school prom, I told my future wife that I was going to be a cartoonist, and she replied that I'd outgrow that when I matured. Fooled her on both counts. But in that halcyon fall, in seven days, I was going to have to put up or shut up: The following Tuesday, on the Teen-Age page of the *Chronicle-Telegram* in Elyria, Ohio, a new comic panel was going to make its debut, a panel about teens written and drawn by yours truly. My first published cartoon in a real bona fide newspaper. It had to be good, because that only happens once.

Now, a teen strip was, frankly, the last thing I ever thought I'd do, or ever want to do. My comic strip tastes had been shaped early on by the comics that my dad would read to me from the *Akron Beacon Journal* and, later, by the pulp sensibilities of comic books. I was in awe of the grandeur of Hal Foster's *Prince Valiant,* the otherworld beauty of Mac Raboy's *Flash Gordon* Sunday strips, and the total bravura insanity of Chet Gould's *Dick Tracy.* Even at that tender age, I was already formulating a plan, because I knew that when the time came to take my shot, I wanted to do stuff like that.

Around that time, I also encountered the movie serial that would spin my head around. Every Friday afternoon, my elementary school in Akron would show old movie serials as a reward, I suppose, for having put up with another week of the drudgery and horrors of second grade. Whatever, it worked for me. For a mere dime, we were exposed to wonders that made going to school totally worth it. On one rainy Friday afternoon, we were treated to the first chapter of a serial that was unlike anything I'd ever experienced before. It was *The Phantom Empire,* starring Gene Autry, the Singing Cowboy, a serial so unique that it almost defies description. So I'm not even going to try. Instead, I'm going to quote from the blurb on the back of the DVD collection (yes, I now own a copy of this classic on DVD and VHS . . . still waiting on the Blu-ray):

> *Hidden deep beneath the earth is the lost civilization of Murania, ruled by the ruthless Queen Tika. When Gene Autry stumbles across the hidden city, the Muranians are determined to silence him and destroy his ranch to protect their secret world. The Queen's masked army of thunder riders hunts down the singing cowboy and brings him to their subterranean city. Teeming with futuristic weaponry and machinery, the unfamiliar land resembles an alien planet. It looks like the last round-up for Gene when deadly robots attack him with flamethrowers. Autry's daring and the Queen's bloodlust escalates to a final confrontation which threatens the entire populace of Murania with total war.*

Cowboys, thunder riders dressed in quasi medieval armor shooting futuristic weapons, robots with flamethrowers—*The Phantom Empire* viewed genre boundaries as mere inconveniences rather than limits. And here's the kicker: Scattered throughout the story, the singing cowboy would periodically have to have to show up at Radio Ranch to sing on his radio broadcast or the evil bankers were going to foreclose on his ranch. It was this dose of realism (defined by me at the time as

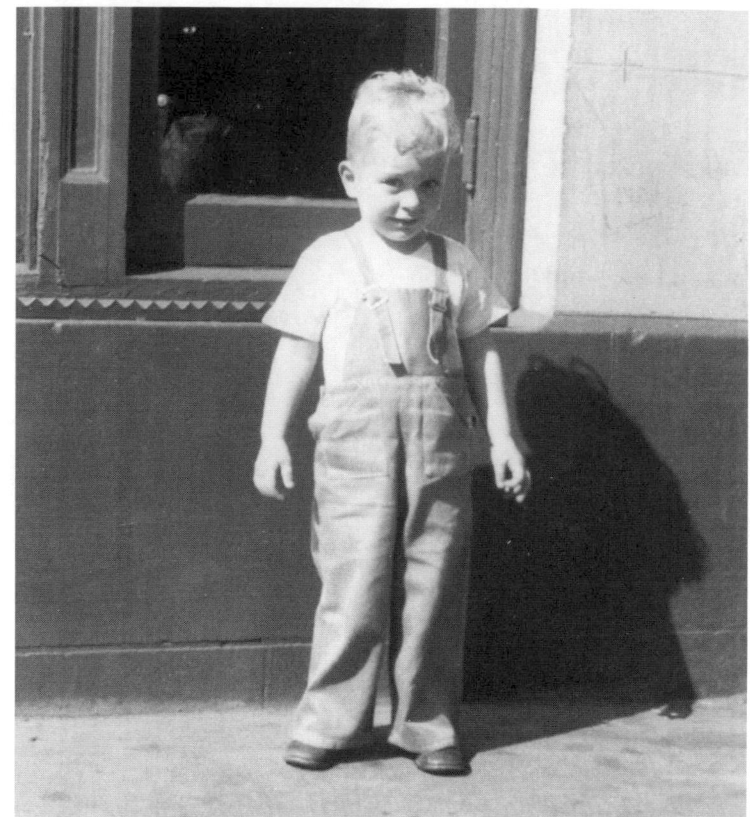

Trying to conjure up a little street cred.

anything that wasn't fun) juxtaposed with the over-the-top fantasy elements that really caught my attention. I became fascinated with the idea of taking what was considered to be a low art form and creating something of substance within those confines, of trying to take what others considered junk and turning it into something more. That thought continued to inform my cartooning choices for the next fifty years. It's hard to overestimate the impact that *The Phantom Empire* has had on my developing brain.

I've long had a theory that there's a certain golden window of opportunity when you're wide open and vulnerable to falling under the magic spell of an art form or a sport or almost any other type of pursuit. Had I been exposed to DeBussy's "Prelude

Above: Our home in Akron, where I was bitten by the cartooning bug.
Right: What more is there to say?

Crouse Elementary, where the dime was dropped.

to the Afternoon of a Faun" at that golden moment, I might have become a composer . . . or a painter, had I seen Monet's luminous Rouen Cathedral paintings. Instead, I walked into that elementary school auditorium and straight into *The Phantom Empire.* Years later, reading a biography of the comics artist Murphy Anderson, I saw that he also mentioned *The Phantom Empire* as an influence. Apparently, if you were of a certain bent, that baby was right in your wheelhouse.

The clincher came when I got my hands on my first comic book. My dad always deflected my early attempts to buy comic books when I'd spot them on the drugstore spinner racks by saying they were too violent. However, one day on a visit to our family dentist, there they were—scattered across a table in his waiting room. My eye was caught by a *Hopalong Cassidy* cover that showed Hoppy on horseback riding after two bandits escaping on rocking horses. *Rocking horses!* Now, I had seen Hopalong Cassidy on television, but never like this. Once again it was the juxtaposition of the real and the fantastic that captured my imagination. I just had to know what was going on there. Unfortunately, I was ushered in to see the dentist before I could read it and find how the writer resolved that seemingly insoluble conundrum. (I wasn't to see that book again until many years later at a comics convention when there it was, just as I'd remembered it. It was late in the con weekend, and the dealer, a purveyor of only western comics, had obviously not been selling too many. I saw an opportunity to pick up that holy grail book at a reasonably inexpensive price. Unfortunately, as I was thinking that thought, I heard myself saying aloud, "I don't believe it! I've been looking for this book my whole life!" The dealer was kind enough to at least let me keep my wallet.)

The dentist visit wasn't a total loss, because by the end of the afternoon I had acquired my first comic book. Our dentist, who obviously was no fool, used to give my sister and me a prescription for an ice cream cone at the end of our exams. The scrip was worth a dime at the drugstore on the corner. That day, as we stood at the ice cream counter, my dad said we could buy anything we wanted. I had him repeat that so there would be no question as to exactly what had been said, and then I responded, "I want one of those," pointing at the comics spinner rack. I left that afternoon with my very first comic book, a copy of *Tom Corbett Space Cadet.* To help cement the deal, I had pointed out to my dad that I was allowed to watch *Tom Corbett* on TV, so the comic book must, by extension, be okay as well. Besides, my dad had specifically said, "Anything you want . . ."

Inside that *Tom Corbett,* I saw my future, and, inspired and empowered, I began buying comics whenever the opportunity presented itself. When the monthlong wait between issues became too much to bear, I began writing and drawing my own comics to bridge the gap. When I wasn't creating cartoons, I was working on my novel. I had a little green notebook in which I chronicled my western opus *The Arizona Ranger.* Its portability allowed me to take it with me on our forced marches every Sunday to visit relatives in Akron, which we had been doing since my dad's job had taken our family about an hour away to North Eaton. While the adults talked and the cousins played baseball, I'd find

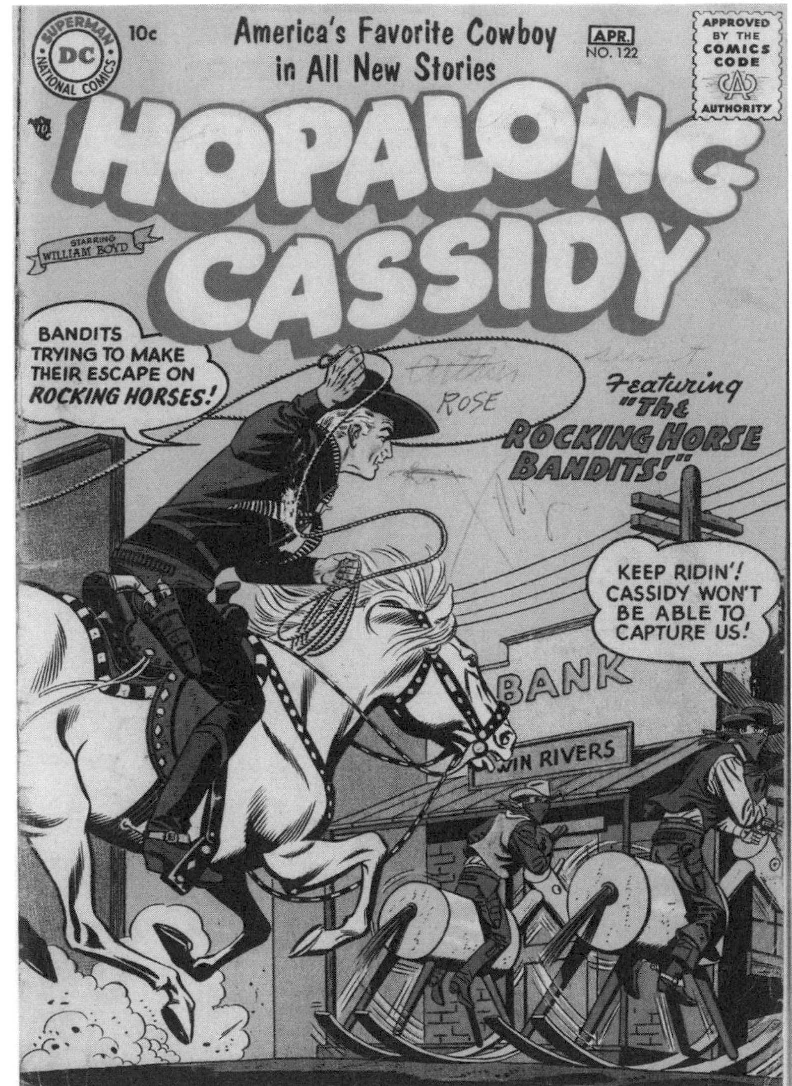

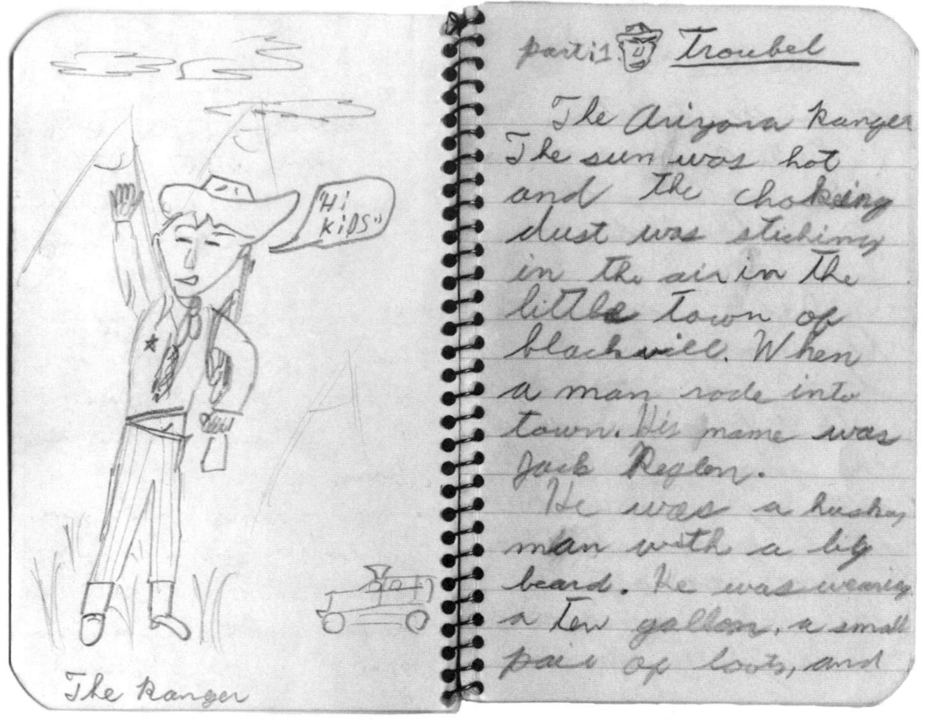

"Hi KIDS"
The Ranger
part 1 Troubel
The Arizona Ranger
The sun was hot and the chokeing dust was sticking in the air in the little Town of blackwill. When a man rode into town. His name was Jack Reglon.
He was a husky man with a big beard. He was wearing a Ten gallon, a small pair of boots, and

Right out of the gate, in my first novel, I break Elmore Leonard's admonition about never opening with weather.

a corner somewhere to work on my story. Occasionally, someone would ask to read what I was writing and would comment approvingly, but mostly I was simply regarded as a curiosity.

One Sunday, to break the tedium of the long ride home, I imagined the giant electrical towers that carried the power lines across the farm fields breaking free and marching toward the city. A few months later, when I saw that exact thing taking place in an issue of *The Flash,* I became more convinced than ever that I had found my calling. It was in the letters section of *The Flash* where I found some kindred spirits among the letter hacks and the editor, Julius "Julie" Schwartz. Julie treated us as equals by paying attention to us and encouraging our precocious commenting. It's interesting, but not surprising, to note that a number of the alumni from Julie's letter columns ended up as writers for comic books, movies, and television.

At the same time, my sense of humor was beginning to be shaped by various influences. It started with my dad, whose punning and wordplay I quickly picked up on. Whenever my mom was doing something and would ask for a hand, my dad would break into applause. My mom never thought that was funny. I, on the other hand, found it endlessly amusing. At other times around the dinner table, my dad, my sister, and

The names of my daring detective duo make Funky Winkerbean seem almost tame by comparison.

NATIONAL COMICS
PUBLICATIONS, INC.

575 LEXINGTON AVENUE
NEW YORK 22, NEW YORK
PLAZA 9-5700

February 24, 1961.

Mr. Tom Batiuk
1383 Durkee Road
R.D. 1
Grafton, Ohio

Dear Mr. Batiuk,

Congratulations! A letter of yours will appear in the June FLASH, for which you have been awarded the original FLASH drawings for the story "The Doomed Scarecrow." The drawings are being mailed to you under separate cover.

Sincerely yours,

Julius Schwartz

Julius Schwartz,
Editor.

I would conduct a conversation consisting of nothing but non sequiturs, with my mom being the odd person out. We all found this to be great fun—again, my mom not so much. My dad's tastes in comedians also led me to the kind of professional comedy I liked. I was never much of a slapstick humor fan, preferring the likes of Jack Benny and Bob and Ray. Later I gravitated toward the work of poet Ogden Nash and comedians Bob Newhart and Woody Allen. Oh, and let us not forget Pogo. My dad and I could sing "Deck Us All with Boston Charlie" by heart and did so every Christmas. As I was growing up and absorbing all of this wordplay, it never really crossed my mind that I'd find it at all useful.

That being said, allow me to waste no time in contradicting myself. In going through my files, collections, and treasured mementos (the junk I had in boxes in the attic) as I was preparing this book, I came across some early cartoons that I had completely forgotten about. My dad was a chemical engineer and subscribed to a magazine called *Chemical Processing*. The magazine was actually drier than it sounds, and apparently I felt it could use a little sprucing up. So when I was in junior high, I sent the editors some submissions consisting of humorous single-panel cartoons. None of them was accepted, primarily because the art looked like it had been done by a seventh grader, which it had been, but I think I can definitely say with a fair amount of equivocation that the writing was really not all that too terribly horribly horrible. So apparently the idea of doing a humorous cartoon wasn't as foreign to me as I had thought.

Note that Julie addressed his letter to "Mister Batiuk." He made you matter.

I continued working on my "serious" cartoons and never really attempted another humor cartoon until my junior year at Kent State University. Being a student at Kent State in the late sixties placed you at the epicenter of the enormous cultural upheaval that was taking place in the nation. For someone who was slowly making his way toward getting a shot at updating the somewhat moribund teen genre strip, it was the perfect environment in which to assimilate all that was happening. For another Kent State student, Chuck Ayers, the environment would lead to a career as a political cartoonist. (More about Chuck in a moment.) At some point my friend Dave Miles and I noticed that the student paper, the *Daily Kent Stater,* wasn't running any cartoons and decided to rectify that. We worked up some cartoons that were typical of the kind you'd find in a college newspaper, with raw-looking art and fairly sophomoric ideas. We took them into the *Stater,* convinced the editors that they ought to be running some cartoons, and soon our cartoons were appearing a couple of times a week. Life was good. We had a nice run of a couple of months until a student named Chuck Ayers (I said we'd get back to him) showed up with his own cartoons. Chuck's cartoons had a certain indefinable

Seeing Mr. Sponge again, I realize that never getting a shot at writing superheroes was perhaps a good thing.

Tom Batiuk
"IT'S CALLED A HUMAN AND IT DOES THE WORK OF SEVERAL ROBOTS."

My attempt to crack the always tough *Chemical Processing* market.

something about them that made ours pale by comparison, but let me take a shot at defining it anyway: They were a lot better. I took some cartoons into the *Stater* office one day, saw several of Chuck's cartoons lying on a desk, and decided to retire. It wasn't so much that the *Stater* let Dave and me go as that we never went back. (The world takes interesting turns, though, because eventually Chuck and I would get a chance to work together and to memorialize those Kent State days in a comic strip called *Crankshaft*. But that's getting ahead of things a bit.) At the time, I simply refocused my attention back on trying to get a gig working on *Batman* or *Spider-Man*.

The summer I graduated from Kent State, I flew to New York City with an illustrated story and several story treatments in an attempt to land a job at DC or Marvel comics. As my plane circled over the city, I was suddenly struck by the realization that I had just crossed a line. If I didn't make the attempt, I'd never fail; but it was too late for that, and the prospect of failure was now a part of the equation. I met with an editor at DC Comics who ripped not only my work up and down but me as well for having had the temerity to show up at his office with it. He must have felt a pang of compassion, though, because as I got up to leave he handed me a piece of original DC art and said, "Here! At least do it at the right size!" But it was only a momentary lapse, because as I reached the door, he yelled after me, "And don't go telling everybody that DC is giving away free art!"

My reception at Marvel was much more gracious, and associate editor and writer Roy Thomas deserves a shout-out for knowing how to treat a neophyte cartoonist with a much gentler touch. (I should note here that Roy was a fellow letter hack from the pages of *The Flash*.) Although he told me basically the same thing that the DC editor had, he left the door open with an invitation to submit more work, and I left feeling more optimistic.

I returned home fully intending to do that very thing, but along the way my focus became somewhat diffused. That fall of 1969 I took a job teaching art at Eastern Heights Junior High in Elyria. I'd get home each day and work on material for Marvel, but I also began work on newspaper comic strip

"Since it has recently been brought to our attention that the Faculty Parking lot beneath the Education Building is sinking into quicksand -- I recommend that it be immediately changed to a student lot!"

Speaking up for the issues that really mattered in this *Daily Kent Stater* cartoon.

submissions and some on-spec spot art for the local paper. At one point I even considered getting part-time work with a local ad agency as a means of gaining some professional experience. My scattergun approach wasn't producing any results, and the ad agency idea was about to send me off in a direction that I knew deep down wasn't the right one. In short, I was at a crossroads.

There are inflection points in life that, for better or worse, send you on a new path, and I was about to arrive at one. My high school art teacher, Jim Mateer, used to hold open sessions for his students in his art room on Saturday mornings. When I was his student, he'd never let me work on cartoons in class. He had various explanations for this, but I suspect that the real one was that he intuitively understood that telling me I couldn't do something was the best possible way to motivate me to do exactly the opposite. Along with being an expert practitioner of reverse psychology, Jim was also a great teacher in the best and broadest sense of the word. Sure, he taught us art, but he also taught lessons about life. He had theories about almost everything, which he delivered in fascinating down-to-earth homilies that were generally right on the money. In my hour of wavering, I found myself heading to his open art room one Saturday morning to seek his counsel.

We spent the morning talking, and, over the course of our conversation, Jim presented his general theory of how people end up doing what they do in life, all the while taking great pains, of course, never to tell me directly what I ought to do. He described the various ways people tend to make decisions or the ways people let decisions make them. "And then, of

And a Choir of Angels Filled the Air

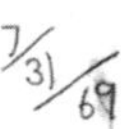

Two eerie, winged creatures hover in space looking out at the earth. They are angels, but they are more ominous and sinister than we usually picture them. They are conversing and their conversation centers on the imminent destruction of the planet Earth. "He was right to decide as He has, "they say, "they have had their opportunity and they have made ill use of it. Soon they shall realize their folly,... too late!" And with that, the two figures descend to the earth to witness man in his final hour.

They land in a ghetto and witness man's intolerance of his own kind. Then they go to a jungle and witness man at war. They view scenes of man's greed, hate, cruelty, and indifference.

"There is no love," they say, "yet in their passing they may yet justify their creation!" And with that they soar off in laser-like flight towards Earth's sun. The two angels plunge into the flaming belly of the sun and it soon glows even hotter, finally exploding and engulfing the solar system. The earth dies in the blazing super nova of it's once life-giving sun.

On an alien planet, five strange humanoids mounted on equally strange looking creatures glance up at the night sky. The sky is filled with a choir of singing angels. Suddenly two more appear , and as they do they point to a certain star which begins to shine more brightly than all of the others.

And one alien turns to the others and says, "It is as it was written in the old books: 'Follow the star and you shall find him!' Come let us ride, for our savior is born tonight!"

Maybe this treatment for Marvel comics wasn't quite as cliché forty years ago.

course," he said, "there's the bulldog approach, where people focus on one goal to the exclusion of everything else." I left his art room that morning having been cleverly nudged back onto the bulldog track. Careerwise, cartooning and only cartooning was where I was going to expend my energy. Sorry, Eastern Heights Junior High.

My next step was to head back to my local paper. My thinking was that I could get a job doing some freelance spot cartoons for them and that some syndicate executive would then see them and say, "That guy should be doing a syndicated comic strip!" Or something like that. I figured I'd work out the details once I'd gotten my foot in the door. This time I'd go there personally, instead of mailing in my submissions, so I could explain why they couldn't live without these cartoon illustrations. I showed up and was ushered to the desk of the managing editor, James Dauble. As luck would have it, I had taken along my sketchbook, and as Dauble looked through it he noticed some of the sketches I'd made while at school. As a way of inculcating the idea with the students that they needed to keep a sketchbook, I'd get mine out from time to time and sketch the students . . . except that I'd add humorous captions or word balloons. When I was in junior high we used the *Reader's Digest* in English class, and the moment I got my copy I'd go through it and add silly word balloons to all the people in the ads. My sketchbook takes were just an extension of that. Dauble liked them and asked if I'd consider doing a cartoon for a new page they were starting called the Teen-Age page. His mouth had barely stopped forming the question when I agreed. He then introduced me to Shannon Kaiser-Jewell, editor of the Teen-Age page, and we set up a time for me to bring in some cartoons. I had gone in seeking a job doing spot art and had left with my own cartoon.

At this point, it probably wouldn't hurt to go back and read my first paragraph again for emphasis. Go ahead, I'll wait.

I decided that this time a little diligence was due, so I bought a book on how to write humor cartoons. The book turned out to be next to useless, focusing on writing a style of humor that I wasn't particularly fond of to begin with. Forced to fall back on my own devices, I resorted to writing the sort of stuff that I used to write on the pictures in *Reader's Digest*. The writing came fairly easily and the drawing fairly painfully, a process that hasn't really changed much over the years. I was a fast writer but an agonizingly slow artist. The previous summer's suntan was the last I would ever have. But before the week was out, I had my first batch of cartoons.

My first meeting with Shannon established the pattern that we followed from then on. I'd show up on a Saturday morning with eight or nine cartoons for her to go through. Chuckling at the appropriate spots, she'd choose the cartoons for the next couple of weeks. It always seemed to me that a good editor was one who sought ways to identify what you were doing well and then challenge you to do more of the same, and this is how Shannon operated. She encouraged my best, and I, in turn, was eager to please. I needed that experience, and it became particularly important in my development, because, as it turned out, Shannon, for better or worse, would be the last true editor I would ever have. The weekly cartoon was a perfect way to break into the process of working with an editor

Eastern Heights Junior High became the reference for Westview High as seen in the May 24, 1972, daily.

and meeting a regular, but not oppressive, creative deadline. People would ask how I came up with the ideas, and I'd say that I didn't really know, but I did know that I had all week.

The day my first cartoon was scheduled to run, I stopped at a drugstore after school and bought a stack of papers to take home, I suppose to reassure myself that my cartoon was actually in every copy of the paper. Plus, I figured it wouldn't hurt to bump up the number of copies that were sold every Tuesday. I imagined the managing editor sitting there each week going over the circulation figures and smiling at the spike in sales as he congratulated himself on having had the foresight

The Chronicle Telegram / Teen-age page

THIS IS THE FIRST TIME OUR SCHOOL HAS CROSSED THE FIFTY YARD LINE ALL NIGHT!
50
TMB

The first band cartoon.

to hire that young cartoonist. As time went on, there was occasionally a week when the cartoon would get bumped by breaking teen news or advertising, so I quickly learned to check first to see that my cartoon was there before I bought my stack. There's nothing quite as deflating as bringing home a stack of papers without your cartoon in them. The panel eventually acquired the name *Rapping Around,* and for the next year it became my home in the newspaper and my training ground.

From the very beginning, I had some definite ideas about how I wanted to approach a teen strip. The crop of teen strips in the early seventies seemed oblivious to the time in which they existed. The enormous changes taking place in the youth culture were quickly making the strips with the jalopies and letter sweaters irrelevant. They'd all been around awhile and were being done by middle-aged men who were viewing things from a rose-colored distance. My new cartoon was going to be an inside job. I was just out of school myself and, even more important, was teaching in one. I decided to avoid the standard teen strip clichés. There would be no teenagers hanging on the phone or parents yelling at them to clean up their rooms; there would be no letter-sweatered football hero trying to decide which cheerleader he wanted to date. Instead, I was going to write about the realities of the school that I knew, from the tedium of being an unheralded and unrecognizable member of the band to the horrors of having to climb the dreaded rope in gym class. Rather than focus on jocks and cheerleaders, I was going to write about everyone else. Avoiding the parent-teen clichés also meant that with one small exception there wouldn't be any parents in the strip. The only

adults would be the teachers—but, again, since I was one, it would be an inside job.

A number of the themes that first appeared on the *Chronicle-Telegram*'s Teen-Age page later showed up in *Funky*. My very first cartoon dealing with a high school band appeared in *Rapping Around,* and several other ideas would later find themselves directly converted into *Funky* strips.

As things progressed, I found that I really enjoyed the challenges of working on a humor panel and, even more important, working on something that was all mine. As a result, all plans of going back to Marvel comics were shelved and replaced by a new one. Since I was starting to get favorable responses to the panel from people other than my mom, I began considering it for national syndication. It so happened that a national newspaper syndicate, the Newspaper Enterprise Association (NEA), was located practically in my backyard, in Cleveland. Over the holidays I gathered the best of my panels and set off to see what sort of reception they'd get in the wider world.

Walking into NEA's offices in an old warehouse on West Third Street was like walking into a time machine. The bulk of NEA's roster was relics of a bygone era. Big blowups of strips like *Our Boarding House* and *Alley OOP* hung on the walls around a large open bullpen filled with desks and drawing boards covered with paper and comic strips. I met with the manager of their comic art department, the guy with the coolest name in the newspaper business, Flash Fairfield. Flash was a lanky character right out of a Hollywood B movie. The only thing missing was an eyeshade and garters on his shirtsleeves.

Freckles and His Friends, created by Merrill Blosser.

Flash was also the perfect guy for a budding young cartoonist to run into. He sat down with me, I showed him my samples, and we spent the rest of the afternoon not only talking about the work I'd brought in but about comics in general and about how a good comic strip was constructed.

From the beginning, Flash stressed the importance of having just a few strong characters with distinguishing traits and appearances. Looking back, I'm sure this is why I did things like have the band director always appear in uniform. With his earnestness and genuine interest in my work, Flash made quite an impression on me. In fact, a note he sent reminding me of these points remained taped to my drawing board for a number of years. Eventually it disappeared, and shortly thereafter I began breaking most of Flash's rules, but at the time it was advice that I needed to hear, and it helped me build a solid foundation for the work. Feeling that my writing style would work better in a strip form, he sent me home with instructions to turn my panels into a comic strip with three or four main characters. He followed up by sending me copies of the samples I'd left graded, marked up, and broken down into strip form.

Once I returned home, I did a little happy dance and then immediately started coming up with characters for a comic strip. Since the work I was doing was only about a quarter-inch removed from real life, I decided not to stray too far for the characters' identities either. So I simply looked to my friends and coworkers as models for my characters.

The main characters, T.D. and Les, were friends from my Kent State days, Thom Dickerson and Les Meyer. Roland, the hippy/revolutionary, was a guy who lived in an apartment across the street from mine, and Livinia was based on one of my art students with a name taken from a magazine. I pulled their looks from some of the characters that I'd used in *Rapping Around.* I used people I knew because the characters then came with established identities that I could immediately plug in and begin working with in the strip. It was a handy way to start things off, and it's remained my work method ever since. My junior high band director became Harry L. Dinkle, the World's Greatest Band Director, and Mrs. McKenzie, the lady in the apartment below mine, would later turn up as the next-door neighbor in *Crankshaft.* The holding title for the strip was *Moondog,* which I apparently was just using until I could come up with an even goofier name.

The pattern that winter was this: I left school in the afternoon, stopping at a Burger King two blocks from my apartment, and then, with no cooking or cleanup necessary, settled down to work on the strips until hitting the sack after the late-night talk shows. It must have been taking a bit of a toll

The rock festival Sunday in *Funky* started with this drawing from my sketchbook.

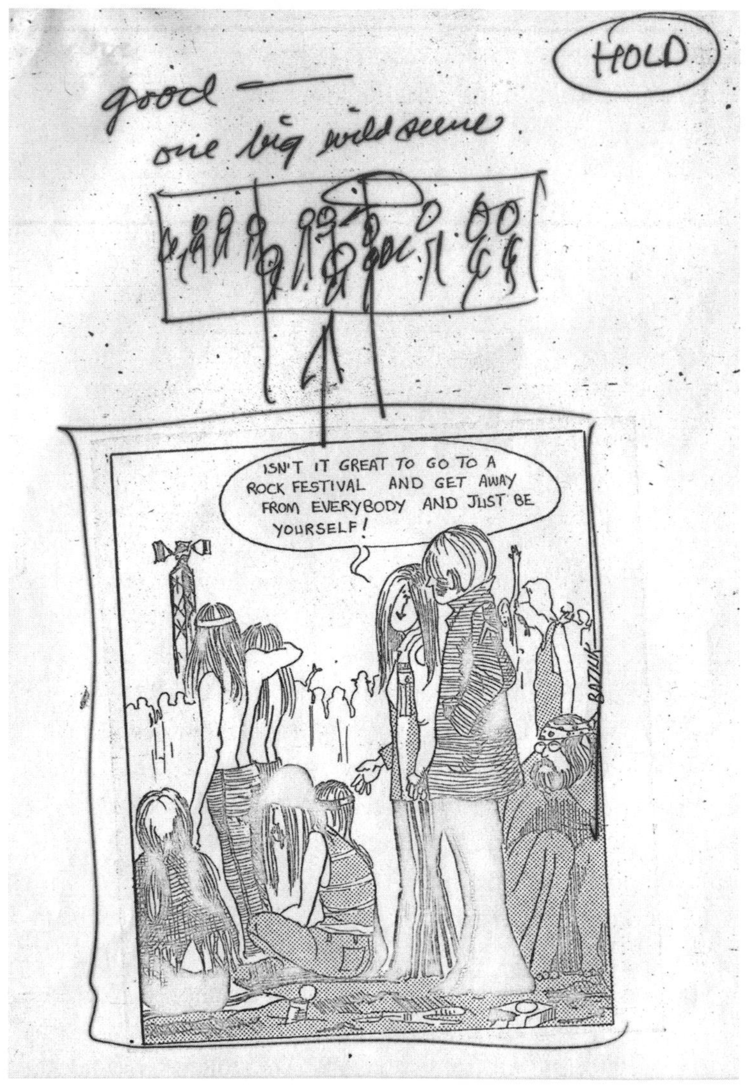

Above: The *Rapping Around* cartoon.
Right: The marked-up copy from Flash Fairfield suggesting how it could work as a strip.

The rock festival as a *Funky* Sunday strip.

on me, because I remember one of my seventh graders coming up to me in class one day and telling me that I needed to get more sleep. In a short while though, I had a batch of strips ready to send off to NEA. And since it was not a given that NEA would pick up the strip, I also made plans for a return trip to New York City to visit the major newspaper syndicates over my spring break. My dad, who traveled quite a bit on business, provided me with maps of the city, gave me a hotel suggestion, and even recommended a syndicate to check out. Our local papers didn't carry *Doonesbury,* but he had seen it in an out-of-town paper and suggested that I might want to visit Universal Press Syndicate while I was there.

I flew to New York and caught a bus to the East Side Terminal. It was pouring rain, so I made the first of what would become many NYC sidewalk umbrella purchases and, with my suitcase and portfolio in hand, marched the breadth

NEWSPAPER ENTERPRISE ASSOCIATION, INC.

1200 WEST THIRD STREET • CLEVELAND, OHIO 44113 • PHONE: (216) 621-7300

JOHN D. FAIRFIELD
Production Manager
Comic Art Department

January 13, 1971

Mr. Tom Batiuk
1383 North Durkee Rd.
Grafton, Ohio 44044

Dear Tom,

I have shown your samples to Tom Peoples, Director of Comic Art, and Phil Pastoret, our Story Editor. They liked both your art and gags. As I stated when you were here, I thought we would be more receptive to your comic in strip form. This proves to be the case.

I have enclosed Xeroxes of the material you left here plus the material you mailed later. I have marked the copies we would like to see worked up in strip form with suggestions for adapting them to the strip format. Others I marked "hold" and others "nix."

Several facts should be considered in a comic strip. First, it is almost mandatory to establish a main character and three or four major characters. These characters should be addressed by name in the balloons when possible to establish their identity. These characters should have distinguishing traits and appearances.

Second, the drawing area will be more limited in a comic strip per frame as compared to a panel. It will require less detail and a stronger line.

Third, I would keep your gags simple and short, just as they are. The art should enhance the gag as much as possible. In some cases it might help the gag to vary the panels from close-up, to silhouette, to long-shot. In other cases, it might work better if the panels were almost the same.

This means the final judgment on characters, gags, wording, panels and art must be yours. I have made suggestions, but please use <u>your</u> judgment.

of Manhattan to my hotel on the West Side. The next day I made Universal Press my first stop. John McMeel met with me and was simply wonderful. While he looked through my work, he gave me a *Doonesbury* book to look at. I was seeing it for the first time, and even though McMeel had some favorable

Funky Winkerbean was born in the second-floor apartment of this house on West Avenue in Elyria, Ohio.

One of the *Moondog* panels I took to the syndicates in New York in 1970.

things to say about my work, from what I was reading, I could see that Universal Press had no need for me. Even so, John McMeel, in his engaging and charming way, left me feeling very positive and encouraged about my prospects.

For the rest of the day, my calls ran the gamut from syndicates where someone would only step out in the hall to talk to me to the McClure Syndicate, where an editor actually pulled out a *Mutt and Jeff* strip with someone slipping on a banana peel and told me that my strip needed that kind of action. At the Chicago Tribune–New York News Syndicate I ran into another gentleman, Henry Raduta, who spent the better part of the morning with me going over my submission in detail. He offered several suggestions, one of which dealt with a way of introducing my characters that eventually became the very first *Funky* strip. The day ended at Publishers-Hall Syndicate, where no one would see me at all and where the best I could do was leave some copies with a receptionist. In later years, the story was told that when Publisher-Hall's editor Richard Sherry saw my submission, he ran out into the hall looking for me. But I tend to discount that version, because I remember walking very slowly and looking back over my shoulder all the way to the elevator. But the day after I got home, an airmail

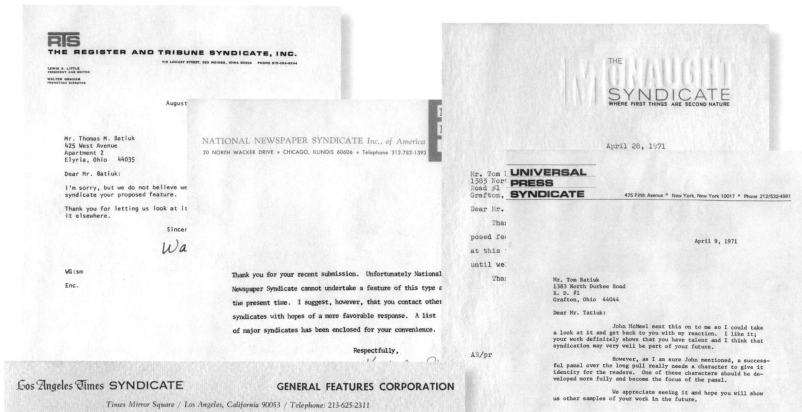

THE REGISTER AND TRIBUNE SYNDICATE, INC.

715 LOCUST STREET, DES MOINES, IOWA 50304 PHONE 515-284-6244

LEWIS A. LITTLE
PRESIDENT AND EDITOR

WALTER GRAHAM
PROMOTION DIRECTOR

August

Mr. Thomas M. Batiuk
425 West Avenue
Apartment 2
Elyria, Ohio 44035

Dear Mr. Batiuk:

I'm sorry, but we do not believe we
syndicate your proposed feature.

Thank you for letting us look at it
it elsewhere.

Sincer

Wa

WG:sm

Enc.

NATIONAL NEWSPAPER SYNDICATE *Inc., of America*

20 NORTH WACKER DRIVE • CHICAGO, ILLINOIS 60606 • Telephone 312-782-1393

Thank you for your recent submission. Unfortunately National Newspaper Syndicate cannot undertake a feature of this type a the present time. I suggest, however, that you contact other syndicates with hopes of a more favorable response. A list of major syndicates has been enclosed for your convenience.

Respectfully,

THE MCNAUGHT SYNDICATE
WHERE FIRST THINGS ARE SECOND NATURE

April 28, 1971

Mr. Tom
1383 Nor
Road #1
Grafton,

Dear Mr.

Tha
posed fe
at this
until we

Tha

AR/pr

UNIVERSAL PRESS SYNDICATE

475 Fifth Avenue • New York, New York 10017 • Phone 212/532-4991

April 9, 1971

Mr. Tom Batiuk
1383 North Durkee Road
R. D. #1
Grafton, Ohio 44044

Dear Mr. Tatiuk:

John McMeel sent this on to me so I could take a look at it and get back to you with my reaction. I like it; your work definitely shows that you have talent and I think that syndication may very well be part of your future.

However, as I am sure John mentioned, a successful panel over the long pull really needs a character to give it identity for the readers. One of these characters should be developed more fully and become the focus of the panel.

We appreciate seeing it and hope you will show us other samples of your work in the future.

Sincerely yours,

Jim Andrews

James F. Andrews
Editor

JFA:rn
Enclosures

u|p|s

Los Angeles Times SYNDICATE   **GENERAL FEATURES CORPORATION**

Times Mirror Square / Los Angeles, California 90053 / Telephone: 213-625-2311

Thank you very much for giving us a chance to see samples of your feature. We have given the material careful study and serious consideration for possible syndication.

We are sorry to report, however, that we will be unable to undertake syndication of your work. While we find considerable merit in your material, we regret that we cannot fit the feature into our syndicate package.

We are returning your samples herewith.

The Editors

letter from Publisher's-Hall arrived. In it Sherry said that they were impressed by the cartoons I had left and that he wanted me to give him a call. I never thought of this until now, but it's quite possible that airmail letter and I flew home together on the same plane.

After another happy dance, I called and Sherry again expressed his interest. I told him that NEA was interested as well, and he asked if he could send me a ninety-day option agreement. I said fine. When we were done talking, I called Flash Fairfield to see where things stood at NEA. Flash said that they had decided to take a pass, so when the option letter from Publishers-Hall arrived, I signed it.

Sherry asked for the originals of the strips I had left with him, followed by a request for some pencil roughs. He apparently liked what he was seeing, and not long after I opened my mailbox to find a contract to produce a comic strip for Publishers-Hall. As I read the contract, though, I stopped in the middle of my third happy dance in as many months. The contract was for a comic strip all right, but the syndicate would own all of my creations in perpetuity throughout the universe (there went my chances in the Andromeda Galaxy), and I had to work for them in perpetuity as well. I called Sherry, and he said that it was really a "gentlemen's agreement" and that if I ever became so unhappy that I wanted to leave, I could. However, it would mean leaving my imaginary friends behind and, even though I'd only been working with them a short time, I'd grown kind of fond of them. So I took the contract to a lawyer, and together we determined that we could both read a contract just fine and that it was pretty

C·T·N·Y·N·S

HENRY RADUTA
MANAGER

August 2,1971

Mr. Thomas Batiuk
1383 N. Durkee Rd.
R.D. #1
Grafton, Ohio 44044

Dear Tom:

I just wanted you to know that I haven't forgotten about you and your work. I've thought of you many times and wondered how you made out with your feature.

I do hope I didn't discourage you too much and I trust you submitted it to other syndicates to get their reactions.

Please keep in touch and if you ever have something to show us please do not hesitate to send it along. Or, if you are planning a trip to N.Y. let me know and I will arrange to give you as much time as you need.

Best regards,

HRaduta

Henry Raduta

HR:ja

CHICAGO TRIBUNE - NEW YORK NEWS SYNDICATE, INC.
220 EAST 42ND ST., NEW YORK, N. Y. 10017 • 212 MU 2-1234

Publishers-Hall Syndicate

30 EAST 42ND STREET
NEW YORK, N. Y. 10017
TELEPHONE (212) 682-5560

RICHARD SHERRY
EDITOR

April 7, 1971

Mr. Tom Batiuk
1383 N. Durkee Road
Grafton, Ohio 44044

Dear Mr. Batiuk:

We are impressed by the cartoons that you left for us to see today. This note, of course, will not reach you until you return to Ohio. Otherwise we could have met while you were here.

When you have the opportunity, perhaps you will call me collect at the above number.

Cordially,

RS:ljt

401 NORTH WABASH AVE. CHICAGO, ILL. 60611 TELEPHONE: (312) 321-2795

much exactly what I thought it was. As I was leaving, he added that I'd probably make a lawyer rich someday getting out of it. (He really should be listed in the Bible alongside the other prophets.) But, for the moment, that contract was my invitation to the dance. I was going to have to kick any problems that I had with it down the road so I could settle in and get to work on my new comic strip.

The summer of '71 was a game changer. I married Cathy, my high school sweetheart and soul mate; I began serious work on my new as-yet-unnamed comic strip; I was still doing my weekly *Rapping Around* cartoon for the *Chronicle-Telegram;* and I could feel a new school year lurking just around the corner. I caught a bit of a break when Publishers-Hall announced that they were moving their offices from New York to Chicago. As a result, *Funky*'s launch got pushed back by several months—time that I was able to use to go on a honeymoon and, after returning home, work on building up material for the strip. When school started up again that fall, I was back to working long days and nights and seeing only darkness at the end of the bat cave. It didn't seem like I was going to be able to teach full-time and do a comic strip full-time in the only one full time that I had.

In the meantime, the strip had developed an identity crisis—a couple of them, actually. *Moondog* had only been a holding name, and nobody at the syndicate even liked it as a holding name. And calling my lead character T.D. wasn't going to cut it either. Again, *Doonesbury* didn't run yet in our area, so I didn't know about the character in that strip called B.D. The syndicate did, however, and they wanted something different for my character. We all started spitballing names for the strip and its lead character, but nothing was really working.

Then one day at school I asked all of my classes to write down funny or interesting names. That night Cathy and I sat at the kitchen table in our apartment and went through the list of names that I had brought home. Out of that collection of names we came up with a few to send off to the syndicate. I made up logos for *Winkerbean & Co., Funky Winkerbean, Three-o-Clock High,* and a couple of others that I no longer recall. The one that came back with the Publishers-Hall seal of approval was *Funky Winkerbean,* the name that has been my blessing and my curse. Had I known that the strip would be around for forty years and the directions that the work would take me, I think I would've spent more time working a little harder on the name. As one newspaper editor put it shortly after the strip was launched, "That's either the worst name or the best name that's ever been given to a comic strip." The jury's still out.

Finally, a launch date of March 27, 1972, was set for *Funky.* I remember coming home from school the day that the sales campaign started, lying down on the bed in our apartment, and realizing that there wasn't anything more I could do. *Funky*'s fate was in the hands of others. The syndicate salesmen are the unsung warriors of the comics business. Without their efforts, there wouldn't be an American comics page, let alone a reason to be doing this book.

As it turned out, *Funky*'s fate was in some excellent hands. Bob Coles was the head of sales for Publisher's-Hall, and his staff of Dick Lafave, Don Lane, Fred Dingman, and Bill McGhee helped Funky launch in more than seventy papers nationwide.

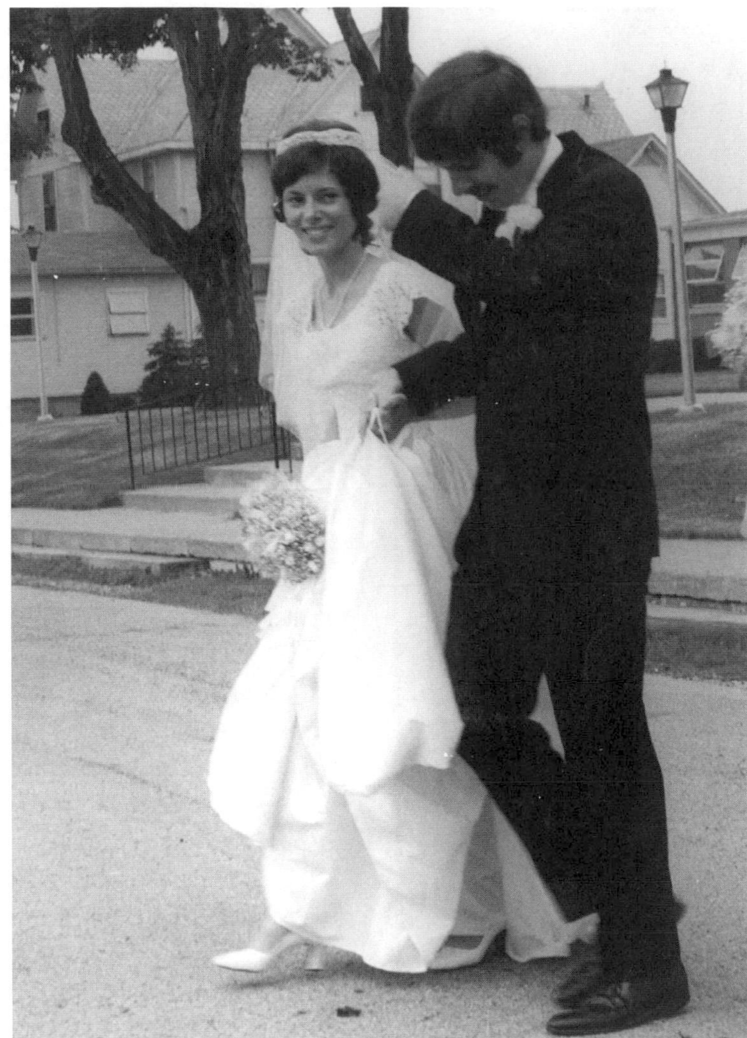

1971 was a game-changer . . . I took on two long-term contracts.

Funky to Debut in PD Comics

Feeling funky? If not, now you can do something about it. Starting tomorrow in The Plain Dealer comic pages, "Funky Winkerbean" debuts. Funky and his hilarious cohorts, Les, Roland, Derek and Livinia, are based on the real-life junior high school group that creator Tom Batiuk of Elyria teaches.

Look for "Funky Winkerbean" tomorrow in the P.D.

THOMAS BATIUK

Teen page cartoonist's comic strip syndicated

Thomas Batiuk, The Chronicle-Telegram's Teen-age Page cartoonist, is now drawing a nationally-syndicated comic strip.

The strip, "Funky Winkerbean," will be distributed by Publishers-Hall Syndicate of Chicago on a daily and Sunday basis.

"Funky" will be carried in the Cleveland Plain Dealer starting Monday, according to Batiuk, who has been drawing the weekly Teen-age Page cartoon, "Rapping Around," for the C-T since September, 1970.

The C-T cartoon will be discontinued until fall.

Batiuk has been an art teacher at Eastern Heights Junior High School for the past three years.

The comic strip will be based on his experiences in teaching and will present a semi-sophisticated, look at young people, he explained.

A 1965 graduate of Midview High School, he received his bachelor of science degree in art from Kent State University in 1969. He and his wife, Cathy, live at 425 West Ave.

Later, the ball would be moved further down the field by the addition to the sales staff of four former teachers: John Killian, Jack Prahl, George Haeberlein, and Bill Weir. Having just left the teaching trenches, these men got *Funky,* and that knowledge translated into a rapidly growing client list. Now the ball was handed back to me. The salesmen were getting *Funky* into papers across the country, but I had to keep it there.

The strip's launch had been pushed back so far that I thought I might be able to finish the school year. But it was now clear that that wasn't going to happen. Something would have to give—the teaching job, the cartooning job, or me. After talking it over with Cathy, we decided I'd leave teaching to focus on the strip. It would leave me without a fallback position in case the strip didn't sell, and, of more importance concerning the work, I'd lose my insider status. When Jim Mateer heard that I'd have to leave my teaching position, he invited me to come out to his classes at Midview, my old high school, to sketch and hang out whenever I wanted. Jim understood perhaps even more than I did at the time how important my being in school was to the particular comic work I was doing. So at least once a week I'd head out to

Sketching in Jim Mateer's art class at Midview High School.

Midview to spend a period or two sketching in Jim's classes. The fact that it was my old high school didn't hurt one bit either. When I'd walk into the gym, it still smelled like the gym did when I was a student there only a few years before. Now, maybe I would have written about Les having to climb the dreaded rope in the gym class anyway, but being in that place surrounded by those memories certainly didn't hurt. It also helped me establish a work pattern of getting close to and researching my subject matter that I follow to this day.

Later, I began subbing for Jim. It was a good fit because I knew the layout and the lesson plans, and the students knew I'd be back and could narc on them if they caused any problems, so I like to think it worked to everyone's benefit. It would have been easy to become isolated from my subject matter, but Jim's foresight and generosity in inviting me into his classroom kept that from happening. When the school year ended, Shannon and I put *Rapping Around* on summer hiatus, intending to pick it up again in the fall. But, as it turned out, I had done my last *Rapping Around.*

For the first few weeks of work on *Funky,* I was sending pencil roughs to the syndicate to get them approved before turning them into strips. I finally asked how long I had to keep doing that and was told that I could stop it whenever I felt comfortable. So, feeling comfortable, I stopped. However, I wasn't without my resources. I would get together with Cathy and my parents for sessions where I'd preview material to cull the best work. Cathy was always there as a sounding board, and she also affected the work in more subtle ways. Countless times over the years an article would slide across the breakfast table accompanied by the words, "You should read this." She never let me get away with anything too easy for too long, and her gentle influence over the years has been profound. Publisher-Hall's editorial stance was extremely laissez-faire when it came to my work. Maybe it was something I said—I don't know. But *Funky* was successful, so they left me alone. Other than the obvious things—like the fact that I couldn't spell *banana* to save my life (the only reason I did just now was because of the spell-checker on my laptop)—there wasn't really any editing being done on my work. Whenever they saw the word *banana,* they had carte blanche to fix it, but otherwise, for the first dozen or so years, I was my own de facto editor. When the opportunity arose for me to codify that editorial control in my contract, I did.

• • •

This volume includes the first three years of *Funky Winkerbean.* I think it's appropriate to say a few words about what you'll find here.

Starting a comic strip is a unique proposition that requires a slightly different skill set from the one you'll hopefully be using a few years later. When I was just beginning with *Funky,* I read a *Peanuts* strip that completely frustrated me. The strip in question had come after a week during which Linus had had his blanket taken away, and he was lying on the ground shaking as he went through withdrawal. In the second panel, Snoopy walks up wearing his WWI flying helmet and scarf. He pauses to look down at Linus shaking on the ground and then walks off saying, "Poor blighter, his kind shouldn't be sent to the front." It was an elegant strip that Schulz had taken twenty years to set up. Twenty years in which he had developed the theme of Linus and his blanket, developed the character of Snoopy and Snoopy's fantasy world as a fighter pilot in WWI—all so he could create the opportunity to eventually dovetail them into that one perfect strip. Twenty years that I didn't have behind me in those first few weeks of *Funky.*

Instead, what you have in a beginning strip is a great deal of expository dialogue trying to establish your characters' names, personalities, and situations. Oh, and have them say something funny. I've often likened it to a stand-up comic who has to win over new audiences each night with a series of individual jokes. Later, if he's lucky, he moves on to a sitcom where the situational humor allows him to extend the comic narrative. Finally, if he's really lucky, he gets to make movies, where there's room for the subtleties of behavioral humor. It takes a long time to establish your characters and develop their personalities. The flip side of the coin is that, once established, the half-life of those ideas is right up there with plutonium. Les hasn't been behind the machine gun at his hall monitor's post in decades, but people will still mention it as if I had drawn him there yesterday.

Before we part company, let me just take a moment to highlight a couple of things nestled among the cartoons you're about to read. First, on page 51 (May 8, 1972) you'll find a rare parent sighting. While there may be a couple of other one-off parent appearances, they have even less significance than this one of Roland's dad. I think I broke my no-parent rule here because Flash Fairfield had made a point of how much he liked the draw-

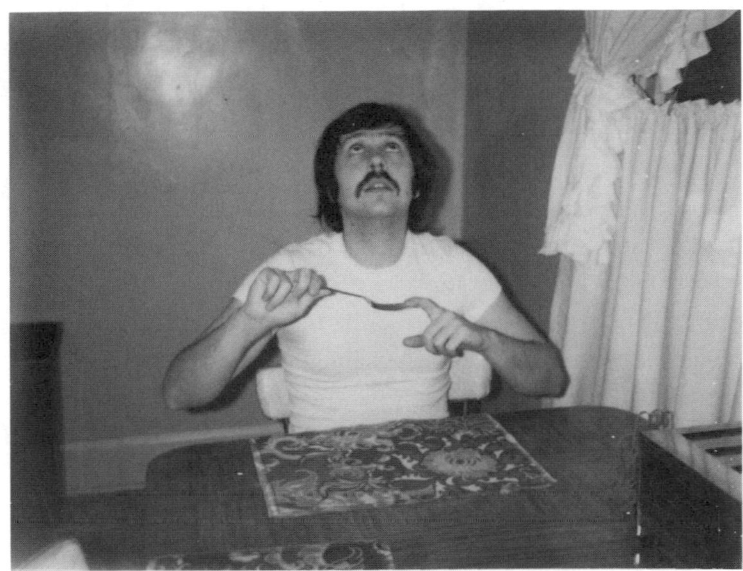

A reference shot for the October 8, 1972, *Funky* Sunday.

ing of Roland's dad when he was reviewing my initial samples. Roland's dad hangs around for a bit but is eventually banished to the cartoon limbo where the other parents in *Funky* live. No parent would play a significant role of any kind in the strip until years later when Funky puts his father in a nursing home.

On page 105 (September 12, 1972) Crazy Harry makes his first appearance. Whether it was playing frozen pizzas on his stereo or playing air guitar or refusing to observe daylight savings time, Crazy Harry became my go-to guy if something slightly off-center needed to be done. Crazy Harry living in his locker first happens on page 135 (November 21, 1972). When you're starting out as a cartoonist, you're an amalgam of your influences, and so I'll leave it up to you to see if you can figure out the source inspiration for that story arc.

This next highlight moment was news to me when I was going through the beginning year of strips for the first time in forty years. On page 111 (September 26, 1972) we find out that Fred Fairgood was previously married and had a child before he met and married Ann. Interesting. That's going to take some serious retconning (that's comic bookese for *retro-continuity*) in the current story line one of these days.

John Darling makes his appearance on page 138 (November 27, 1972). John was the first of my attempts to create a character who was a winner after reading an interview with Charles Schulz in which he proclaimed that only losing was funny. I was only partially successful. While John had the trappings of success, he really was a loser. He just didn't know it. I based John on a local TV anchor and seven years later he would spin off into his own strip.

In the Christmas Sunday strip on page 149 (December 24, 1972), I began a tradition of hiding Cathy's name somewhere in the holiday strip. When our son, Brian, came along, I began putting him in as well, and it's something that I've carried on in every Christmas strip to this day.

On page 211 (May 13, 1973) I finally found my winner who was funny. This Sunday strip marks the first appearance of Harry L. Dinkle, the World's Greatest Band Director. Harry was not only a winner as a band director but as a character as well. Avoiding the usual suspects, I instead drew on my junior high band experience for this inside send-up of the typical type-A band director. His take-charge personality struck a chord (pun intended) with band directors, band students, and band parents and led to a long and rewarding relationship with music educators across the country. It's the kind of character you hope to someday create when you're starting out. I left this Sunday version open for coloring, but soon, even in the Sunday strip, he'd assumed his distinctive black uniform. Staying with the band for just a moment, Holly Budd, the band's majorette, makes her first appearance on page 427 (September 23, 1974). A couple of strips later, we see Funky talking with her, both of them unaware at this early stage that she would one day become Mrs. Winkerbean with Funky's second marriage.

Finally, on page 391 (July 2, 1974), we have the first appearance of Tony Montoni in his pizzeria. Montoni's was based on a pizza shop in Kent from my college days, and its beginnings don't fully foreshadow the major stage it will one day become in the strip. Montoni's will play a key role in a number of pivotal events, including turning into the wedding chapel of love for a number of Funky characters. But that backstory will have to wait for another day.

Looking back on *Funky*'s opening scenes, I can see a young cartoonist beginning to feel his way into the intricacies of creating a daily comic strip. The art slowly simplifying until the view is straight through the proscenium arch, the writing drawing on adolescent feelings and emotions to propel it. With more than a little luck, I had fallen into a subject matter and work method that both allowed me and forced me to draw heavily from my own experience, which in turn enabled my readers to be able to identify with it and trust it. That trust is important, because, eventually, it permits you to be able to ask your readers to follow you to new places. For now, however, in the strips you're about to encounter, the characters and I are both growing up together in a world that's naive, innocent, and relatively carefree. Whatever cares they have at this point are adolescent cares, not adult cares. Those are still down the road.

1972

MY NAME IS **FUNKY**! I'M JUST AN AVERAGE KID TRYING TO FIGURE OUT A CONFUSING WORLD,... NOT TO MENTION PLANE GEOMETRY! MEET MY FRIENDS!
I'M **ROLAND**, AND I REJECT ALL SYMBOLS OF THE ESTABLISHMENT,... WITH THE EXCEPTION OF PLAYBOY MAGAZINE!
I'M **LES**! I REALLY WANT TO BE FAR OUT LIKE ROLAND,... BUT NOT TOO FAR SINCE I HAVE TO BE HOME BY 11:00!
AND I'M **LIVINIA**, THE ONLY GIRL IN THIS STRIP BUT WHAT WOMEN'S LIB DOESN'T KNOW WON'T HURT 'EM!
Publishers-Hall Syndicate, 1972
BATIUK 3-27

YOU DON'T HAVE TO PLAY IT COOL KID! YOU'RE PROBABLY AS ANXIOUS TO MEET ME AS I AM TO MEET YOU!
RIGHT?
WRONG!
3-28
Publishers-Hall Syndicate, 1972
BATIUK

3-29

YOU KNOW LES, POPCORN TASTES A LOT BETTER WITH A GIRL'S HAND IN IT!

YA KNOW FUNKY, WITH ALL OF THIS POLLUTION, POLITICAL UNREST, AND THE DRAFT, WE SURE HAVE ENOUGH TO WORRY ABOUT!
3-30

OF ALL THE PROBLEMS WE FACE, WHICH DO YOU CONSIDER TO BE THE MOST CRUCIAL?
NO PARKING
BATIUK
Publishers-Hall Syndicate, 1972

ACNE!

I WANT YOU TO THINK OF ME, NOT AS A COUNSELOR, BUT AS A FRIEND YOU CAN RAP WITH! A SOUL BROTHER!

FEEL FREE TO SHARE ANY PROBLEM WITH ME, NO MATTER HOW PERSONAL! NOW WHAT SEEMS TO BE THE TROUBLE?
BATIUK 3-31
Publishers-Hall Syndicate, 1972

MY LOCKER'S JAMMED!

SAY, I JUST GOT MY T-SHIRT FROM THE "FRATERNAL ORDER OF OPTIMISTIC LOSERS"!
Publishers-Hall Syndicate, 1972

HEY! IT FITS!
I AM A F.O.O.L.
4-1

I'LL SAY!
I AM A F.O.O.L.
BATIUK

FUNKY WINKERBEAN
115
COUNSELOR

COME IN FUNKY! WHAT SEEMS TO BE TROUBLING YOU?

WE'RE NOTHING BUT COMPUTER NUMBERS AT THIS SCHOOL, MR. FAIRGOOD!

BATIUK

NOBODY CARES ABOUT US AS PERSONS!

I'M TIRED OF BEING JUST A NUMBER!

4-2

I WANT A CHANCE TO MAKE SOME OF MY OWN DECISIONS!

OKAY! WHAT WOULD YOU LIKE TO BE,... ODD OR EVEN?

SOMETHING TELLS ME FUNKY, THAT THIS IS ONE SEX-EDUCATION COURSE MY FOLKS WON'T HAVE TO WORRY ABOUT!
BATIUK
4-3

YOU SAY YOUR DATE WITH THAT NEW GIRL WENT OKAY TILL YOU RAN OUT OF THINGS TO SAY?

WELL DON'T WORRY LES! THAT ALWAYS HAPPENS ON FIRST DATES!

YEAH FUNKY, BUT WHEN IT HAPPENED WE WERE ONLY AT THE END OF HER DRIVEWAY!
BATIUK
4-4

THIS SCHOOL NEWSPAPER IS THE BIGGEST COLLECTION OF TRITE GARBAGE I'VE EVER SEEN!
BATIUK

WHY DON'T YOU DO AN ISSUE ON SOMETHING RELEVANT, ... LIKE WHAT'S HAPPENING WITH MY BROTHERS AND SISTERS AT THIS SCHOOL?
4-5

STRANGE ..., I THOUGHT YOU WERE AN ONLY CHILD!

ARE YOU LISTENING TO ME GLORIA?

OF COURSE I AM LES!

SAY WHAT'S A SIX LETTER WORD FOR A LARGE SOUTH AMERICAN RIVER?
BATIUK
4·6

BAH! YOU'RE ALWAYS WATCHING TELEVISION!
BATIUK 4·7

TV IS NOTHING BUT A DECADENT ESTABLISHMENT TOOL USED TO PACIFY THE MASSES!

OH, ... WHO'S WINNING?

ROLAND, DOES YOUR DAD EVER BUG YOU ABOUT YOUR LONG HAIR?

NO FUNKY! IN FACT HE LIKES IT THIS WAY!
HE DOES!? WHY?
BATIUK 4-8

IT HIDES THE EARRINGS!

FUNKY WINKERBEAN

I DIDN'T REALIZE IT WAS SO WONDERFUL, FUNKY!

I KNOW WHAT YOU MEAN, LIVINIA!
BATIUK
Publishers-Hall Syndicate, 1972

JUST BEING ABLE TO GET OUT AND COMMUNE WITH NATURE!

ISN'T IT GREAT TO GET AWAY FROM EVERYONE AND JUST BE YOURSELF?
4-9
← ROCK FESTIVAL

GO DIRECTLY TO JAIL!

YOU WILL NOT BE RELEASED ON BAIL, BUT YOU COULD GET A REDUCED SENTENCE IF YOU WILL NAME YOUR FELLOW CONSPIRATORS.

SOMEONE'S BEEN GETTING CUTE WITH THE COMMUNITY CHEST CARDS!

AH! MY CHANCE FOR REVENGE!

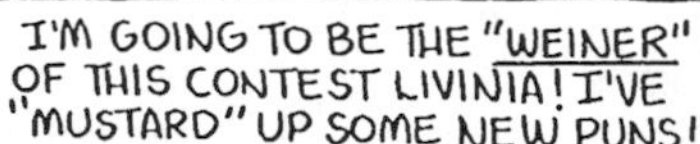

I'M GOING TO BE THE "WEINER" OF THIS CONTEST LIVINIA! I'VE "MUSTARD" UP SOME NEW PUNS!

I "RELISH" YOUR CHALLENGE FUNKY, BUT I'M AFRAID YOU'LL NEVER "KETCHUP" TO ME!

WE HAVEN'T CROSSED PUNS FOR THE LAST TIME YOU FIEND!

AREN'T YOU GOING TO DO ANYTHING ABOUT THAT BIG CLOD WHO'S BEEN PUSHING YOU AROUND, LES?
NO FUNKY!

WELL, YOU KNOW WHAT THEY SAY: 'A COWARD DIES A THOUSAND DEATHS, A HERO ONLY ONE'!

I KNOW! WE COWARDS TAKE A LOT OF PRIDE IN OUR ENDURANCE!

SAY FUNKY, WOULD YOU TURN UP THE VOLUME ON MY AMPLIFIER?
SURE ROLAND!
4-13 BATIUK
Publishers-Hall Syndicate, 1972

LET'S SEE NOW... THAT SHOULD DO IT!

IT'S ALWAYS NICE TO SEE SOMEONE TRANSFIGURED BY BEAUTIFUL MUSIC!

WHAT ARE YOU READING LES?
THE SENSUOUS SPARROW FUNKY!

OH YEAH? HOW IS IT?
BATIUK

IT'S FOR THE BIRDS!
4-14
Publishers-Hall Syndicate, 1972

BOY! WAS THAT TEST A BEAR! I MISSED THE LAST QUESTION COMPLETELY, FUNKY!

I DIDN'T PUT ANYTHING ON MY PAPER FOR THAT ONE EITHER, LES!
Publishers-Hall Syndicate, 1972 BATIUK
4-15

I KNOW!

FUNKY WINKERBEAN
PRINCIPAL

WAITING TO SEE THE PRINCIPAL, HUH LES?

WELL DON'T LET HIM SCARE YOU!

HE COMES ON STRONG, BUT IT'S MOSTLY A LOT OF YAK!

WHY ARE YOU HERE ANYWAY?.. SMOKING? FIGHTING? GIVING LIP TO A TEACHER?
BATIUK 4-6
Publishers-Hall Syndicate, 1972

NO! I'M SUPPOSED TO TELL HIM MY MOM WILL BAKE FOR THE P.T.A.

BAKING, LIVINIA ?
YOU'RE QUITE PERCEPTIVE FUNKY!

BUT YOU TOLD ME THAT YOU WERE GOING TO SPEND THIS WEEKEND DOING SOMETHING TO HELP THOSE LESS FORTUNATE THAN YOU!
BATIUK Publishers-Hall Syndicate, 1972 4-17

I AM! I'M BAKING A FRUITCAKE FOR HOWARD HUGHES!

YOU GIRLS' LIBBERS CAN'T INTIMIDATE ME!

AND I WON'T BE SWAYED BY MERE THREATS OF VIOLENCE!

CRAAAK!

HOWEVER, ACTUAL VIOLENCE ITSELF WILL SWAY ME QUICKER THAN ANYTHING I KNOW!
Publishers-Hall Syndicate, 1972 4-18 BATIUK

I'VE JUST APPLIED FOR THE JOB AS EDITOR OF THE SCHOOL NEWSPAPER
Publishers-Hall Syndicate, 1972

BUT LES, YOU'VE NEVER HAD ANY NEWSPAPER EXPERIENCE!
BATIUK 4-19

YEAH, BUT I'VE SEEN 'CITIZEN KANE' TWELVE TIMES!

FUNKY, CAN YOU IMAGINE WHAT IT WILL BE LIKE WHEN THE POPULATION OF THE EARTH DOUBLES IN THE NEXT THIRTY YEARS?

YEAH!
BATIUK Publishers-Hall Syndicate, 1972 4-20

IT'LL BE A LOT EASIER TO MEET GIRLS!

ISN'T SPRING NICE FUNKY? MOTHER NATURE'S RENEWAL OF LIFE!
THE SEASON OF LOVE AND HAPPINESS
BATIUK 4-21

BUT WHY CAN'T WE HAVE LOVE AND HAPPINESS EVERY SEASON LIVINIA?

WHAT ARE YOU TRYING TO DO? UPSET THE ECOLOGY OR SOMETHING?

I READ THAT AIR POLLUTION CAN TRAP THE SUN'S HEAT AND CAUSE THE POLAR CAPS TO MELT!

DO YOU KNOW WHAT THAT MEANS FUNKY?

SURE LIVINIA, WE CAN JUST DRIVE TO PITTSBURGH TO GO SURFING!
BATIUK 4-22

FUNKY WINKERBEAN
7

I'D GIVE THAT GIRL A FOUR LES!
NAW! I'D SAY A TWO FUNKY!

THAT ONE IN THE RED IS A NINE IF I EVER SAW ONE!

I THINK IT'S ROTTEN FOR YOU GUYS TO STAND HERE AND RATE GIRLS!

YOU'RE JUST A COUPLE OF CRUEL AND INSENSITIVE CHAUVINISTS!

HEY! THERE'S MARY SUE!
BATIUK 4-23
Publishers-Hall Syndicate, 1972

WOW! TEN!
TEN PLUS!
ONE! ONE!

POWER TO THE PITCHER!
SOCK IT TO 'EM!

RIGHT ON!

IT APPEARS WE'VE JUST ENTERED THE ERA OF RELEVANT BASEBALL CHATTER.
BATIUK

WHAT'S THIS PASS FOR, DEREK?
HALL MONITOR

THE RESTROOM!

I NEED A REST!
BATIUK

WHY DO YOU HAVE TO SIT LIKE THAT TO MEDITATE FUNKY?
IT HELPS ME TO BLOCK OUT THE WORLD AND CLEAR MY THOUGHTS!
BATIUK

WHAT ARE YOU THINKING OF?
HOW PAINFUL THIS IS!

YOU KNOW, FUNKY, THE YOUTH CULTURE REALLY CHANGES QUICKLY!

IT'S HARD TO TELL WHAT DIRECTION IT WILL TAKE NEXT!

I KNOW, LIVINIA, IT MUST BE DRIVING THEM NUTS ON MADISON AVENUE!
BATIUK 4·27

HALL MONITOR

HALL MONITOR

TWELVE O'CLOCK AND ALL'S WELL!
HALL MONITOR
BATIUK 4·28

HMMM...

!?

HEY! WHAT RHYMES WITH RELEVANT?

FUNKY WINKERBEAN
115
COUNSELOR

HI THERE!

WHAT CAN I DO FOR YOU FUNKY?

MAY I USE YOUR PHONE MR. FAIRGOOD?

CERTAINLY! YOU'RE WELCOME TO USE IT!

HELLO, TONY'S? I'D LIKE TO ORDER A SMALL MUSHROOM AND SAUSAGE PIZZA!
BATIUK
4-30

IF I DON'T STUDY FOR MY BIOLOGY TEST I CAN REVIEW FOR MY MATH FINAL!

BUT IF I DO THAT I'LL FLUNK MY 'BIO' TEST!

IN THAT CASE, I WON'T STUDY FOR EITHER ONE!

I PREFER TO GIVE EQUAL WEIGHT TO EACH OF MY ACADEMIC SUBJECTS!
BATIUK
5-1

YOU HAVE TWO MINUTES LEFT BEFORE I COLLECT YOUR TESTS!

OKAY! LET'S START WRAPPING IT UP!

BOY! TIME REALLY FLIES WHEN YOU'RE HAVING FUN!
BATIUK 5-2

WELL, LES, THAT BIG CLOD, BULL BUSHKA, HAS BEEN PICKING ON YOU FOR A FULL WEEK NOW!
BATIUK 5-3

YEAH! I HATE TO DO IT, BUT I GUESS THERE'S ONLY ONE COURSE OF ACTION OPEN TO ME!

WHO DO I SEE ABOUT DROPPING OUT OF SCHOOL?

I'M NOT LOOKING FORWARD TO THIS T.B. TEST, FUNKY!
T.B. TEST

OH! IT WON'T BE THAT BAD, LES!

I DON'T KNOW! I REALLY DIDN'T HAVE A CHANCE TO STUDY FOR IT!

WHAT DO YOU THINK OF MY PAINTING, FUNKY?

YOU'VE BROUGHT NEW MEANING TO THE WORD TRITE!

WHAT ARE YOU DOING, ROLAND?

I'M TRYING TO BOIL AN EGG WITH MENTAL ENERGY, FUNKY!
HAS ANYTHING HAPPENED?

YEAH! SO FAR I'VE MANAGED TO BRING IT UP TO ROOM TEMPERATURE!

FUNKY WINKERBEAN

YOU KNOW FUNKY, OUR SOCIETY REALLY HAS ME BUGGED!

IN WHAT WAY ROLAND?

I'M SICK AND TIRED OF ALL THE SILLY CUSTOMS AND TRADITIONS WE HAVE TO FOLLOW!

I'VE DECIDED I'M NOT GOING TO TAKE PART IN THEM ANY MORE!
© Field Enterprises, Inc., 1972
BATIUK

DOES THAT INCLUDE CUSTOMS LIKE DATING?
5-7

I SAID SILLY CUSTOMS AND TRADITIONS!

IT'S NOT MY FAULT I HAVE PROBLEMS!

MY SOCIETY HAS FAILED ME!

ACCORDING TO THIS... SO HAS YOUR MATH TEACHER!

HI THERE!

I'M MR. FAIRGOOD, THE NEW COUNSELOR FOR THE IMPROVEMENT AND UNDERSTANDING OF STUDENT-FACULTY INTER-RELATIONSHIPS!

WHOOPEE!

IF THIS NEXT SCHOOL LEVY DOESN'T PASS, THEY'LL HAVE TO SHUT DOWN THE SCHOOLS!

THEY CAN'T DO THAT!!

I'VE JUST BEEN MOVED NEXT TO MARY SUE SWEETWATER IN STUDY HALL!

THERE'S NOTHING LIKE LYING DOWN IN THE DARK AND LISTENING TO YOUR FAVORITE L.P.
STATE

STATE

I CAN'T WAIT TILL I GET A RECORD PLAYER!
STATE
BATIUK 5-11

CAN I COPY YOUR MATH HOMEWORK, FUNKY?
© Field Enterprises, Inc., 1972

WHY? YOU COPIED IT LAST NIGHT, LES!

THAT'S RIGHT! SOMETIMES I FORGET HOW CONSCIENTIOUS I REALLY AM!
BATIUK 5-12

I'M WRITING A SONG THAT WILL EMBODY THE HISTORY OF ROCK N' ROLL IN ALASKA!
© Field Enterprises, Inc., 1972

WHAT DO YOU PLAN TO CALL IT, FUNKY?

ESKIMO PIE!
BATIUK 5-13

FUNKY WINKERBEAN

WHAT'S UP LES?

I'VE BEEN THINKING ABOUT THE DRAFT FUNKY!
BATIUK

SO I'M WRITING TO FIND OUT WHAT MY CHANCES WILL BE WHEN MY YEAR COMES UP FOR THE LOTTERY!

THAT'S A GOOD IDEA LES!
5-14

WHO ARE YOU WRITING TO? THE DRAFT BOARD?

NO! JIMMY THE GREEK!

WHAT'S THAT ON YOUR FINGER, FUNKY?
IT'S MY PET BAT, LES!

ARE YOU KIDDING? WHY WOULD ANYONE WANT A PET BAT?
5-15
BATIUK

HE'S A WATCH BAT! IF I'M EVER ATTACKED, HE FLIES FOR HELP!

TELL ME, FUNKY, ARE ALL BATS THAT SAME UGLY GRAY COLOR?

OF COURSE NOT, LIVINIA! THEY ALSO COME IN RED FOR FESTIVE OCCASIONS!

WE BAT ENTHUSIASTS CAN GET QUITE SARCASTIC!
5-16
BATIUK

WHAT'S YOUR PET BAT DOING, FUNKY?
OH, HE'S SLEEPING!

BUT I THOUGHT BATS HUNG UPSIDE DOWN WHEN THEY SLEPT!
HE CAN'T!

THE BLOOD RUNS TO HIS HEAD!
BATIUK 5/17

YOU'RE MY CHEMISTRY PARTNER, DEREK?
SOMETHING WRONG?

WELL, I WAS KIND OF HOPING FOR A GIRL!

I'M NOT TOO CHOKED UP ABOUT THE DEAL MYSELF!
BATIUK 5-18

IS THIS A HEAVY RECORD, MAN?

OH YOU BET! IT'S HEAVY HEAVY, FAR OUT, RIGHT-ON, AND GROOVY!
5-13
BATIUK

SMILE WHEN YOU SAY THAT!

SOLVING THE PROBLEMS MANKIND FACES, WILL BE UP TO YOU PEOPLE IN THIS VERY CLASSROOM!

SMALL WONDER I'VE BEEN SO DEPRESSED LATELY
5-20
BATIUK

FUNKY WINKERBEAN
EDUCATIONAL FACILITATOR

YOU KNOW FUNKY, SOME OF THE NEWER IDEAS IN EDUCATION ARE REALLY EXCITING!

I KNOW WHAT YOU MEAN, LES!

HOWEVER, WE JUST CAN'T THROW AWAY ALL OF THE OLD METHODS!

IN FACT THERE ARE SOME THINGS I KIND OF MISS!
© Field Enterprises, Inc., 1972
BATIUK

LIKE WHAT?

WELL, LIKE A MILK AND COOKIE BREAK!

IS THAT THE SAMPLE OF POLLUTED WATER THAT YOU'RE TAKING TO SCHOOL, LES?
YEAH, FUNKY!

IT'S HARD TO BELIEVE THAT WATER FROM A STREAM CAN BE THAT BLACK AND POLLUTED!

WELL NOT QUITE! I THREW IN A LITTLE FOOD COLORING TO GIVE IT SOME PUNCH!

I'D LIKE TO SEE A FAR-OUT PSYCHEDELIC SHIRT THAT'LL REALLY MAKE ME LOOK MOD AND "IN"!

YEAH! FAR OUT! THAT'S IT!

UH, ... DO YOU HAVE ONE WITH A BUTTON-DOWN COLLAR?

BOY! THREE BIG TESTS TO CRAM FOR THIS WEEKEND!

OF COURSE THE IMPORTANT THING IS WHAT WE GET OUT OF IT!

YEAH! AN ULCER AND A NERVOUS TWITCH!

WHAT ARE YOU THINKING ABOUT, FUNKY?

OH, I WAS JUST THINKING ABOUT SCHOOL AND WHERE I GO FROM HERE, LES!

I USUALLY GO HOME!
© Field Enterprises, Inc., 1972
BATIUK
5-25

© Field Enterprises, Inc., 1972
I'D LIKE TO KNOW IF YOU HAVE A BOOK THAT WILL MAKE ME A POISED AND CONFIDENT LADY KILLER!
BATIUK

HAVE YOU TRIED THE SCIENCE FICTION SECTION?
5-26

YOU KNOW, FUNKY, OUR GENERATION IS PROBABLY THE MOST LITERATE AND WELL READ IN HISTORY!

HEY! MY COMIC BOOK FINALLY CAME!

OF COURSE, THERE'LL ALWAYS BE ROOM FOR A LITTLE IMPROVEMENT!
© Field Enterprises, Inc., 1972
BATIUK
5-27

FUNKY WINKERBEAN
HI!

BEFORE YOU SHOOT ME DOWN, LIVINIA, HEAR ME OUT!

FIRST, I'LL TAKE YOU TO THE LATEST NEW MOVIE!
BATIUK 5-28
© Field Enterprises, Inc., 1972

THEN WE'LL HIT THAT NEW SPOT, THE PSYCHEDELIC ARMPIT!

AND HEAR THAT GREAT NEW BAND THE RADIANT RADISH!

WOW!

NO!

I WAS AFRAID OF THIS!
© Field Enterprises, Inc., 1972

THE COUNTY HEALTH BOARD HAS CONDEMNED MY LOCKER!
UNSAFE
5-29
BATIUK

YOU KNOW, FUNKY, THAT MARY SUE SWEETWATER IS REALLY SOMETHING!
5-30

I SWEAR, WHEN SHE WALKED INTO HOMEROOM THIS MORNING, I COULD HEAR BELLS RING!

SHE WAS ALMOST TARDY AGAIN, HUH?
© Field Enterprises, Inc., 1972
BATIUK

SURELY YOU GIRLS LIBBERS MUST BE WILLING TO MAKE SOME COMPROMISES!

WELL... WHAT'S YOUR ANSWER?
© Field Enterprises, Inc., 1972

CRAAK!
5-31

A CLASSIC EXAMPLE OF NEGATIVE FEEDBACK!
BATIUK

I THINK YOU SHOULD STAND UP TO THAT BIG OX WHO KEEPS BUGGING YOU, LES!
6-1

AND IF YOU NEED ANY HELP PAL, ... YOU KNOW WHERE TO GET IT!
© Field Enterprises, Inc., 1972
BATIUK

THE PRINCIPAL'S OFFICE IS JUST DOWN THE HALL!

I'M SORRY, LES, BUT I CAN'T GO OUT WITH YOU FRIDAY!

HOW LONG CAN YOU KEEP ME WAITING, LIVINIA?
© Field Enterprises, Inc., 1972
BATIUK
6-2

I DON'T KNOW! LET'S TRY FOR A RECORD!

FOR THE LAST TIME, LES, I WILL NOT GO OUT WITH YOU! NOW WILL YOU GET OFF MY BACK YOU CREEP?!!
6-3
BATIUK

© Field Enterprises, Inc., 1972

YOU'VE JUST GIVEN MY HUMILITY A TERRIFIC BOOST!

FUNKY WINKERBEAN

WELL, LES, YOU FINALLY GOT A DATE WITH MARY SUE SWEETWATER!

© Field Enterprises, Inc., 1972
BATIUK 6-4
HOW DO YOU FEEL?

I'M SO NERVOUS, I CAN'T EAT ANYTHING, FUNKY!

.. AND I HAVEN'T BEEN ABLE TO SLEEP ALL WEEK!

AND ALL OF MY GRADES ARE STARTING TO DROP!

I'VE NEVER BEEN SO HAPPY IN MY WHOLE LIFE!

IS YOUR DAD'S COMPANY GOING TO DO ANYTHING ABOUT INDUSTRIAL POLLUTION, FUNKY?
BATIUK
© Field Enterprises, Inc., 1972
6-5

THEY EXPECT TO IN THE NEAR FUTURE, LIVINIA!
WHAT ARE THEY WAITING FOR?

MANDATORY LEGISLATION!

I'VE DECIDED TO FURTHER MY EDUCATION WITH AN ENRICHMENT PROGRAM THIS SUMMER, FUNKY!
6-6

WHAT ARE YOU GOING TO BE DOING, LES?
BATIUK

I'M TAKING REMEDIAL MATH IN SUMMER SCHOOL!
© Field Enterprises, Inc., 1972

DON'T FEEL BAD ABOUT GOING TO SUMMER SCHOOL, LES!

JUST LOOK ON IT AS A DIFFERENT AND ENRICHING EXPERIENCE!
© Field Enterprises, Inc., 1972
BATIUK
6-7

WHY DON'T YOU SIGN UP WITH ME, FUNKY?

AND GO TO SCHOOL IN THE SUMMER!? ARE YOU NUTS?

THIS IS INTERESTING...
© Field Enterprises, Inc., 1972
6-8

IT SAYS THAT PEOPLE WITH LOWER INCOMES AND LESS EDUCATION TEND TO WATCH BASEBALL!

STRIKE THREE!
BATIUK

BOY! YOU SURE CAN FIND SOME INTERESTING THINGS WHEN YOU CLEAN UP A RIVER!

WHAT'S THAT YOU'VE GOT THERE, FUNKY?
© Field Enterprises, Inc., 1972
BATIUK
6-9

OH, IT'S JUST AN OLD ECOLOGY BUTTON!

YOU KNOW, I REALLY FEEL CLOSE TO YOU, DEREK!
© Field Enterprises, Inc., 1972
BATIUK

WE BOTH KNOW WHAT IT FEELS LIKE TO BE REJECTED!
6-10

WHAT'S YOUR EXCUSE?

FUNKY WINKERBEAN
Hi!

MR. FAIRGOOD! YOU'RE GOING TO BE MY MATH TEACHER IN SUMMER SCHOOL?
THAT'S RIGHT, LES!
BATIUK

BUT I THOUGHT YOU WERE A COUNSELOR!
6-11
© Field Enterprises, Inc., 1972

I AM, LES, BUT OCCASIONALLY I LIKE TO GET BACK INTO THE CLASSROOM!

IT GIVES ME A BETTER UNDERSTANDING OF THE PROBLEMS AND FRUSTRATIONS THAT CONFRONT YOU STUDENTS!

IT HELPS ME TO RELATE TO YOU STUDENTS IN A MORE MEANINGFUL WAY!

YOU NEED THE MONEY HUH?
DESPERATELY!

DAD! THIS IS MY FRIEND, FUNKY WINKERBEAN!
6-12

© Field Enterprises, Inc., 1972

DO I SALUTE HIM, OR SING THE STAR SPANGLED BANNER?
BATIUK

LES, DO YOU EVER LIE BACK AND IMAGINE THAT YOU CAN SEE THINGS IN THE SHAPES OF THE CLOUDS?
BATIUK

SURE FUNKY! FOR INSTANCE THAT ONE LOOKS LIKE A BIG GRAPEFRUIT!
6-13

THAT'S THE SUN!
© Field Enterprises, Inc., 1972

WHEN YOU'RE LYING ALONE IN YOUR ROOM, YOU HAVE TIME TO THINK!
STAT
© Field Enterprises, Inc., 1972
6-14

WHEN YOU'RE LYING ALONE IN YOUR ROOM, YOU HAVE TIME TO FIGURE OUT HOW YOU RELATE TO THE VAST UNIVERSE!
STAT
BATIUK

WHEN YOU'RE LYING ALONE IN YOUR ROOM, YOU DON'T HAVE TO MOW THE LAWN!
STAT

I PUT AN AD IN THE PAPER FOR A SUMMER JOB AND I ONLY GOT ONE REPLY!
BATIUK
6-15

WHO FROM?

MY MOM!
© Field Enterprises, Inc., 1972

THE OLDER GENERATION HAS DONE NOTHING BUT LIE TO US, LES!
6-16

THAT'S FOR SURE, DEREK!
© Field Enterprises, Inc., 1972
BATIUK

TAKE THAT BUSINESS ABOUT THE TOOTH FAIRY!

HAS ALL OF THIS MEDITATING DONE YOU ANY GOOD, FUNKY?
© Field Enterprises, Inc., 1972

CERTAINLY, ROLAND!
6-17

IT'S OPENED MY EYES TO A WHOLE NEW WORLD OF THINGS I CAN'T UNDERSTAND!
BATIUK

FUNKY WINKERBEAN

WHAT ARE YOU DOING THIS SUMMER, FUNKY?

I JUST PLAN TO GO SWIMMING EVERY DAY, DEREK!

MAN! IS THAT EVER A SELFISH ATTITUDE!
© Field Enterprises, Inc., 1972
6-18

YOU'RE JUST GOING TO IGNORE ALL OF THE PROBLEMS WE FACE?
BATIUK

WHAT WOULD IT BE LIKE IF EVERYONE FELT THAT WAY?

THE POOLS WOULD BE VERY CROWDED!

LOOK AT THAT SPIDER, LES!

HE HAS THAT FLY CAUGHT IN HIS WEB, BUT HE WON'T GO NEAR IT! HE JUST STAYS IN THE MIDDLE!

MAYBE HE DOESN'T WANT TO GET INVOLVED!
© Field Enterprises, Inc., 1972
BATIUK 6-19

THESE GOLF TOURNAMENTS ARE REALLY FUN, FUNKY!
BATIUK

WOW! LOOK UP THE FAIRWAY! THAT'S JACK NICKLAUS!
6-20

WHAT DO YOU THINK OUR CHANCES ARE OF TALKING TO HIM?

PRETTY GOOD! YOU'RE STANDING ON HIS GOLF BALL!
© Field Enterprises, Inc., 1972

DOES THAT CUTE BLOND LIFEGUARD MAKE YOU NERVOUS, LES?
© Field Enterprises, Inc., 1972
6-21

ARE YOU KIDDING, FUNKY? I DON'T GO TO PIECES JUST BECAUSE I SEE A PRETTY GIRL!

THAT'S GOOD, BECAUSE I THOUGHT YOU WORE YOUR SHOES INTO THE POOL BECAUSE YOU WERE NERVOUS!
BATIUK

WELL, I DID WHAT YOU SAID! I ASKED THAT NEW LIFE-GUARD OUT AND TOLD HER I WOULDN'T TAKE NO FOR AN ANSWER!
6-22

WAY TO GO, LES!

I TOOK 'GET LOST' FOR AN ANSWER INSTEAD!
BATIUK

THIS UNDERGROUND PAPER OF MINE IS GOING TO EXPOSE THE FALLACIES OF OUR MATERIALISTIC, CAPITALISTIC SOCIETY!

WHERE ARE YOU GETTING THE FUNDS TO PRINT IT?
6-23

WE'RE HOLDING A CARWASH AND BAKESALE SATURDAY!
BATIUK

I CAN'T GO WITH YOU, FUNKY! I'VE GOT TO FINISH THIS HOMEWORK!

SUMMER SCHOOL ONLY LASTS TILL NOON! WHY DON'T YOU DO IT IN THE AFTERNOON?
6-24

AND MISS MY SOAP OPERAS?
BATIUK

FUNKY WINKERBEAN

LOOK AT THIS, FUNKY!

MY FIRST ORGANICALLY GROWN FOOD!

IT WAS GROWN WITHOUT ANY INSECTICIDES OR UNNATURAL CHEMICALS!
© Field Enterprises, Inc., 1972
6-25

THAT'S TERRIFIC, LES!

YOUR FIRST ORGANICALLY GROWN STRAWBERRY!

THAT'S A TOMATO!
BATIUK

WHAT'S THIS?!
WHAT DOES IT LOOK LIKE?

A FLAG!
© Field Enterprises, Inc., 1972

YOU WIN!
6-26
BATIUK

WHY ARE YOU WEARING YOUR SHADES, DEREK?

IT'S COMPLETLY OVERCAST TODAY!
© Field Enterprises, Inc., 1972

SOMETIMES I LIKE TO MOVE AROUND INCOGNITO!
6-27
BATIUK

ISN'T IT ROMANTIC TO SIT ON A BEACH AT NIGHT, FUNKY?
6-28

OUT UNDER A FULL MOON!
© Field Enterprises, Inc., 1972

LISTENING TO THE SOUNDS OF FROGS AND CRICKETS COUGHING IN THE NIGHT AIR!
BATIUK

MOST OF THESE ORGANIC FOOD RECIP ES ARE PRETTY COMPLICATED!
© Field Enterprises, Inc., 1972

DO YOU HAVE ANY THINGS THAT ARE EASY TO PREPARE?
HOME SWEET HOME

HOW ABOUT ONE OF OUR ORGANIC T.V. DINNERS!
BATIUK 6-29

DO YOU HAVE ANY GUM, LIVINIA?
YEAH, JUST A SECOND, FUNKY!
© Field Enterprises, Inc., 1972

HEY! THIS PIECE HAS ALREADY BEEN CHEWED!
6-30

I KNOW! THAT'S MY LOANER PIECE!
BATIUK

YOU SHOULDN'T EAT SO MUCH CANDY ALL THE TIME, ROLAND!
© Field Enterprises, Inc., 1972
7-1

WHAT HAPPENED TO YOUR ORGANIC FOOD CAMPAIGN?

THIS IS A CHOCOLATE COATED SOY BEAN BAR!
BATIUK

FUNKY WINKERBEAN
SWIMMING POOL

WHAT?! 'SWIMMERS WITH LONG HAIR MUST WEAR BATHING CAPS'!
POOL RULES:

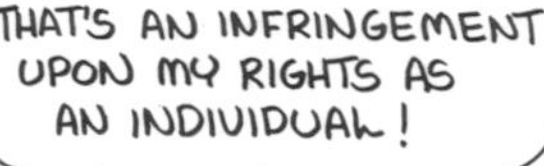
THAT'S AN INFRINGEMENT UPON MY RIGHTS AS AN INDIVIDUAL!

© Field Enterprises, Inc., 1972
BATIUK

I'D LIKE TO SEE ONE GOOD REASON WHY I SHOULD WEAR ONE!

UH,... LET ME GUESS!

YOU'LL TOSS ME OUT ON MY EAR RIGHT?
RRR-RIGHT!
7-2

I'M ALWAYS OPEN TO A LOGICAL DISCUSSION OF AN ISSUE!

SIR! I'D LIKE YOU TO TAKE A LOOK AT MY UNDERGROUND PAPER!

IT EXPLAINS HOW THE WORKING CLASS IS BEING EXPLOITED AND WHAT CAN BE DONE ABOUT IT!

PERHAPS I SHOULD CONSIDER HIRING A PAPER BOY!

THE POLICE! WELL, I GUESS I SHOULD HAVE EXPECTED THIS!

MY PAPER HAS BEEN MAKING THINGS A LITTLE TOO HOT FOR THE LOCAL POLITICAL FAT CATS, HUH?

NO, ACTUALLY WE'RE HERE TO PRESENT YOU WITH THIS JUNIOR ACHIEVEMENT AWARD!

WHAT HAPPENS IF YOU DON'T DEVELOP THESE PICTURES RIGHT?

I'M TAKEN OUT BACK AND FLOGGED TO YOUR SATISFACTION!

MY COMPLIMENTS TO YOUR CUSTOMER RELATIONS DEPARTMENT!

WHAT A BEAUTIFUL DAY!
© Field Enterprises, Inc., 1972

IT'S JUST GREAT TO BE ALIVE! WHAT COULD POSSIBLY SPOIL IT?
BATIUK 7-6

IT'S HERE AT LAST! THE BOOK THAT'S GOING TO CHANGE MY LIFE AND MAKE ME PART OF THE 'IN' CROWD!

PETER SMOOTH'S ADVICE TO THE MODERN TEENAGER.

BATIUK 7-7
© Field Enterprises, Inc., 1972
COPYRIGHT 1941

I CAN'T BELIEVE ALL OF THIS BARBARISM IN OUR CITY STREETS!

IT'S DISGUSTING! THEY SHOULD CUT HAIR IN THE SHOPS!

BATIUK 7-8
© Field Enterprises, Inc., 1972
THE SCARY PART IS,... I THINK HE WAS SERIOUS!

FUNKY WINKERBEAN

WHAT ARE YOU DOING, LIVINIA?

I'M WRITING A LETTER TO A CONVICT IN PRISON, FUNKY!

IT'S PART OF A PROGRAM WHERE PEOPLE IN PRISON CAN CORRESPOND WITH SOMEONE IN THE OUTSIDE WORLD!

IT GIVES THEM INFORMATION ABOUT WHAT'S GOING ON, AND HELPS CHEER THEM UP!
THAT'S VERY COMMENDABLE!
OF COURSE, DURING THE SCHOOL YEAR, THEY WRITE LETTERS TO CHEER ME UP!
BATIUK
7-9

YOU KNOW, LES, THERE'S NOTHING LIKE GETTING OUT TO THE OLD POOL!

SLIP!

WIPE OUT!
© Field Enterprises, Inc., 1972
BATIUK 7-10

AND NOW WE LEAVE THE CONVENTION FLOOR AND GO TO THE MOUNT PALOMAR OBSERVATORY...
© Field Enterprises, Inc., 1972

WHERE WE WILL HEAR A REPORT ON HOW RECENT SUNSPOT ACTIVITY COULD AFFECT THE VOTING!
BATIUK 7-11

THAT'S WHAT I LIKE,... IN-DEPTH REPORTING!

NOW REMEMBER, LIVINIA!
BATIUK 7-12

IN CHESS, THE KING CAN ONLY MOVE ONE SQUARE AT A TIME, WHILE THE QUEEN CAN MOVE AS MANY AS SHE WANTS!

GLORIA STEINEM WOULD LIKE THAT!
© Field Enterprises, Inc., 1972

THESE PICTURES AREN'T WHAT I WANTED FOR MY UNDERGROUND PAPER, FUNKY!

THESE ARE ALL PICTURES OF GIRLS IN BIKINIS! I WANT SOMETHING RELEVANT!

IT APPEARS WE'RE DEALING WITH VAST IDEOLOGICAL DIFFERENCES!
BATIUK 7-13

WHAT'S GOING ON, FUNKY?
7-14
BATIUK

I'M CANVASSING THE NEIGHBORHOOD TO REGISTER AS MANY NEW VOTERS AS I CAN, LES!

THAT SOUNDS GOOD!

WHAT KIND OF PRIZE DO YOU GET?

WHO'S AT THE DOOR, ROLAND?
7-15
BATIUK

THERE'S A GUY SELLING SOME STUPID THING!

TELL HIM WE'VE ALREADY GOT ONE!

FUNKY WINKERBEAN
HEY!

ROLAND! I DIDN'T EXPECT TO SEE YOU AROUND!

WHAT HAPPENED?

I THOUGHT YOU WERE GOING TO 'DO YOUR OWN THING' AND TRY LIVING OFF OF THE LAND THIS SUMMER!
BATIUK

AWAY IN YOUR OWN CABIN IN THE WILDERNESS SOMEPLACE!
7-16
© Field Enterprises, Inc., 1972

I WAS!

BUT THERE WASN'T ANY PLACE TO PLUG IN MY NITE-LIGHT!

JUST THINK, ROLAND! THREE WHOLE DAYS AT A ROCK FESTIVAL!

NOTHING BUT GOOD MUSIC AND GOOD VIBES! WHERE'S LES?
© Field Enterprises, Inc., 1972
BATIUK 7-17

WELL IT MIGHT RAIN YA KNOW!

WELL, IT LOOKS LIKE THE MUSIC HAS STOPPED FOR THE NIGHT!

WE MIGHT AS WELL SACK OUT!
© Field Enterprises, Inc., 1972
BATIUK 7-18

OKAY! I'LL TAKE THE FIRST WATCH!

FAR OUT MAN! ARE YOU PART OF SOME NEW RELIGIOUS SECT?

NO! I JUST WORE THIS IN CASE IT RAINS!
BATIUK 7-19
© Field Enterprises, Inc., 1972

THE PEOPLE AT THESE ROCK FESTIVALS ARE GETTING FREAKIER ALL THE TIME!

HEY, LOOK, LES!
© Field Enterprises, Inc. 1972

THEY'RE UNPLUGGING SIXTEEN OF THE THIRTY-FOUR AMPLIFIERS!
BATIUK 7-20

THEY MUST BE PLANNING TO DO SOME BALLADS!

YOU KNOW, ROLAND, THEY SAY THAT HEARING CAN BE IMPAIRED BY LOUD ROCK MUSIC!

DO YOU THINK THE SOUND HAS DAMAGED YOUR HEARING?
© Field Enterprises, Inc. 1972
BATIUK 7-21

CLEARING? YEAH I THINK IT IS CLEARING!

HOW DO MOVIE PRODUCERS EXPECT PEOPLE TO SIT THROUGH SADISTIC AND VIOLENT MOVIES LIKE THIS?

I AGREE! IT'S SICKENING!
© Field Enterprises, Inc. 1972
BATIUK 7-22

WANT SOME MORE POPCORN?

FUNKY WINKERBEAN
PARK

YOU KNOW, I HAVE TO ADMIRE YOU, FUNKY!

YOU REALLY ACT NATURAL ON A DATE!

YOU DIDN'T TRY TO IMPRESS ME BY TAKING ME TO EXPENSIVE PLACES!

AND YOU DIDN'T TRY TO SHOW-OFF OR ACT PHONY!

YOU JUST RELAXED AND LET YOUR OWN PERSONALITY COME THROUGH!
© Field Enterprises, Inc., 1972
BATIUK 7-23

OF COURSE IT WASN'T MUCH FUN!

WHEN YOU'RE IN A PARK, LES, IT'S NICE TO JUST SIT BACK AND OBSERVE 'MOTHER NATURE'!
BATIUK 7-24

SHE'S PUT ON A LITTLE WEIGHT!
. . .

YOU KNOW, DEREK, SUMMER VACATION IS KIND OF BORING!

IN FACT, IN SOME WAYS, I SORT OF MISS GOING TO SCHOOL!

HOMEWORK!

THANKS! I NEEDED THAT!
BATIUK 7-25

PAPERBACK

HANDBOOK FOR THE OVERTHROW OF THE ESTABLISHMENT
BATIUK 7-26

LIBRARY OF CONGRESS CATALOG CARD NUMBER: 3066-75

WOULD YOU LIKE TO GO TO THE DANCE AT THE REC CENTER, ROBIN?

YOU WOULD? TERRIFIC!

I WAS GETTING WORRIED! YOU'RE THE THIRD GIRL I'VE ASKED!
© Field Enterprises, Inc., 1972
BATIUK 7-27

CLICK!

I LIKE TO BE WITH YOU, LIVINIA!

YOU'RE NOT LIKE OTHER GIRLS!

BATIUK 7-28
THIS BETTER BE GOOD!

I SAY YOU'RE WRONG FUNKY!
BATIUK 7-29

SOUTH IS THAT DIRECTION!

SEE? THE MOSS IS GROWING ON THE
SIDE!

FUNKY WINKERBEAN
UNDER-GROUND PAPER

ROLAND, I'VE GOT A COUPLE OF THINGS TO TALK ABOUT!

SHOOT, FUNKY!

FIRST, I FINISHED THAT ARTICLE FOR YOUR UNDERGROUND PAPER ON HOW WORKERS ARE EXPLOITED WHILE THE BOSSES GET RICHER!

TERRIFIC! WE'LL USE THAT ON THE FRONT PAGE!

BATIUK 7-30

WHAT ELSE DID YOU WANT?

A RAISE!

YOU KNOW, ROLAND, IT WON'T BE LONG BEFORE WE'LL HAVE THE DRAFT TO THINK ABOUT!

IF YOU WERE DRAFTED, WHAT WOULD YOU TRY TO GET INTO?
BATIUK 7-31

CANADA!
© Field Enterprises, Inc., 1972

THAT'S A TYPICAL JULY SKY UP THERE, FUNKY!
© Field Enterprises, Inc., 1972

THIS IS AUGUST LES!
BATIUK 8-1

NOW THERE'S SOMETHING YOU DON'T SEE EVERY DAY,... A TYPICAL JULY SKY IN AUGUST!

HEY!

THERE ISN'T ANY MEAT IN THIS BUN!!
BATIUK 8-2
© Field Enterprises, Inc., 1972

PARTICULAR, AIN'T HE?

I'M FILLING OUT MY PUNCH CARD FOR THE COMPUTER DANCE!

WHAT DO YOU THINK I SHOULD PUT DOWN, FUNKY?
BATIUK 8-3

FRUIT PUNCH WOULD BE NICE!

TELL ME SOMETHING, DEREK!

WHO'S A BLACK THAT YOU REALLY LOOK UP TO?
BATIUK 8-4

WILT CHAMBERLAIN!
© Field Enterprises, Inc., 1972

WICKED WANDA, YOUR HOSTILITY AND AGGRESSION STEM FROM THE FACT THAT YOU CAN'T COMMUNICATE OPENLY!

YOU'VE GOT TO LEARN TO RAP!
© Field Enterprises, Inc., 1972

RAP!

I'D BITE MY TONGUE BUT I THINK I ALREADY DID!
BATIUK 8-5

FUNKY WINKERBEAN
HEAD FOODS
HEAD LETTUCE

WHAT'S SO GREAT ABOUT ORGANIC FOODS ANYWAY?

THEY DON'T ADD ANY POISONS TO YOUR BODY!

AND THEY AREN'T LOADED WITH ALL KINDS OF FATS AND GREASES WHICH LACK NUTRITION!

THEY'RE GROWN FREE OF ANY UNNATURAL CHEMICALS AND ARE JUST THE WAY NATURE INTENDED THEM TO BE!
BATIUK 8-6
© Field Enterprises, Inc., 1972

HURRY UP JOHN! YOUR PIZZA'S GETTING COLD!!

AMAZING!
WANTED FOR HIJACKING

YOU'D THINK WITH ALL OF THE HIJACKERS AROUND ...
BATIUK
8-7

THEY WOULDN'T NEED TO ADVERTISE!
WANTED FOR HIJACKING

IT SAYS HERE THAT MENTAL ILLNESS STRIKES ONE OUT OF EVERY THREE PEOPLE!

YOU LOSE, BUCKWHEAT!
BATIUK 8-8

HEY, FUNKY, FEAST YOUR EYEBALLS ON THAT GIRL IN THE PINK BIKINI!

EENY, MINY, MO AND MEENY,
I'LL TAKE THE GIRL IN THE PINK BIKINI!
BATIUK 8-9

THAT'S PRETTY GOOD!
BIKINIS ALWAYS BRING OUT THE POET IN ME!

THIS IS A BLACK AND WHITE T.V. DINNER! ARE YOU SURE YOU DON'T WANT A COLOR T.V. DINNER?

WHAT'S THE DIFFERENCE?
© Field Enterprises, Inc., 1972
BATIUK 8-10

IN A COLOR T.V. DINNER, THE PEAS ARE ORANGE, THE MEAT IS BLUE AND THE GRAVY'S MAGENTA!

SMOKY THE FISH
SAYS:
OIL SLICKS CAN BE FIRE HAZARDS!
BE CAREFUL!!
BATIUK
8-11

SMOKY THE FISH?

DOESN'T WRITING SUCH A NASTY LETTER TO THE PRESIDENT WORRY YOU?

NO! I FEEL THAT IT'S A CITIZEN'S DUTY TO LET THE ADMINISTRATION KNOW EXACTLY HOW HE FEELS!
© Field Enterprises, Inc., 1972
BATIUK 8-12

BESIDES, I SIGNED YOUR NAME!

FUNKY WINKERBEAN
EYES RIGHT, SPORTS FANS!

BOY! I SURE WISH I KNEW THAT CUTE BLOND LIFEGUARD, FUNKY!

WELL, WHY DON'T YOU PADDLE ON OVER AND TALK TO HER, LES!
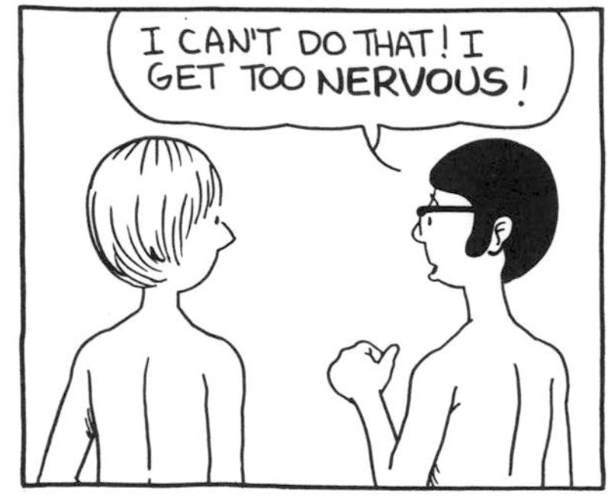
I CAN'T DO THAT! I GET TOO NERVOUS!

LOOK, YOU'LL DO OKAY IF YOU JUST REMEMBER TO ACT CONFIDENT...

AND BE YOURSELF!
© Field Enterprises, Inc., 1972
BATIUK 8-13

WILL YOU MAKE UP YOUR MIND?

HERE I AM NEGOTIATING MY LUNAR ROVER ACROSS THE DESOLATE SURFACE OF THE MOON!

HERE I AM APPROACHING MYSTERIOUS CRATERS!

HERE I AM IN THE FLOWER BED!
BATIUK 8-14
© Field Enterprises, Inc., 1972

WELL, HERE I STAND ON THE HIGH DIVE!

IF I DIVE OFF HERE, I'LL REALLY IMPRESS THAT CUTE BLOND LIFEGUARD!
BATIUK 8-15
© Field Enterprises, Inc., 1972

FAT LOT OF GOOD THAT'LL DO ME IN THE HOSPITAL!

I'VE BEEN DEBATING WHETHER OR NOT TO JUMP FROM THIS HIGH DIVE FOR A LONG TIME! I WONDER IF ANYONE HAS NOTICED?

YOU IN TROUBLE, MAC?

THEY'VE NOTICED!
BATIUK 8-16
© Field Enterprises, Inc., 1972

LES, WE'VE GOT TO HELP YOU OVERCOME YOUR SHYNESS WITH GIRLS!

YEAH, FUNKY, A GIRL NEVER GETS A CHANCE TO KNOW THE REAL ME!
BATIUK 8-17

YEAH,... WELL WE'VE GOT TO THINK POSITIVE AND IGNORE THAT POSSIBILITY!

PEOPLE BETTER GET ON THE STICK AND START DOING SOMETHING ABOUT OVERPOPULATION!
BATIUK 8-18

YEAH, I AGREE!

I WISH I'D HAVE STARTED SOONER MYSELF!

GET A LOAD OF THIS, FUNKY!
BATIUK 8-19

I ENTERED A CONTEST IN OUR LOCAL PAPER AND GOT TWO TICKETS TO A BASEBALL GAME!

WHAT DID THE WINNER GET?

FUNKY WINKERBEAN

LOOK, LES, I JUST DON'T WANT TO GO OUT WITH YOU!

NOR WILL I WANT TO GO OUT WITH YOU IN THE FUTURE!

I WILL **NEVER** WANT TO GO OUT WITH YOU!

ABSOLUTELY, POSITIVELY, NEVER!

NEVER, NEVER, NEVER, NEVER, NEVER!
BATIUK 8-20
© Field Enterprises, Inc., 1'72

YOU WANT MORE TIME TO THINK ABOUT IT, RIGHT?

SO WHAT'S WRONG, FUNKY? LOT'S OF PEOPLE HAVE PET S!

I DIDN'T SAY THERE WAS ANYTHING WRONG, LES!

IT'S JUST THAT I NEVER HEARD OF A MOSQUITO-FARM BEFORE!
BATIUK 8-21
© Field Enterprises, Inc., 1972

I HATE DARTS, LES! I JUST CAN'T GET ANY ACCURACY!
OH, I'M ACCURATE ENOUGH, DEREK!

BATIUK 8-22
© Field Enterprises, Inc., 1972
MY PROBLEM IS DISTANCE!

THAT SURE DOESN'T SMELL LIKE SUNTAN LOTION, LES!

BATIUK 8-23
© Field Enterprises, Inc., 1972
OH! WELL WHAT DO YOU KNOW, FUNKY, ... IT'S NOT!

HOWEVER MY ENTIRE BODY IS NOW PROTECTED AGAINST ATHLETE'S FOOT!

I NEVER CEASE TO BE AMAZED, ROLAND!

WHAT DO YOU SUPPOSE IT IS THAT COMPELS MAN TO GAZE AT THE STARS AT NIGHT?

BECAUSE YOU CAN'T SEE THEM DURING THE DAY!
BATIUK 8-24
© Field Enterprises, Inc., 1972

LIVINIA!

THIS SURE IS A SURPRISE! I NEVER THOUGHT YOU'D COME OVER TO SEE **ME**!

I NEVER THOUGHT **YOUR** FOLKS WOULD GET AIR CONDITIONING!
BATIUK
© Field Enterprises, Inc., 1972
8-25

I'D LIKE WHATEVER SIZE CONE I CAN GET FOR A DIME!
BIG DIPPER 45¢

BIG DIPPER 45¢
BATIUK 8-2
© Field Enterprises, Inc., 1972

BIG DIPPER 45¢

FUNKY WINKERBEAN

DO YOU THINK ANYONE PAYS ATTENTION TO THESE DEMONSTRATIONS, ROLAND?

THEY'D BETTER, FUNKY! TODAY'S YOUTH HAS A LOT TO SAY!

WE'RE PROBABLY THE MOST EDUCATED AND AWARE GENERATION IN HISTORY!
© Field Enterprises, Inc., 1972
BATIUK 8-27

THE HOPE OF THE WORLD RESTS ON OUR SHOULDERS!

WORKERS OF THE WORLD UNTIE!

THAT JUST SET US BACK TWENTY YEARS!

I'M TRYING TO SEE WHAT OLD SCHOOL MATERIALS MIGHT COME IN HANDY THIS YEAR, FUNKY!

DO YOU THINK ECOLOGY WILL STILL BE IN?
BATIUK 8-28

HEH! HEH!

YEAH! RIGHT-ON!
BATIUK 8-29

I'M SURE GOING TO MISS OL' CAPTAIN KANGAROO WHEN I GO BACK TO SCHOOL!

GIMME A CHOCOLATE CONE, GEORGE!

YOU LOOK DOWN, LES! GIRL PROBLEMS?
BATIUK 8-30

YEAH! MAYBE YOU'D BETTER MAKE THAT A DOUBLE!

IT'S REALLY HARD TO BELIEVE THAT SCHOOL IS JUST AROUND THE CORNER, LES!
BATIUK 8-31

I'LL SAY, FUNKY!
© Field Enterprises, Inc., 1972

I THOUGHT IT WAS ON THE OTHER SIDE OF TOWN!

WELL, FRED, IN A FEW DAYS THE SCHOOL WILL BE FILLED WITH STUDENTS IN PURSUIT OF AN EDUCATION!
PRINCIPAL

HOW RIGHT-ON YOU ARE, MR. BURCH! EAGER AND INQUISITIVE YOUNG MINDS FILLED WITH ENTHUSIASM FOR NEW EXPERIENCES!

HEAVEN ONLY KNOWS WHAT THE LITTLE DEVILS HAVE IN STORE FOR US THIS YEAR!
© Field Enterprises, Inc., 1972
BATIUK 9-1
PRINCIPAL

OKAY, THE PURPOSE OF OUR WOMEN'S CLUB 'RAP CELLAR' IS TO LET YOU KIDS GET TOGETHER TO DISCUSS THE RELEVANT ISSUES OF THE DAY!

WOULD ANYONE LIKE TO KICK THINGS OFF?
© Field Enterprises, Inc., 1972
BATIUK 9-2

YES! IS IT TRUE THAT NOT ALL ASPIRINS ARE ALIKE?

FUNKY WINKERBEAN
WATER-TESTING KIT

STILL PLAYING WITH YOUR 'MR. WIZARD SCIENCE-LAB,' LES?

VERY HUMEROUS! THIS HAPPENS TO BE MY NEW WATER-TESTING KIT, FUNKY!
BATIUK 9-3

WITH THIS KIT, YOU CAN CHECK RIVERS AND STREAMS FOR SIGNS OF INDUSTRIAL POLLUTION!

NOT ONLY THAT, BUT YOU GET HALF THE FINE LEVIED AGAINST ANY COMPANY YOU CATCH!

WHAT HAPPENS IF THE COMPANY CATCHES YOU?

THEY GET TO KEEP YOUR WATER-TESTING KIT!

YOU KNOW, FUNKY, EVERY GENERATION ALWAYS THINKS THAT THEY KNOW WHERE IT'S AT!
© Field Enterprises, Inc., 1972
BATIUK 9-4

YEAH, THAT'S TRUE, LES!

ISN'T IT FUNNY THAT OUT OF ALL THE GENERATIONS, WE'RE THE ONES WHO REALLY KNOW?

WELCOME BACK
REGISTER
I HAVE HERE A LIST OF STUDENT DEMANDS!
NOT YET! NOT YET!
SIGN UP HER
© Field Enterprises, Inc., 1972
BATIUK 9-5

AHH! ONCE AGAIN THE HALLS OF THE ACADEMY FILL WITH YOUNG PEOPLE EAGER FOR NEW ADVENTURE IN LEARNING!

HONK!
HONK!
© Field Enterprises, Inc., 1972
BATIUK 9-6

AND ONCE AGAIN THE HALLS EMPTY BECAUSE THAT CLOWN WHO PULLS THE FIRE ALARM IS STILL AT IT!

HI! WHAT CAN I DO FOR YOU, FUNKY?
POSITIVELY NO CLASS SCHEDULE CHANGES
BATIUK 9-7

I WANT TO CHANGE ONE OF MY CLASSES!
POSITIVELY NO CLASS SCHEDULE CHANGES

WOULD YOU LIKE TO GO WITH ME TO THE GAME FRIDAY, JOYCE?

SORRY, LES, BUT I'M BOOKED UP THROUGH TRACK SEASON!
BATIUK 9-8

AND SO WE START ANOTHER YEAR OF SCHOOL!

I QUIT! I'M TIRED OF BEING DEHUMANIZED AND TREATED LIKE AN ANIMAL!
17
14

NONSENSE, FUNKY! YOU'RE PROBABLY JUST NOT FEELING WELL!
14

BATIUK 9-9
SEE? YOUR NOSE IS DRY AND WARM!

FUNKY WINKERBEAN
THE JOY'S OF SCHOOL

GETTING UP EARLY...
BUUZZZZZZ

MEETING THE PRINCIPAL...
DON'T YOU KNOW THIS SCHOOL HAS A DRESS CODE?
SURE! I'M A TEACHER!

GETTING LOST...
THIS CAN'T BE MATH CLASS!
HOW WAS LUNCH?

I'M SORRY, BUT ACCORDING TO THE COMPUTER, YOU DON'T EXIST!

MAKING NEW FRIENDS...
Hi
THE DRESS CODE DOESN'T BOTHER ME! I DON'T WEAR DRESSES!
AND BEST OF ALL...
GETTING HOME!
AHHHHH!!
© Field Enterprises, Inc., 1972
BATIUK 9-10

HERB SHOP
© Field Enterprises, Inc., 1972
BATIUK
9-11

HEY! WHAT GIVES? I THOUGHT THIS WAS SUPPOSED TO BE AN HERB SHOP!

IT IS! I'M HERB!

I'VE REALLY BEEN LOOKING FORWARD TO THE CHALLENGE OF A BRAND NEW YEAR OF TEACHING!
© Field Enterprises, Inc., 1972
9-12

HI, I'M CRAZY HARRY YOUR NEW STUDENT!
BATIUK

LUCKILY, SUMMER VACATION IS ONLY NINE MONTHS AWAY!

YOU'RE NEW HERE AREN'T YOU?

YEAH! I'M CRAZY HARRY! I'M BEING BUSSED TO YOUR SCHOOL UNDER A COURT ORDER!
© Field Enterprises, Inc., 1972
BATIUK
9-13

REALLY? HOW MANY KIDS ARE BEING BUSSED HERE?

JUST ME!

HEY! MARY SUE SWEETWATER HAD THIS BOOK BEFORE ME!
9-14

JUST THINK! ALL THIS YEAR I'LL BE USING MARY SUE SWEETWATER'S OLD ALGEBRA BOOK!
BATIUK

I JUST KNEW THIS WAS GOING TO BE MY YEAR!

BUT YOU'VE GOT TO MAKE AN EXCEPTION AND CHANGE MY SCHEDULE, MR. FAIRGOOD!

THE COMPUTER HAS ME DOWN FOR FOOTBALL INSTEAD OF GIRL'S GYM!
9-15
BATIUK

LOOK HONEY! WE'VE ALL GOT TO MAKE SACRIFICES!

THEY'RE GOING TO PUT A NEW SURFACE ON THE FOOTBALL FIELD FOR THIS YEAR, LES!
9-16

IT'S SUPPOSED TO REALLY CUT DOWN ON INJURIES!
WHAT'S IT CALLED, FUNKY?

GRASS!
BATIUK

FUNKY WINKERBEAN

THIS SCHOOL YEAR WE PLAN TO PROVIDE YOU STUDENTS WITH A MORE UNSTRUCTURED LEARNING ENVIRONMENT!

OUR NEW PROGRAM OF MODULAR SCHEDULING WILL ALLOW FOR GREATER STUDENT DECISION-MAKING!
9-17

FOR ONE THING, UNDER THIS SYSTEM, YOU WILL BE ABLE TO ENTER OR LEAVE A CLASSROOM AT YOUR OWN DISCRETION!
© Field Enterprises, Inc., 1972
BATIUK

FUNNY THIS DIDN'T OCCUR TO SOMEONE WHEN WE WERE CREATING THE PROGRAM!

CATCH THIS, FUNKY!

THIS NATIONAL GEOGRAPHIC HAS A FOLD-OUT MAP!

YEAH, I KNOW! THAT'S THE PENINSULA OF THE MONTH!

WELL, MISS WRIGHTON, HOW ARE THINGS GOING FOR OUR BEGINNING TEACHER?

TERRIBLE! THIS IS COMPLETELY BACKWARD AND ARCHAIC!
YOU MEAN OUR CURRICULUM?

NO! THIS PAY SCALE!

I DON'T WANT TO TEACH USELESS FACTS FROM SOME OLD HISTORY BOOK, MR. BURCH!
PRINCIPAL

I WANT TO TEACH LIFE!

CERTAINLY, MISS WRIGHTON! SHALL WE ORDER A SUBSCRIPTION FOR YOU, OR FOR EACH STUDENT?

THE RETURN TO SCHOOL ALWAYS BRINGS THE BRUTAL CONTACT OF WELL-TRAINED PHYSICAL SPECIMENS EXECUTING THEIR PROWESS ON THE PRACTICE FIELD!
COACH
BATIUK
9-21

THEY'RE TOUGH ALL RIGHT!

I WISH WE COULD GET SOME OF THOSE GIRLS ON THE FIELD HOCKEY TEAM TO GO OUT FOR FOOTBALL!

WELL, MR. FAIRGOOD, HAS THE NEW COMPUTER SYSTEM SPEEDED UP STUDENT SCHEDULING?

OH DEFINITELY, MISS WRIGHTON!
9-22
BATIUK

IT FOULS THINGS UP IN MINUTES THAT USED TO TAKE US ALL DAY!

OKAY, MEN! LISTEN UP! STARTING TODAY WE'RE GOING BACK TO THE FUNDAMENTALS!
11
14
BATIUK
9-23

NOW, THIS IS A FOOTBALL!
71

UH, COULD WE GO BACK OVER THAT AGAIN COACH?
71

FUNKY WINKERBEAN

YOU WANTED TO SEE ME, DEREK?

YOU BET I DO!
40

THIS FOOTBALL TEAM PRACTICES DISCRIMINATION!

THERE SHOULD BE THE SAME PROPORTION OF BLACKS ON THE TEAM AS THERE ARE IN THE STUDENT BODY!
© Field Enterprises, Inc., 1972
BATIUK

WELL? WHAT DO YOU PLAN TO DO ABOUT IT?

THIS ISN'T EXACTLY WHAT I HAD IN MIND!
9-24

WELL, KIDS, WHAT SHALL WE RAP ABOUT DURING TONIGHT'S 'RAP CELLAR' MEETING?
BATIUK • 9-25
© Field Enterprises, Inc., 1972

SEX!
(GASP)! HIC!

NOW LOOK WHAT YOU DID! YOU GAVE HER THE HICCUPS!
HIC! HIC! HIC!

BULL, I'M GOING TO GET YOU SOME HELP SO THAT YOU CAN REMAIN ELIGIBLE FOR FOOTBALL!

I'VE TAKEN A VERY PERSONAL INTEREST IN YOUR PROBLEM!
© Field Enterprises, Inc., 1972
BATIUK
9-26

ESPECIALLY SINCE THE COACH KIDNAPPED MY DAUGHTER!

FUNKY, WE'D LIKE YOU TO HELP TUTOR OUR STAR FULLBACK, BULL BUSHKA!
BATIUK 9-27

HERE'S THE BOOK HE'S USING AND SOME RAW HAMBURGER!
RAW HAMBURGER?!

THAT'S JUST TO GET HIS ATTENTION!

OKAY, BULL, I'M GOING TO HELP YOU WITH YOUR MATH!
9-28

NOW THIS IS A HEXAGON!
PRETTY!
BATIUK

THIS IS GOING TO TAKE A LITTLE LONGER THAN I THOUGHT!

PROTESTING LIKE THIS WON'T SOLVE MUCH, ROLAND!
9-29

I'M SURPRISED YOU DON'T REALIZE THAT YOU CAN DO MORE BY USING APPROVED AND ESTABLISHED PROCEDURES WITHIN THE SYSTEM!

BATIUK

WE ARE! WE'RE ON STRIKE!

WHAT ARE YOU WATCHING NOW?
9-30

THE PACKERS-BEARS GAME!
BATIUK

DIDN'T YOU SEE THAT ONE LAST YEAR?

FUNKY WINKERBEAN

BOINK!

OKAY, CRAZY HARRY! COME UP HERE!

WELL YOUNG MAN, SCHOOL HAS ONLY BEEN IN SESSION A LITTLE WHILE AND ALREADY YOU'VE PROVEN YOURSELF TO BE A CONSTANT DISRUPTIVE FORCE!
10-1

BUT BELIEVE ME, YOU'RE NOT GOING TO MAKE ME LOSE MY COOL!

I'M GOING TO HANDLE THIS SITUATION LIKE THE SKILLED PROFESSIONAL I AM!
© Field Enterprises, Inc., 1972
BATIUK

GO TO THE OFFICE!

I DON'T CARE WHAT YOU SAY!
10-2

NOT WITHOUT A HALL-PASS!
HALL MONITOR
14
BATIUK

DARN IT!

I'VE GOT THE ANSWER TO THIS QUESTION RIGHT ON THE TIP OF MY TONGUE!
BATIUK
10-3

I'VE HEARD OF CRIBBING, BUT THAT'S RIDICULOUS!

THERE'S SOMETHING I'D LIKE TO KNOW, MR. BURCH!
STUDENT SUGGESTION BOX
10-4

JUST HOW MANY PEOPLE HAVE KEYS TO THIS SUGGESTION-BOX?
STUDENT SUGGESTION BOX
BATIUK

YOU MEAN THERE'S A KEY?
STUDENT SUGGESTIO BOX

COME ON! LET'S PLAY BALL!
© Field Enterprises, Inc., 1972
10-5

BATIUK

I HOPE HE'S HAD HIS SHOTS!

DOES YOUR 'FREE SCHOOL' HAVE ANY COURSES ON FARMING, ROLAND?
YEAH, WE HAVE THREE, FUNKY!
FREE SCHOOL SIGN-UP

WHAT DOES THE FIRST COURSE COVER?
© Field Enterprises, Inc., 1972
10-6

HOW TO ORDER FROM A BURPEE CATALOG!
BATIUK
FREE SCHOOL SIGN-

JUST BECAUSE YOU BELIEVE IN WOMEN'S LIB, WICKED WANDA, ...THAT DOESN'T MEAN YOU CAN'T BEHAVE IN A MORE FEMININE WAY!
© Field Enterprises, Inc., 1972
10-7

(WHAM)

NOW THAT'S A DANDY BEGINNING!
BATIUK

FUNKY WINKERBEAN
CAFETERIA

THWIP
MISSED!

I THINK YOU'RE RAISING YOUR HEAD ON YOUR 'THWIP'!

ALL RIGHT! WHAT'S GOING ON HERE?

IT'S A GAME WE MADE UP CALLED 'MEATING'! YOU PUT SOME MEAT ON YOUR FORK...
BATIUK

© Field Enterprises, Inc., 1972
..AND TRY TO FLIP IT ONTO THE CEILING!

WELL I'M AFRAID YOU GUYS CAN'T GO ON 'MEATING' LIKE THIS!
10-8

LOOK AT THAT, FUNKY! CHRISTMAS DECORATIONS

SON OF A GUN!
© Field Enterprises, Inc., 1972
10-9

IT'S HARD TO BELIEVE IT'S OCTOBER ALREADY!
BATIUK

I HEARD YOU WERE SELECTED TO RUN FOR STUDENT COUNCIL PRESIDENT, FUNKY!
10-10

THAT'S QUITE A DISTINCTION!
© Field Enterprises, Inc., 1972

YEAH, I WAS THE ONLY ONE WHO DIDN'T SAY 'NO' FAST ENOUGH!
BATIUK

I WAS WONDERING IF YOUR UNDERGROUND PAPER WAS GOING TO SUPPORT ME FOR STUDENT COUNCIL PRESIDENT, ROLAND!
10-11

WE PLAN TO SUPPORT THE CANDIDATE WE FEEL IS BEST SUITED FOR THE JOB, FUNKY!
© Field Enterprises, Inc., 1972

I ALMOST HATE TO ASK THE NEXT QUESTION!
BATIUK

I'D LIKE TO SEE THIS STUDENT COUNCIL ELECTION BE A GOOD CLEAN FIGHT!

I SEE NO REASON WHY WE CAN'T TAKE THE HIGH ROAD AND BEHAVE LIKE GENTLEMEN!

SO I PLAN TO REFRAIN FROM ALL MENTION OF MY OPPONENT'S POOR GRADES, LOUSY ATTENDANCE RECORD, OR LOW IQ SCORES!
BATIUK

I'D LIKE TO KNOW WHAT MY OPPONENT PLANS TO DO ABOUT THE VIETNAM SITUATION!
STUDENT COUNCIL DEBATE

BUT I CAN'T DO ANYTHING ABOUT THE VIETNAM SITUATION!

HA!
STUDENT COUNCIL DEBATE
BATIUK

I WOULDN'T FEEL BAD ABOUT LOSING THE STUDENT COUNCIL ELECTION, FUNKY! YOUR OPPONENT JUST HAD AN UNFAIR ADVANTAGE!

HE HAD THE SUPPORT OF THE PRINCIPAL, THE TEACHERS WERE BEHIND HIM, HE HAD MORE MONEY TO SPEND ...

... AND HE HAD MORE VOTES!
BATIUK

FUNKY WINKERBEAN

BEGINNING A WEEK FROM TODAY WE'LL HOLD OUR MOCK NATIONAL CAMPAIGN AND ELECTION!
10-15

A WEEK FROM TODAY?!

BUT WE'RE NOT PREPARED, WE'RE NOT ORGANIZED!
BATIUK
© Field Enterprises, Inc., 1972

WE HAVEN'T PICKED A CANDIDATE YET!

RIGHT ON...THAT'S THE KIND OF REALISM WE'RE LOOKING FOR!

MISS WRIGHTON, I'D LIKE TO DO SOME EXTRA-CREDIT WORK IN THE CLASS!
10-16

WELL, HAROLD, YOU'D LIKE TO DO A LITTLE RESEARCH AND PERSONAL EXPLORATION INTO AN AREA THAT INTERESTS YOU?
BATIUK
© Field Enterprises, Inc., 1972

NO! I'D LIKE TO DO A BOOK REPORT TO PULL UP MY GRADE!

I'M DOING A COLUMN FOR THE SCHOOL PAPER TO KEEP THE STUDENTS INFORMED ON ANY NEW POLITICAL DEVELOPMENTS...
© Field Enterprises, Inc., 1972
10-17

SO THAT THEY WILL KNOW WHAT THE ISSUES ARE WHEN THE POLLS OPEN IN DECEMBER!

HAVE I GOT A SCOOP FOR YOU!
BATIUK

I THOUGHT YOU MIGHT WANT THIS STORY FOR YOUR UNDERGROUND PAPER, ROLAND!
© Field Enterprises, Inc., 1972
10-18

HEY! THIS IS GREAT, FUNKY WE'LL USE IT ON THE FRONT PAGE!
BATIUK

STOP THE MIMEOGRAPH MACHINE!!

I'M SORRY, WICKED WANDA, BUT IF YOU WISH TO SEE A COUNSELOR, YOU SHOULD GO SEE THE GIRLS' COUNSELOR!
© Field Enterprises, Inc., 1972

SMASH!
10-19

HAVE A SEAT!
BATIUK

OKAY MEN, IT'S NEARLY TIME FOR THE GAME!
72
18
11
14

LET'S GO OUT THERE AND REALLY STICK IT TO'EM!
COACH
© Field Enterprises, Inc., 1972
10-20

THOSE GUYS THAT NEED HELP TYING THEIR SHOES, LINE UP HERE!
COACH
BATIUK

© Field Enterprises, Inc., 1972
FUNKY!
10-21

WHY IS IT I CAN NEVER FIND HIM WHEN I NEED HIM?

ALL IT TAKES IS A LITTLE PRACTICE!
BATIUK

FUNKY WINKERBEAN
CHEMISTRY LAB

WELL, DEREK, ONE FINAL STEP AND WE'LL HAVE COMPLETED OUR FIRST LAB EXPERIMENT!
YIPPY-DO!
10-22

ALL WE HAVE TO DO IS ADD THESE TWO SOLUTIONS TOGETHER AND RECORD THE RESULTS!
BATIUK
© Field Enterprises, Inc., 1972

KA-BLAAM!

DOES `KABLAAM' HAVE ONE `L' OR TWO?

I CAN'T GET TO SLEEP THINKING ABOUT THAT BIG CLOD, BULL BUSHKA!

I JUST DREAD GOING TO SCHOOL AND HAVING HIM PICK ON ME!
10-23

STICKS AND STONES CAN BREAK MY BONES BUT NAMES CAN NEVER HURT ME!

I WISH HE'D CALL ME MORE NAMES!
BATIUK

I GOT RID OF EVERY COPY OF YOUR PAPER THAT I HAD, ROLAND!

TERRIFIC, FUNKY! HOW MUCH MONEY DID WE TAKE IN?
10-24
BATIUK

WE'RE CHARGING FOR 'EM?

'CRAZY HARRY', THIS IS THE THIRD TIME YOU'VE BEEN SENT TO THE OFFICE THIS WEEK!

I'M GIVING YOU A DETENTION!
BATIUK
10-25

OKAY! BUT I'M BOOKED UP TILL APRIL THIRD!
PRINCIPAL

JUST LOOK AT ALL OF THIS... SAY YOUNG MAN, ARE YOU A REAL HIPPIE?

YES MA'AM!

SEE GEORGE... I TOLD YOU THIS WAS AN ORGANIC SHOP!
BATIUK
10-26

I'D LIKE A BOX OF WHEAT GERM, PLEASE!

ARE YOU INTO ORGANIC FOODS, LADY?
BATIUK

HEAVENS NO! THIS IS FOR MY SON... HE'S A FREAK!
10-27

BOY! I'M REALLY LOOKING FORWARD TO YOUR HALLOWEEN PARTY, FUNKY!

ALL THE FUN OF CIDER AND DOUGHNUTS, AND BOBBING FOR PUMPKINS!

BOBBING FOR PUMPKINS?
BATIUK
10-28

FUNKY WINKERBEAN

OKAY, BULL BUSHKA, I'VE HAD IT WITH YOU!

YOU'VE BEEN PICKING ON ME FOR A LONG TIME NOW!

YOU'VE HARASSED ME, EMBARRASSED ME, AND BEATEN ME UP!

YOU'VE DONE EVERYTHING YOU COULD TO STRIP ME OF MY PRIDE!
BATIUK

WHAT MORE CAN YOU DO TO ME?
10-29

ONE OF THESE DAYS HE'S GOING TO PUSH ME TOO FAR!

I COMPLETELY FORGOT TO GET A HALL PASS, LES, BUT YOU'LL LET ME THROUGH WON'T YOU?
ALL
TOR
© Field Enterprises, Inc., 1972

SURE! THAT'S OKAY, MARY SUE!
BATIUK

I CAN ALWAYS SPOT AN HONEST FACE!
ALL
ITOR
10-30

THAT'S INTERESTING, LES!
10-31

IT'S REALLY UNIQUE!
© Field Enterprises, Inc., 1972
BATIUK

I DON'T THINK I'VE EVER SEEN A HALLOWEEN WATERMELON BEFORE!

THERE MUST BE A HUNDRED THINGS THIS SCHOOL INSURANCE DOESN'T COVER!

WHAT'S IT GOOD FOR?
© Field Enterprises, Inc., 1972
BATIUK

THE COMPANY THAT SELLS IT!
11-1

HOW'S IT GOING, DEREK?

OKAY, MAN!
© Field Enterprises, Inc., 1972

I WONDER HOW HE KNEW IT WAS ME?
BATIUK
11-2

WELL, CRAZY HARRY, WHAT ARE YOU WAITING TO SEE THE PRINCIPAL FOR?

PRINCIPAL?! WELL I'LL BE ...
BATIUK
11-3

I THOUGHT THIS SEEMED LIKE KIND OF A SMALL CLASS!

DO YOU LIKE PIERCED EARS, FUNKY?

NOT REALLY, LIVINIA!
BATIUK
© Field Enterprises, Inc., 1972
11-4

IN FACT, MOST FRENCH FOOD TURNS ME OFF!

FUNKY
WINKERBEAN

YOU KNOW, LES, OUR SOCIETY JUST SEEMS TO BE GETTING SO COMPLEX!

IT'S REALLY FRUSTRATING!

I JUST WANT TO GET BACK TO A SIMPLER WAY OF LIVING!

11-5

CAN YOU UNDERSTAND WHAT I'M INTO?

OH SURE, LIVINIA!

I'M VERY SIMPLE-MINDED MYSELF!
BATIUK

I'D LIKE TO KNOW SOMETHING, MR. BURCH!

IS THIS UNION OR NON-UNION LETTUCE?

NEITHER! IT'S CABBAGE!
BATIUK
11-6

HOW DID LES DO ON THE ROPE CLIMB YESTERDAY, FUNKY?

WELL ... HE WENT UP OKAY BUT HE HAD A LITTLE TROUBLE COMING DOWN!
DID HE FALL?
BATIUK

HELP!
WE DON'T KNOW YET!
11-7

LOOK, WE'VE GOT TO GET LES DOWN FROM THE ROPE, FUNKY!
10

WELL I THINK WE ALL AGREE ON THAT!
BATIUK 11-8

BUT I THINK WE CAN COME UP WITH A BETTER SOLUTION THAN SETTING FIRE TO THE ROPE!
71
10

JUST CALM DOWN, LES!

ALL YOU'VE GOT TO DO IS COME DOWN THE SAME WAY YOU WENT UP!

WELL... HERE GOES NOTHING!
BATIUK
11-9

OKAY, LES, START CLIMBING DOWN THE ROPE...
11-10

...AND REMEMBER TO TAKE IT SLOW SO YOU DON'T GET ANY...
BATIUK

YAA-HAAAA
WHAM!

...ROPE BURNS ~

'CLICK' THIS IS A RECORDING...

WHEN YOU HEAR THE TONE, PLEASE STATE YOUR NAME AND THE DAY FOR WHICH YOU ARE REQUESTING A DATE! THANK YOU!
BATIUK

THAT MARY SUE IS A VERY POPULAR GIRL!
11-11

FUNKY WINKERBEAN
WOW! DID I EVER GET A LUCKY BREAK!

I FINALLY GOT SOME TICKETS FOR THE **PURPLE FUDGE** CONCERT, FUNKY!

BUT THEY CANCELLED AND THE **MAHOGANY ANTEATERS** TOOK THEIR PLACE!

THEN THEY GOT BUSTED FOR LITTERING, SO THE **ENAMEL ESOPHAGUS** CAME IN ...

...BUT THEIR INSTRUMENTS WERE SENT TO BRAZIL BY MISTAKE!
BATIUK
11-12

SO WHO'S GOING TO APPEAR AT THE CONCERT?

THE **PURPLE FUDGE**!

BOY! AM I STARVED!
11-13

I JUST CAN'T WAIT TO DIG INTO A SACK OF ...

... GYM CLOTHES !
BATIUK

BULL, THE RESULTS OF YOUR I.Q. TEST GIVE US A GENERAL IDEA OF YOUR STRONG AND WEAK AREAS!

FIRST WE'LL LOOK AT YOUR STRONG POINTS ...
BATIUK
11-14

YOU SCORED FIFTY OUT OF A HUNDRED ON THE NAME GRID!

WELL, BULL ... HAVE YOU GIVEN ANY THOUGHT TO GOING TO COLLEGE AFTER HIGH SCHOOL ?

COLLEGE ?
BATIUK
11-15

... THAT'S A BIG SCHOOL WITH MANY BUILDINGS!

TOMORROW WE'LL BEGIN AN INTERDISCIPLINARY, TEAM-TEACHING PROGRAM UTILIZING THE OPEN SPACE CONCEPT!

WHAT DO YOU SUPPOSE THAT IS, FUNKY?
BATIUK
11-16

A STUDY-HALL IN THE GYM!

OKAY, CLASS, BEFORE YOU START THE TEST, ARE THERE ANY QUESTIONS?

YEAH, WHO WAS THAT GUY YOU WERE WITH AT THE MALL SATURDAY?

I WONDER IF THEY HAVE ANY OPENINGS AT THE PICKLE FACTORY?
BATIUK
11-17

WOW! LOOK AT ALL OF THOSE CUTE CHEERLEADERS, CHRIS!
11-18

SAY... AREN'T THEY SOMETHING, BUD? AND HOW ABOUT SOME OF THOSE PRETTY GIRLS IN THE STANDS!

HEY CHRIS, ONE OF THOSE TEAMS DOWN THERE SEEMS TO HAVE SCORED OR SOMETHING!
BATIUK

I'LL CHECK AND SEE IF WE CAN GET SOME INFORMATION ON THAT FOR YOU FANS DURING HALFTIME!

FUNKY
WINKERBEAN
RAILROAD
PRICE $200

HOW CAN YOU TWO ALWAYS SIT THERE AND PLAY MONOPOLY?
© Field Enterprises, Inc., 1972
BATIUK

DON'T YOU REALIZE HOW CAPITALISTIC AND MATERIALISTIC IT IS?
11-19

IT REINFORCES CORRUPT AND DECADENT VALUES!

WHY DON'T YOU PUT A HOTEL ON BALTIC AVE., DUMMY?

I'D LIKE TO WELCOME YOU PARENTS TO TONIGHT'S P.T.A. MEETING!

I'M SURE ALL OF YOU HEAR QUITE A BIT ABOUT WHAT WE DO AROUND HERE FROM YOUR KIDS ...
BATIUK

... THE PURPOSE OF TONIGHT'S MEETING IS TO DENY ALL THAT!
11-20

HAVE YOU SEEN CRAZY HARRY, FUNKY?
NO! BUT HE WAS IN SCHOOL THIS MORNING, LIVINIA!
11-21
BATIUK

I WONDER WHY WE HAVEN'T SEEN HIM ALL DAY?

BECAUSE I'M TOO EMBARRASSED TO YELL FOR HELP, THAT'S WHY!

WOW!
THAT'S REALLY FAR OUT!
11-22

IT REALLY FREAKS YOUR MIND DOESN'T IT?

CRAZY HARRY JUST LOVES TO SHOW OFF HIS BLACK-LIGHT POSTER!
BATIUK

SINCE IT'S THANKSGIVING, FUNKY, I THOUGHT I'D MAKE UP A LIST OF THE THINGS I HAVE TO BE THANKFUL FOR!

THAT'S VERY COMMENDABLE, LES!
11-23

SAY, DO YOU THINK I SHOULD COUNT MY HEADPHONES SEPARATELY OR AS PART OF MY STEREO?
BATIUK

NOW, LES, AS PART OF YOUR STUDENT PROFILE WE HAVE TO DETERMINE IF YOU ARE A FOLLOWER OR A LEADER!
BATIUK 11-24

HOW WOULD YOU RATE YOURSELF?

SPECTATOR!

WELL, BUD, THAT WAS QUITE A FOOTBALL GAME!

HAVE YOU CHOSEN WHO IS TO RECEIVE THE NEW CAR FOR THEIR PERFORMANCE TODAY?
BATIUK
11-25

YES, CHRIS! I'VE PICKED THAT LITTLE BLOND CHEERLEADER ON THE END!

FUNKY WINKERBEAN
SPLIT-P FORMATION

LISTEN UP, MEN!

AS YOU KNOW, WE PLAY OUR LAST GAME OF THE YEAR AGAINST OUR ARCH-RIVAL, BIG WALNUT TECH!
BATIUK

NOW DON'T LET THEIR REPUTATION AS A POWERHOUSE SCARE YOU!

THEY MAY SEEM BIG, TOUGH, AND UNBEATABLE ... BUT REMEMBER THIS ...

THEY ONLY PUT THEIR PANTS ON ONE LEG AT A TIME!
COACH

NOW HE TELLS US!
11-26

HI THERE! WE, OF THE LOCAL TV MEDIA, ARE DOING A SERIES ON TYPICAL STUDENTS IN A TYPICAL LOCAL SCHOOL!
© Field Enterprises, Inc., 1972
11-27

WELL, HELLO ALL YOU GROOVY PEOPLE OUT THERE IN TV LAND!
BATIUK

DON'T HAM IT UP, KID!

EXCUSE ME, TYPICAL STUDENT...

WE, OF THE LOCAL TV MEDIA, ARE LOOKING FOR STUDENTS WHO EXEMPLIFY THE OPEN PERMISSIVENESS OF THE NEW MORALITY!
© Field Enterprises, Inc., 1972
11-28
BATIUK

SO AM I!

HI, TYPICAL STUDENT! WHAT'S YOUR NAME?

FUNKY WINKERBEAN!
© Field Enterprises, Inc., 1972
BATIUK
11-29

LISTEN TO THAT, FOLKS! WHAT A SENSE OF HUMOR!

YOUNG MAN, DO YOU FEEL THAT YOUR SCHOOL SUFFERS FROM INSTITUTIONAL PARALYSIS ?
BATIUK
11-30

YES, I DEFINITELY DO!

HAVE YOU ANY IDEA WHAT CAUSES IT ?

I THINK IT'S THE LUNCHES!

WHAT'S THAT FOR, MR. FAIRGOOD ?
12-1

DIDN'T YOU HEAR THE ANNOUNCEMENT...?
BATIUK

THERE'S A STAFF MEETING AFTER SCHOOL TONIGHT!

AT TONIGHT'S 'RAP CELLAR' MEETING, I THOUGHT WE COULD DISCUSS HOW ROLES ARE CHANGING IN TODAY'S SOCIETY!
BATIUK
12-2

I'VE NOTICED THAT!

THEY'RE NOT PUTTING IN AS MUCH JELLY AS THEY USED TO!

FUNKY WINKERBEAN
HOW TO PICK UP GIRLS BY CHARLES ATLAS
GEO

YOUR PROBLEM IS THAT YOU'RE TOO UPTIGHT AROUND GIRLS, LES...

JUST WATCH MY STYLE AND YOU CAN PICK UP A FEW POINTERS!

HI THERE!

12-3

BATIUK

I ALREADY KNOW HOW TO DO THAT!

MR. FAIRGOOD, WOULD YOU SHOW ME MY STUDENT PROFILE?
12-4

CERTAINLY, FUNKY! LET ME GET IT OUT OF THE FILE!

HERE IT IS!
BATIUK
© Field Enterprises, Inc., 1972

HERE I AM IN THE PRINCIPAL'S OFFICE AGAIN! WHY DOES THIS HAPPEN TO ME?
© Field Enterprises, Inc., 1972
BATIUK

BECAUSE I REFUSE TO KNUCKLE UNDER TO THE SYSTEM AND BECAUSE NO ONE TRYS TO UNDERSTAND ME OR MY PROBLEMS!

AND BECAUSE SOMEBODY RATTED ON ME AGAIN!
12-5

MR. BURCH! THERE'S A RUMOR GOING AROUND THAT THE STUDENTS ARE PLANNING A **MASS WALKOUT** AT TWO O'CLOCK!

WHAT DO YOU THINK WE SHOULD DO?
PRINCIPAL
12-6
© Field Enterprises, Inc., 1972

LET'S TALK TO 'EM AND SEE IF WE CAN GET IT MOVED UP TO **NOON**!
BATIUK

I CAN'T BELIEVE IT, FUNKY!
© Field Enterprises, Inc., 1972
BATIUK

THERE I WAS TALKING TO MARY SUE SWEETWATER ... AND I ACTED LIKE A TOTAL **IDIOT**!
12-7

WELL, LES, MAYBE SHE'LL ADMIRE YOU FOR YOUR HONESTY!

OKAY, KID, I WANT FIVE HUNDRED THOUSAND DOLLARS AND A PARACHUTE!
HALL
NITOR
12-8

BUT I'M ONLY A HALL MONITOR!
© Field Enterprises, Inc., 1972
BATIUK

IN THAT CASE, SCRATCH THE PARACHUTE!

WELL, FRED, THE KAWANGA TECH BASKETBALL TEAM HASN'T BEEN SCORED UPON THIS YEAR!
12-9

THAT'S RIGHT, BILL!
ISN'T THAT RATHER UNUSUAL?
BATIUK

© Field Enterprises, Inc., 1972
NO! NOT FOR THE SEASON OPENER!

FUNKY WINKERBEAN
PRINCIPAL

MR. BURCH, I'M TIRED OF BEING TREATED AS A SECOND CLASS CITIZEN!
PRINCIPAL

AROUND HERE ... THE TEACHERS HAVE ONE SET OF RULES AND THE STUDENTS ANOTHER!
12-10

THIS SCHOOL IS BEING RUN UNDER A DOUBLE STANDARD!

THAT'S VERY TRUE, ROLAND!

BATIUK
WE NOT ONLY STRIVE FOR HIGHER STANDARDS IN EDUCATION ...

... BUT MORE OF THEM TOO!!

ABOUT THIS ATHLETIC BANQUET TOMORROW, COACH...
12-11

ARE WE SUPPOSED TO WEAR FORMAL ATTIRE ?
COACH
BATIUK

DEFINITELY! GOLF SHIRTS BUTTONED TO THE TOP BUTTON!

12-12

DARN IT!

BATIUK

I JUST COULDN'T STUDY WITH THIS PUDDING MAKING ALL THAT NOISE IN THE REFRIGERATOR!

LOOK, FUNKY!
BATIUK

ISN'T THAT ROMANTIC ?
12-13

SOMEONE'S SPRAY-PAINTED THEIR INITIALS ON THIS TREE!
TB + CW

SPROING!
BATIUK

I'M GOING TO HAVE TO GET THAT RECORD CHANGER ADJUSTED!
12-14

WELL, MR. FAIRGOOD, FRIDAY WE ALL GET OFF FOR A PERSONAL GROWTH DAY!
12-15

WHAT DO YOU PLAN TO DO?

I THINK I'LL START A MOUSTACHE!

DAD, I THINK WE COULD RESOLVE SOME OF OUR DIFFERENCES IF WE'D SIT AND TALK ABOUT IT!
12-16

GOOD IDEA!
BATIUK

WHAT ARE YOU DOING DURING HALFTIME?

FUNKY
WINKERBEAN

IN THIS ISSUE OF MY UNDERGROUND PAPER, FUNKY, I SHOW HOW MADISON AVE. HAS EXPLOITED AND COMMERCIALIZED THE SPIRIT OF CHRISTMAS FOR GREEDY PROFITS!

INSTEAD, I'D LIKE TO SEE A RETURN TO THE VIRTUES OF PEACE, LOVE, AND CHARITY TOWARDS OUR FELLOW MAN!
12-17
© Field Enterprises, Inc., 1972
BATIUK

THAT'S PRETTY GOOD ADVICE FOR TEN CENTS, ROLAND!

WELL, NOT EXACTLY...

OUR CHRISTMAS ISSUE IS TWENTY-FIVE CENTS!

MR. BURCH, I FEEL THAT IF SCHOOLS CAN GRADE STUDENTS, THEN THE STUDENTS SHOULD GRADE THE SCHOOLS!
12-18

IN MY OPINION, YOU'VE FAILED TO MEET MY NEEDS AND HERE'S THE GRADE YOU'VE EARNED!
PRINCIPAL
BATIUK

CAN I DO A BOOK REPORT FOR EXTRA CREDIT?
F

SEE THIS SNOWBALL, LES?
YES!

WOULD YOU LIKE IT SHOVED DOWN YOUR BACK?
NO!

DO YOU KNOW WHAT I'M GOING TO DO WITH IT?
BATIUK

I THINK I'M ABOUT TO GET A PERFECT SCORE!

WHAT'S THIS, LES...? THE NORTH POLE...?

YOU MEAN TO TELL ME THAT YOU'RE SENDING A LETTER TO SANTA CLAUS?
© Field Enterprises, Inc., 1972

WHAT DO YOU TAKE ME FOR, DEREK? THAT WAS FOR MY LITTLE COUSIN!

I MAILED MINE WEEKS AGO!
BATIUK
12-20

LIVINIA, WOULD YOU LIKE TO GO TO THE CHRISTMAS CONCERT WITH ME?
© Field Enterprises, Inc., 1972

ARE YOU KIDDING? GET SERIOUS, KNUCKLEHEAD!

BY THE WAY, MERRY CHRISTMAS!
BATIUK
12-21

I JUST CAN'T BELIEVE HOW WELL YOU'VE FIXED UP THE INSIDE OF YOUR LOCKER, CRAZY HARRY!

IF YOU THINK IT'S NICE NOW, JUST WAIT, FUNKY!
© Field Enterprises, Inc., 1972

I'M HAVING THE STUDY CORNER PANELLED IN CHERRY WOOD OVER THE CHRISTMAS BREAK!
BATIUK
12-22

I'VE HAD IT WITH YOU, WICKED WANDA!

© Field Enterprises, Inc., 1972
BATIUK
YOU'RE NOTHING BUT A BIG DUMB ROLLER DERBY REJECT!
SMASH!
LUCKILY, I WASN'T STANDING ON MY HEAD OR SHE WOULD HAVE BROKEN ALL MY TOES!
12-23

FUNKY WINKERBEAN

GOD REST YE MERRY GENTLEMEN...

HEY! LOOK! UP ON THE ROOF!
12-24

WHY IT'S A JOLLY OLD MAN IN A RED SUIT TRYING TO CLIMB DOWN THE CHIMNEY!
BATIUK

AND HE HAS A SHINY RED NOSE!
© Field Enterprises, Inc., 1972

LOOKS LIKE YOUR UNCLE FRED HAS HAD A LITTLE TOO MUCH CHRISTMAS CHEER AGAIN!

WHAT'S UP, ROLAND?
I'M SITTING HERE, FUNKY, CONTEMPLATING ON HOW GREED HAS BECOME SO MUCH A PART OF THIS SPIRITUAL HOLIDAY!
HAVE YOU FOUND ANYTHING FOR YOU THERE?
ONLY SIX MEASLY PRESENTS SO FAR!
BATIUK
12-25

AHH!

THERE'S NOTHING LIKE SLEEPING IN DURING THE CHRISTMAS BREAK...

...AND HEARING YOUR DAD GET UP TO GO TO WORK!
BATIUK
12-26

I THINK THAT ONE OF THE PROBLEMS THESE DAYS IS THAT LIFE DOESN'T SEEM TO HAVE ANY REAL MEANING!
12-27

THAT'S BECAUSE YOU NEED TO FILL YOUR LIFE WITH MEANINGFUL GOALS!
BATIUK

TAKE MYSELF FOR EXAMPLE! I SAVE GREEN STAMPS!

YOU KNOW, 'CRAZY,' IT'S A FUNNY WORLD! MADISON AVE. EXECUTIVES WEAR LONG HAIR AND THE RICH DRESS LIKE PAUPERS!

THERE'S NO LONGER ANY WAY TO REBEL AGAINST THE ESTABLISHMENT!

I AM, ROLAND! I'M STILL OBSERVING DAYLIGHT SAVINGS TIME!

SAY, CHRIS, WOULD YOU LIKE TO GO TO A NEW YEAR'S EVE PARTY WITH ME?

OH...

WELL, SAY, WHAT ARE YOU DOING NEXT YEAR?

DO YOU LIKE YOUR WIFE'S FRIED CHICKEN, SIR?
SURE DO!

LET'S CALL HER UP AND FIND OUT WHAT SHORTENING SHE USES!

HONEY, A LADY HERE WANTS TO KNOW WHAT KIND OF SHORTENING YOU USE!

HAVE YOU BEEN DRINKING AGAIN, FRED?

FUNKY WINKERBEAN

CRAZY HARRY, WITH THIS NEW TEST...

I CAN GET A BETTER PICTURE OF YOUR PSYCHOLOGICAL MAKE-UP!
12-31

NOW WHAT DOES THIS PICTURE REMIND YOU OF?

IT LOOKS LIKE JACKIE ONASSIS AND MICK JAGGER SITTING IN A HUGE PEANUT BUTTER JAR...

...SMOKING THE ODD NUMBERED PAGES FROM THE READER'S DIGEST!
BATIUK

HOW ABOUT THAT! I'VE HIT THE JACKPOT ON THE FIRST CRACK!

1973

HI, ... SAY DO YOU COME TO THESE NEW YEAR'S PARTIES OFTEN?

OH, I'D SAY ABOUT ONCE A YEAR!
BATIUK
1-1

OH REALLY? THAT OFTEN?

I THOUGHT I'D TAKE A SAMPLING OF SNOW FROM MY BACKYARD AND SEE HOW MANY IMPURITIES I COULD FIND IN IT DEREK!

DID YOU FIND ANYTHING, LES?

YEAH, I FOUND MY OLD BASEBALL!
BATIUK
1-2

I THOUGHT I'D SHOW SOME SLIDES OF MY VACATION TO THE BAHAMAS AT OUR NEXT 'RAP CELLAR' SESSION!
BATIUK
1-3

BUT, MARCIA, SOME OF THOSE SLIDES SHOW YOU IN YOUR BIKINI!

LISTEN, JAN, WE'RE JUST GOING TO HAVE TO TAKE THE PLUNGE AND BE SEXUALLY HONEST WITH THESE KIDS!

ATTENDANCE HAS REALLY FALLEN OFF WITH THE YOUNG PEOPLE AT OUR 'RAP CELLAR', MARCIA!
1-4

WE'VE GOT TO DO SOMETHING THAT WILL REALLY SPARK THEIR INTEREST!
© Field Enterprises, Inc., 1973

SAY! WHY DON'T WE HOLD A TUPPERWARE PARTY?
BATIUK

YOUNG PEOPLE SURE SEEM TO LIKE THESE CHEAP HAMBURGER COUNTERS!
1-5

SURE, WHY DO YOU THINK THEY'RE CALLED THE COUNTER CULTURE?

REAL CUTE, FELLA!
© Field Enterprises, Inc., 1973
BATIUK

SSSSSS
1-6

SSSSSS

S?
SSSSSS
© Field Enterprises, Inc., 1973
BATIUK

FUNKY WINKERBEAN
HEX

I'M SO NERVOUS I CAN'T STAND IT, FUNKY!

EVERY TIME I'M AT A GAME, SOMEONE SPILLS THEIR DRINK ON ME!

IT'S UNBELIEVABLE! IT'S NEVER FAILED TO HAPPEN YET!
1-7

I JUST KNOW SOMEONE'S GOING TO SPILL SOMETHING ON ME TODAY, TOO!
BATIUK
© Field Enterprises, Inc., 1973

SLOP!

THERE! NOW YOU CAN RELAX!

MR. BURCH, I WANTED TO TALK TO YOU THIS MORNING, BUT YOU SAID TO WAIT AND COME IN AFTER SCHOOL!
1-8

OKAY, CRAZY HARRY! WHAT DID YOU WANT TO SEE ME ABOUT?

YOU LEFT YOUR CAR LIGHTS ON!
PRINCIPAL
BATIUK

THAT'S INTERESTING!
1-9

DO YOU WRITE UP ALL YOUR LESSON PLANS ON YELLOW PAPER?

NO, THEY JUST GET THAT WAY OVER THE YEARS!
BATIUK

FUNKY, YOUR TEST RESULTS INDICATE AN APTITUDE FOR A JOB AS A MANAGEMENT ANALYSIS CONSULTANT!
1-10

WHAT'S THAT, MR. FAIRGOOD?

I DON'T KNOW, I LOST MY ANSWER KEY!
BATIUK

HOW ABOUT THIS BOOK FOR YOUR BOOK REPORT, FUNKY?

ARE YOU KIDDING?
BATIUK 1-11

HOW CAN I DO A BOOK REPORT ON A BOOK THAT DOESN'T HAVE A DUST-JACKET?

WHAT WAS YESTERDAY'S ASSEMBLY ABOUT, LES?

THIS GUY TALKED ABOUT HOW EVERY-ONE WORRIES MORE ABOUT A CRIMINAL THAN ABOUT THE
BATIUK
1-12

DID HE OFFER ANY SOLUTIONS?

YEAH, NO-FAULT MUGGING INSURANCE!

I'D LIKE SOMETHING FOR BLEMISHES THAT REALLY WORKS!

SOMETHING THAT WILL COMPLETELY CHANGE THE WAY I LOOK!

HAVE YOU CONSIDERED GROWING A BEARD?
BATIUK

FUNKY WINKERBEAN

YOU LOOK KINDA DOWN, LES! WHAT'S BUGGING YOU?

MY DAD JUST TOLD US THAT HIS COMPANY MIGHT RELOCATE HIM, FUNKY!
1-14

THAT MEANS WE MIGHT HAVE TO MOVE TO ANOTHER STATE!
BATIUK

WELL, LOOK AT THE BRIGHT SIDE!

IT COULD BE AN EXCITING NEW ADVENTURE!

YEAH, BUT I HATE THE THOUGHT OF LEAVING ALL MY PASSING ACQUAINTANCES!

THERE'S MARY SUE SWEETWATER AT THE DOOR!

NOW'S MY CHANCE TO REALLY MAKE A GOOD IMPRESSION!
BATIUK
1-15

WHO WERE YOU TALKING TO ?

I THINK MY NEW HALL MONITOR'S CHAIR IS GOING TO MAKE ME ONE HUNDRED

I REALLY DON'T SEE HOW A NEW
MUCH OF A HELP, LES!
BATIUK
1-16

I SEE HOW A NEW CHAIR COULD REALLY HELP!

THE BLACK STUDENTS IN THIS SCHOOL WANT TO SEE MORE BLACKS IN POSITIONS OF AUTHORITY AND POWER!
1-17

BUT WE HAVE BLACKS IN THE ADMINISTRATION AND ON THE SCHOOL BOARD, DEREK!

WHAT WE WANT IS A BLACK IN COMPUTER SCHEDULING!
BATIUK

THE FIRST ITEM ON OUR FACULTY MEETING AGENDA CONCERNS OUR TEACHERS' ORGANIZATION DUES!

SEVERAL TEACHERS HAVEN'T PAID YET ...
BATIUK
1-18

AND UNLESS THEY HAVE A NOTE FROM THEIR PARENTS, THEY'LL ALL BE SERVING DETENTIONS NEXT WEEK!

THE TASK WE FACE AS EDUCATORS IS NOT AN EASY ONE ...

IT WILL REQUIRE HARD WORK, SACRIFICE, AND DEDICATION! THEREFORE ...
BATIUK
1-19

THIS IS THE PART I LIKE ... WHERE HE DRAWS THE LINE ON THE FLOOR WITH HIS SWORD!

LISTENING TO YOUR STEREO AT FULL VOLUME IS PEACE ITSELF!

YOU CAN SHUT OUT THE WORLD AND ALL OF ITS PROBLEMS!

BATIUK

UNLESS, OF COURSE, YOU'RE LISTENING TO A JOAN BAEZ RECORD!
1-20

FUNKY WINKERBEAN
I SEE IT, BUT I DON'T BELIEVE IT!

YOU MEAN YOUR MOM MADE YOU WEAR A TIE FOR YOUR SCHOOL PICTURE?

BOY, ARE YOU EVER OUT OF IT, FUNKY!

NOBODY WEARS TIES FOR THEIR SCHOOL PICTURES ANYMORE!

YOU'LL BE THE LAUGHING STOCK OF THE ··· WHOLE ···
BATIUK
© Field Enterprises, Inc., 1973

OUR CHANCES LOOK PRETTY GOOD THIS YEAR, HUH, COACH?
1-22

THAT'S RIGHT, FRED! OUR BASKETBALL TEAM IS A CINCH TO MAKE IT TO THE STATE FINALS!
BATIUK

ONE MORE PAPER DRIVE AND WE'LL HAVE ENOUGH TO BUY TICKETS FOR THE WHOLE TEAM!
COACH

LET'S SEE ... I WAS GOING TO MAKE A NOTE TO DO SOMETHING ...
'73
1-23

YEOOWW!
'73
BATIUK

OH YEAH, ADJUST THE HOT WATER LINE TO THE SHOWER!
'73

TELL ME, FUNKY!

DID YOUR PARENTS CHECK YOUR EYES BEFORE YOU LEFT FOR SCHOOL?

YEAH, AS A MATTER OF FACT THEY DID, DEREK!
BATIUK

THE P.T.A. MUST HAVE HAD ANOTHER LECTURE ON DRUGS AGAIN!

HAROLD, YOU STILL HAVE SOME OUTSTANDING FEES FROM THE FIRST OF THE YEAR!

WHY THANK YOU, MISS WRIGHTON!
BATIUK

IT'S ALWAYS NICE TO BE NOTED FOR ONE'S ACCOMPLISHMENTS!
1-25

I DID JUST WHAT YOU SUGGESTED, FUNKY!

I SAW THAT MARY SUE WAS BUYING LUNCH SO I ASKED IF I COULD JOIN

..BUT I JUST COULDN'T GO THROUGH WITH IT!
YOU WERE TOO NERVOUS,
BATIUK
1-26

NO! THEY WERE HAVING MACARONI AND CHEESE AGAIN!

OH, OH ··· HERE COMES MARY SUE SWEETWATER!

EVERY TIME I TALK TO HER, I ALWAYS END UP SAYING SOMETHING STUPID!
BATIUK

HI, MARY SUE! BOY! YOU SURE LOOK NICE OUTSIDE TODAY!

THEN AGAIN, I SOMETIMES START OFF WITH SOMETHING STUPID!
1-27

FUNKY WINKERBEAN
COUNSELOR
REMEDIAL COUNSELIN

FUNKY, I HAVE THE RESULTS OF YOUR VOCATIONAL APTITUDE PROFILE!

IT INDICATES THAT YOU'RE OF EQUAL ABILITY IN TWO DIFFERENT FIELDS!
© Field Enterprises, Inc., 1973

WELL, HOW DO WE CHOOSE THE BEST ONE FOR ME, MR. FAIRGOOD?

FEAR NOT! THAT SITUATION IS COVERED BY SECTION (D) OF THE INTERPRETATION GUIDE!

BATIUK 1-28

LET'S SEE NOW...

SAY, I DON'T SUPPOSE YOU'D HAVE A COIN ON YOU?

WHY DID I HAVE TO GET A DETENTION TONIGHT?

I WAS GOING TO WALK MARY SUE TO HER BUS AND ASK HER TO THE GAME!
BATIUK

HERE I SIT AT THREE SIXTEEN, WHILE MY GIRL RIDES AWAY ON BUS FIFTEEN!
© Field Enterprises, Inc., 1973

I WONDER IF I COULD SELL THAT TO BUCK OWENS?
1-29

I CAN'T BELIEVE IT, HARRY!

YOU MEAN YOU'VE JUST LISTENED TO 'MY SWEET ANGEL' ONE HUNDRED AND SIX TIMES AT FULL VOLUME?
BATIUK
1-30

© Field Enterprises, Inc., 1973

ONE HUNDRED AND SEVEN!

CRAZY HARRY IS GOING TO LISTEN TO 'MY SWEET ANGEL' AT FULL VOLUME UNTIL HIS SPIRIT TRANSCENDS THE PHYSICAL WORLD!

HAS ANYTHING HAPPENED SO FAR, LES?

YEAH, HE'S HAD THREE NOSEBLEEDS!
BATIUK
© Field Enterprises, Inc., 1973
1-31

HOW CAN WE TELL WHEN CRAZY HARRY REACHES THE OUTER LEVEL OF HIS SPIRITUAL CONSCIOUSNESS, LES?

WELL, FUNKY, THE EYES TAKE ON A GLASSY VACANT LOOK AND THE MOUTH FORMS SORT OF A WARM IDIOTIC SMILE!
BATIUK
2-1

THAT'S WHAT I MEAN! WITH CRAZY HARRY, HOW CAN YOU TELL?

HOW'S CRAZY HARRY'S LITTLE MIND TRIP COMING?

HE'S INTO LEVELS OF CONSCIOUSNESS FEW MORTALS HAVE EVER EXPERIENCED, BUT HE HASN'T REACHED PEAK AWARENESS YET!
2-2

THE BANANA IS MIGHTIER THAN THE PEEL!
BATIUK

I TAKE IT HE'S BROKEN THROUGH!
SIGH!

HE DID IT!!

CRAZY HARRY LISTENED TO 'MY SWEET ANGEL' AT FULL VOLUME, AND REACHED NIRVANA ON THE TWO HUNDREDTH REPLAY!
2-3

BATIUK
WELL, SPORT, WHAT DO YOU HAVE TO SAY?

IT'S GOT A GOOD BEAT AND IT'S GOOD TO DANCE TO! I'D GIVE IT AN EIGHTY-FIVE!

FUNKY WINKERBEAN
HOME SWEET HOME

OKAY, 'CRAZY HARRY', THIS IS YOUR LAST WARNING!

I KNOW THAT YOU'RE IN THAT LOCKER AND I WANT YOU OUT IMMEDIATELY!

WHAT MAKES YOU THINK I'M IN HERE?

I HAPPEN TO HAVE RELIABLE WITNESSES WHO SAW YOU GO IN!
BATIUK

I KNEW I COULDN'T FAKE YOU OUT!
© Field Enterprises, Inc., 1973

MR. BURCH, I'M HERE TO INTERVIEW YOU FOR THE SCHOOL PAPER!
FINE!
BATIUK
2-5

TO WHAT DO YOU OWE THE DEVELOPMENT OF YOUR ARCH-CONSERVATIVE AND REPRESSIVE IDEAS IN SCHOOL ADMINISTRATION?

DON'T YOU ASK QUESTIONS LIKE WHAT MY FAVORITE COLOR IS ANYMORE?

I THOUGHT I'D BAKE SOMETHING FOR OUR NEXT 'RAP CELLAR' MEETING, JAN!
2-6

ARE YOU GOING TO MAKE IT FROM SCRATCH, MARCIA?

NO! I TRIED IT ONCE, BUT THE GRAVEL RUINED MY MIXER!
BATIUK

BULL, I'M GOING TO LET YOU START THESE MATH PROBLEMS...

...AND YOU LET ME KNOW WHEN YOU'RE STUCK! FIRST NUMBER YOUR PAPER FROM ONE TO TEN!

I'M STUCK!
BATIUK
2-7

THERE'S BEEN A LOT OF TROUBLE IN THE CAFETERIA STUDY HALL AND CRAZY HARRY SEEMS TO BE AT THE BOTTOM OF IT!
2-8

WELL, LET'S CALL HIM IN AND ASK HIM ABOUT IT!
PRINCIPAL

ARE YOU KIDDING? THAT'S LIKE ASKING THE FOX WHAT HAPPENED IN THE CHICKEN COOP!
PRINCIPAL
BATIUK
© Field Enterprises, Inc., 1973

THE COMMITTEE ON REVISING THE GRADING STRUCTURE HAS MADE ITS PROPOSAL!

DURING THE NEXT SIX WEEKS WE WILL DO AWAY WITH REPORT CARDS AND INSTEAD EMPHASIZE POSITIVE REINFORCEMENT!
BATIUK
2-9
© Field Enterprises, Inc., 1973

A LARGE BARREL OF JELLY BEANS WILL BE PLACED IN EACH HOMEROOM FOR THIS PURPOSE!

THAT'S PRETTY GOOD, FUNKY!
2-10

I USED TO PLAY A LOT MYSELF...
© Field Enterprises, Inc., 1973
BATIUK

...UNTIL THAT LITTLE CRANK ON MY GUITAR BROKE!

BATIUK © Field Enterprises, Inc., 1973

alumnus

alumni

alumnox
BATIUK
2-12

I'M ONE OF THE FEW PEOPLE AROUND WHO CAN CONJUGATE A NOUN!
© Field Enterprises, Inc., 1973

WHO'S WINNING, SPORTS FANS?

I AM, DEREK! I'VE GOT TWO OF HIS HORSES AND HE ONLY HAS ONE OF MY WATCHTOWERS!

SHE'S NEW AT THE GAME!
I'M HIP!
BATIUK
2-13

LOOK, LIVINIA! I AGREE WITH YOU THAT CHEERLEADERS DO TEND TO PERPETUATE

AND I THINK YOUR PROPOSED SOLUTION WAS MOTIVATED BY SINCERE INTENTIONS!
BATIUK

BUT SOMEHOW, POM POM PERSON JUST DOESN'T HAVE THE RIGHT RING TO IT!
2-14

THE STUDENTS HATE ME, DON'T THEY, FRED?

WHY? WHAT MAKES YOU SAY THAT?

THE OTHER DAY A KID OFFERED TO BUY ME LUNCH IN THE CAFETERIA!
BATIUK
2-15

WANNA PLAY SOME PING PONG TONIGHT, LES?

WELL, ACTUALLY I WAS GOING TO SEE IF MARY SUE WOULD GO TO THE GAME WITH ME, FUNKY!

IF I GET SHOT DOWN, I'LL STOP BY, OKAY?
BATIUK
2-16

SURE! SEE YOU TONIGHT!

WICKED WANDA, YOU'RE NOTHING MORE THAN A SNOBBISH, FEMALE CHAUVINIST BULLY!

WHAT DO YOU HAVE TO SAY TO THAT, SWEETHEART?

SWISH!
I SHORTENED HER STICK!
2-17

FUNKY WINKERBEAN
A+
Blank Verse

SOMETIMES I WISH I WAS BACK IN GRADE SCHOOL!

REMEMBER THOSE LITTLE REWARDS WE USED TO GET?

YEAH, FUNKY! THE TEACHER USED TO STICK A LITTLE BRIGHT COLORED PICTURE OF AN ANIMAL OR PIECE OF FRUIT ON OUR PAPERS!

I ALWAYS USED TO GET DUCKS AND APPLES!
BATIUK
2-18

I'D GET A LOT OF BUNNIES AND ORANGES!

I USED TO GET TURKEYS AND LEMONS!

IT'S HOPELESS, FUNKY! THE STUDENT BODY IS JUST TOO APATHETIC TO JOIN ME IN MY FIGHT AGAINST THE TYRANNY OF THE SCHOOL ADMINISTRATION!

POWER TO THE PEOPLE!
2-19

WITH THE EXCEPTION, OF COURSE, OF THE LUNATIC FRINGE!
BATIUK

THIS SCHOOL IS REALLY GETTING TO BE A GRIND, 'CRAZY'!
2-20

QUIZZES, READING ASSIGNMENTS, PAPERS TO DO, ... IT'S ONE SHOT IN THE HEAD AFTER ANOTHER!

WHAT'S THE PURPOSE OF ALL OF THIS, ANYWAY?
BATIUK

IT'S SORT OF A MOUSE RACE THAT PREPARES YOU FOR THE RAT RACE!

I HATE WRITING THESE STAFF NOTICES!

I'M SURE THERE ARE THOSE WHO RESENT THESE LITTLE REMINDERS!
2-21

AND YET IT'S MY RESPONSIBILITY TO SEE THAT DISCIPLINE AND ORDER ARE MAINTAINED!

BESIDES, THIS IS THE THIRD TIME SOME-ONE HAS PARKED IN MY SPACE THIS WEEK!

AS YOU KNOW, EACH WEEK I PREPARE A STAFF BULLETIN!

FOR THOSE OF YOU WHO WOULD LIKE TO KEEP YOUR BULLETINS IN MINT CONDITION, AND AT YOUR FINGERTIPS FOR READY REFERENCE...
BATIUK
2-12

I'M SELLING THIS GOLD EMBOSSED, SIMULATED LEATHER BINDER WHICH NEATLY HOLDS A YEAR'S COLLECTION!
BULLETINS
© Field Enterprises, Inc., 1973

FUNKY, ABOUT THIS BOOK REPORT YOU DID ON A SPIDERMAN COMIC BOOK...

I KNOW WHAT YOU'RE GOING TO SAY...

I SHOULD'VE READ THE WHOLE THING, RIGHT?
© Field Enterprises, Inc., 1973
BATIUK
2-13

YIIEEEE

SIGH!
© Field Enterprises, Inc., 1973
BATIUK

BOY! SCRATCHES ARE MURDER AT FULL VOLUME!
2-24

FUNKY WINKERBEAN

NOW THIS PIECE IS THE BISHOP, LIVINIA!

THE BISHOP CAN ONLY MOVE DIAGONALLY!

THE QUEEN, ON THE OTHER HAND, CAN MOVE BOTH DIAGONALLY AND IN A STRAIGHT LINE!

OKAY, FUNKY, I THINK I UNDERSTAND ALL THE RULES!

ARE YOU READY TO START?
BATIUK
© Field Enterprises, Inc., 1973
2-25

YEP! PLUG IT IN!

THERE'S A FASCINATING ARTICLE IN 'GRADEBOOK MAGAZINE' THIS MONTH!
PRINCIPAL
2-26

IT SAYS THAT THE PRIME MOTIVATION FOR THE MAJORITY OF TEENAGERS IS SEX!
BATIUK

I WISH THAT WERE TRUE!
© Field Enterprises, Inc., 1973

IT WOULD SURE SAVE US A BUNDLE ON SCHOOL BUSES!
PRINCIPAL

MAY I HELP YOU?

THIS IS A CHECK-OUT COUNTER, ISN'T IT?
THAT'S RIGHT!

WELL, I'M CHECKING YOU OUT!
© Field Enterprises, Inc., 1973
BATIUK
2-27

I'D LIKE TO GET THE CHEAPEST PHONE I CAN FOR MY UNDERGROUND PAPER HERE!

WELL, YOU HAVE A CHOICE BETWEEN OUR REGULAR CHEAP MODEL AND OUR DELUXE CHEAP MODEL!
© Field Enterprises, Inc., 1973
2-28

WHAT'S YOUR DELUXE CHEAP MODEL?

WE ATTACH BALING WIRE INSTEAD OF STRING TO YOUR TIN CAN!

HI! REMEMBER ME?
© Field Enterprises, Inc., 1973

I SURE DO!
BATIUK

YOU'RE THE ONE WHO BUYS CHEWING GUM WITH A MASTER CHARGE!
3-1

I'M SORRY, BUT I HAVE PLANS FOR SUNDAY AFTERNOON TOO!

WELL, LET'S SEE ··· THAT RULES OUT SUNDAY, MONDAY, TUESDAY, WEDNESDAY, THURSDAY, FRIDAY ···

BEGINNING TO PICK UP A PATTERN, ARE YA?
BATIUK
3-2

HI! SAY, WHAT HAPPENED TO THE GIRL THAT WAS HERE YESTERDAY?

OH, ··· SHE'S ON VACATION AND WON'T BE BACK FOR A WEEK!
A MONTH!

··· ER, A MONTH!
© Field Enterprises, Inc., 1973
BATIUK
3-3

FUNKY WINKERBEAN

THIS IS A PRETTY GOOD HORROR MOVIE, FUNKY!

I LIKED THE PART WHERE THE GUY TORTURED HIS VOODOO DOLL BY GETTING ACUPUNCTURE TREATMENTS!

THEY'LL PROBABLY KNOCK OFF THE MONSTER BY LURING HIM TOWARDS THE HYDROELECTRIC PLANT!

NAW! THEY WOULDN'T USE AN OLD TRITE, CLICHE ENDING LIKE THAT!

3-4
BATIUK

I'VE GOT A PLAN! OUR LAST HOPE IS TO LURE IT TOWARDS THE HYDROELECTRIC PLANT!

THEN AGAIN, WHY MESS AROUND WITH A PROVEN CROWD PLEASER?

WHAT DO YOU MEAN I CAN'T GET INTO THE GAME WITHOUT AN I.D. CARD?
TICK
STUDEN
ADULTS

I'M STILL ME! JUST BECAUSE I DON'T HAVE SOME SILLY CARD, DOESN'T MEAN I DONT EXIST!
TICK
STUDENT
ADULTS
3-5

WHO SAID THAT?
TICK
STUDENT
ADULTS
BATIUK
© Field Enterprises, Inc., 1973

I'D LIKE TO WELCOME YOU PARENTS TO TONIGHT'S P.T.A. MEETING!

BEFORE WE GET DOWN TO OUR FILM AND PANEL DISCUSSION ON THE SEXUAL BEHAVIOR OF THE MODERN TEENAGER...
BATIUK

... I'D LIKE TO APOLOGIZE TO ALL OF YOU PARENTS WHO HAVE TO STAND OR SIT IN THE AISLES!
© Field Enterprises, Inc., 1973
3-6

TOMORROW WE WILL BE ADMINISTERING THE FRINKER AND BLOTTMEYER COMPREHENSIVE TEST OF BASIC SKILLS!
© Field Enterprises, Inc., 1973
3-7

NOW, YOU'LL NEED TO BRING TWO NUMBER TWO LEAD PENCILS!

ANYONE WHO DOES NOT HAVE TWO NUMBER TWO LEAD PENCILS WILL BE BLACKBALLED AT EVERY UNIVERSITY IN THE STATE!

IF YOU SHOULD HAVE A QUESTION AT ANYTIME DURING THIS TEST ...

... JUST RAISE YOUR HAND!
BATIUK
© Field Enterprises, Inc., 1973

THIS SHOULD ALLOW ENOUGH BLOOD TO DRAIN FROM YOUR ARM TO YOUR BRAIN TO ENABLE YOU TO SOLVE THE PROBLEM YOURSELF!
3-8

NEXT ON OUR AGENDA IS A REPORT FROM THE STUDENT COUNCIL 'WAYS AND MEANS' COMMITTEE!

I WOULD LIKE TO REPORT THAT OUR HALLOWEEN CANDY SALE IS JUST ABOUT FINISHED! THE RESULTS HAVE BEEN GOOD EXCEPT FOR SOME COMPLAINTS ABOUT STALE CANDY!
BATIUK

THEREFORE, I WOULD SUGGEST THAT WE CHANGE CANDY COMPANIES NEXT YEAR!
© Field Enterprises, Inc., 1973
3-9

YOU SURE GET SOME PRETTY WILD SOUNDS FROM YOUR STEREO, CRAZY!

WHAT'VE YOU GOT ON THERE RIGHT NOW?

A FROZEN PIZZA!
© Field Enterprises, Inc., 1973

STICK AROUND! THERE'S A GREAT PEPPERONI SECTION COMING UP!
BATIUK
3-10

FUNKY WINKERBEAN

YOU LOOK LIKE SOMETHING'S BUGGING YOU, LES!

IT'S REALLY NOTHING, FUNKY!
3-11

IT'S JUST ONE OF THOSE INSOLUBLE PROBLEMS THAT SORT OF KEEP NAGGING AT YOU!

WHY DON'T YOU TELL ME ABOUT IT?

MAYBE I CAN GIVE YOU A DIFFERENT PERSPECTIVE ON IT!
BATIUK

OKAY,... WHY DO COWBOY HATS HAVE DENTS IN THEM?

THE HALL MONITOR'S LOT IS ONE OF LONG LONELY VIGILS!
3-12

OFTEN THERE'S A FAINT BREEZE IN AN EMPTY HALLWAY, AND SOMETIMES IT SEEMS AS IF THE LOCKERS ARE WHISPERING TO ONE ANOTHER!
BATIUK

THAT'S WHEN YOU FIRST REALIZE YOU'RE STARTING TO GO OFF YOUR COOKIE!
© Field Enterprises, Inc., 1973

I KNOW WHAT YOU MEAN ABOUT WOMEN'S ROLES CHANGING, LUVINIA!

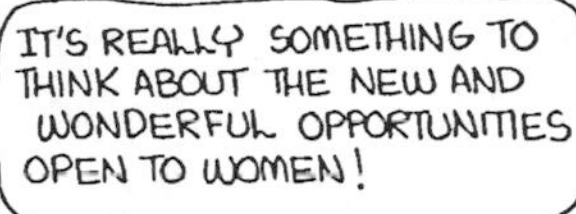
IT'S REALLY SOMETHING TO THINK ABOUT THE NEW AND WONDERFUL OPPORTUNITIES OPEN TO WOMEN!

3-13

WHO WOULD HAVE EVER THOUGHT THE DAY WOULD COME WHEN WE'D BE COOKING VEGETABLES IN LITTLE PLASTIC BAGS!
© Field Enterprises, Inc., 1973

ROLAND, DO YOU EVER WORRY THAT YOU MAY BE FORCED TO DISCLOSE YOUR NEWS SOURCES?
3-14

NOT A BIT, DEREK!
BATIUK

I MAKE THEM ALL UP!

AS YOU KNOW, DEREK, IT WAS MY IDEA TO TRY COMPUTERIZED SCHEDULING THIS YEAR, AND I WAS WONDERING WHAT YOU THOUGHT OF IT?

© Field Enterprises, Inc., 1973
IT WAS REALLY FANTASTIC!

I NEVER GOT TO BE IN A GIRL'S GYM CLASS BEFORE!
3-15
BATIUK

TELL ME, COACH ...
COACH
3-16

HOW DO YOU GET YOUR TEAM UP FOR A GAME?

OH, WE USE ALARM CLOCKS, COLD WATER ... WHATEVER'S HANDY!
COACH
BATIUK
© Field Enterprises, Inc., 1973

HI, JOHN DARLING HERE, ASKING PASSERSBY OUR TYPICAL INANE QUESTION OF THE DAY!
© Field Enterprises, Inc., 1973

HI, PASSERBY! WHAT WITH THE NEW PERMISSIVENESS AND ALL, DO YOU THINK THE WORD '▬▬' WILL EVER BE ALLOWED IN A NEWSPAPER COMIC STRIP?
BATIUK
3-17

I DOUBT IT!

FUNKY WINKERBEAN
AAAGH!

SURE IT HURTS! BIG DEAL... WHAT ARE YOU? A QUITTER?

YOU'VE GOT TO LEARN TO PLAY WITH PAIN!!

THAT'S DISGUSTING! I THINK THAT THE WAY THE COACH TREATS HIS ATHLETES IS BRUTAL AND DEHUMANIZING!

THAT'S NOT THE COACH!
3-18

THAT'S THE BAND DIRECTOR TRYING TO GET MARY ELLEN FREEGLY TO PLAY THE TUBA WITH HER BRACES!
BATIUK

HERE I AM AT MY HOME AWAY FROM HOME!

THIS MARKS MY NINETY-EIGHTH TRIP TO THE PRINCIPAL'S OFFICE THIS YEAR!
3-19

TWO MORE AND I GET MY FOOTPRINTS PLACED IN THE SIDEWALK IN FRONT OF THE SCHOOL!
BATIUK
© Field Enterprises, Inc., 1973

THE PRINCIPAL ALWAYS LIKES TO KEEP YOU WAITING A WHILE TO SEE IF HE CAN MAKE YOU SWEAT!
TAKE ONE!

WHAT'S THIS? A BOX OF LEAD BULLETS WITH TEETH MARKS ALL OVER THEM!
TAKE ONE!
BATIUK

THAT'S A REAL CUTE TOUCH!
TAKE ONE!
3-20
© Field Enterprises, Inc., 1973

SOFT DRINKS
15¢
© Field Enterprises, Inc., 1973

HA! DID YOU SEE THAT, FUNKY?
3-21

I HIT THE JACKPOT! I FINALLY GOT ICE, CARBONATED WATER, AND SYRUP ... ALL IN THE SAME DRINK!
BATIUK

WAY TO GO! TOO BAD THE CUP DIDN'T COME DOWN!

I WAS TOLD TO COME TO YOUR OFFICE, MR. BURCH!

WHO SENDS YOU?
3-22

JOEY HEATHERTON!
BATIUK
© Field Enterprises, Inc. 1973

YES, THIS IS THE YOUTH COUNSELING CENTER!
EMERGENCY RAP-LINE

OKAY, NOW JUST STAY CALM! BELIEVE ME THERE'S REALLY NOTHING TO WORRY ABOUT...
© Field Enterprises, Inc. 1973
BATIUK
3-23

NO... IF YOU'RE STILL IN THE TUB WHEN YOU PULL OUT THE PLUG, YOU WON'T GO DOWN THE DRAIN!
EMERGENCY RAP-LINE

STILL PLAYING FROZEN PIZZAS ON YOUR STEREO, CRAZY?
3-24

YEAH, FUNKY, BUT I'M NOT GETTING THE KIND OF SOUND I WANT!
BATIUK

I'M GOING TO HAVE TO INVEST IN AN ANCHOVY FILTER!
© Field Enterprises, Inc. 1973

FUNKY WINKERBEAN

STUDENT FILES

MR. BURCH! I DEMAND TO BE ALLOWED TO SEE MY STUDENT FILE!

IT'S MY RIGHT TO SEE WHATEVER INFORMATION YOU'VE COLLECTED ABOUT ME!
BATIUK

IF YOU DENY ME MY RIGHTS, I'LL TAKE IT TO COURT AND MAKE A TEST CASE…
ENOUGH!

YOUR REQUEST SEEMS MATURE AND REASONABLE ENOUGH, ROLAND! HERE!

© Field Enterprises, Inc., 1973
3-25

SEE, FUNKY?

SON OF A GUN! YOU DID HAVE FRECKLES IN YOUR FIRST GRADE PICTURE!

EVERY TIME I'M SENT TO SEE THE PRINCIPAL, HE CALLS ME A HOOD!
3-26

HE DOESN'T REALIZE HOW DEEPLY THAT HURTS! I MEAN I CAN BE EMOTIONALLY SCARRED BY ATTITUDES LIKE THAT! HE DOESN'T UNDERSTAND ME! I'M NOT A HOOD!

I'M AN ANARCHIST!
BATIUK

SAY, I'LL BET YOU'VE NEVER HAD YOUR PALM READ, LIVINIA!

HERE, LET ME READ IT FOR YOU!
SIGH!

IT SAYS ... QUIT BUGGING ME, CREEP!

I WONDER HOW SHE DID THAT?
BATIUK
3-27

I MADE UP A FEW SLOGANS FOR YOUR EDITORIAL AGAINST STUDENT SMOKING, LES!
LET'S HEAR ONE, LIVINIA!

OKAY... SMOKE AND DIE YOU CLOWN!

SUBTLETY NEVER WAS ONE OF YOUR STRONG SUITS, WAS IT?
BATIUK

BIG WALNUT TECH SURE HAS PUT ON SOME INTERESTING HALFTIME SHOWS DURING THE BASKETBALL GAMES THIS YEAR, FUNKY!
BATIUK
3-29

I WONDER WHAT TONIGHT'S WILL BE LIKE ?

I HEARD THEY WERE DOING A VALVE JOB ON A '62 CHEVY!

ANOTHER FRIDAY NIGHT AT HOME ALONE AND I'M GETTING AN IRRESISTIBLE URGE TO DROWN MY SORROWS IN A PIZZA!

WELL, I'M NOT GOING TO GIVE IN AND ORDER ONE!

HERE'S WHERE I SHOW MY TRUE METTLE!

HELLO, MONTONI'S ?
BATIUK
3-30

I'M DEFINITELY NOT GOING TO ORDER A PIZZA TONIGHT!

I'M NOT GOING TO LET MY STOMACH DICTATE TO THE REST OF MY BODY!

AFTER ALL, WHAT AM I, A MAN ... OR A MOUSE ?

YEAH! A LARGE ONE ... WITH LOTS OF CHEESE!
BATIUK
3-31

FUNKY WINKERBEAN
HALL MONITOR

HALL MONITOR
HEY, WHY DON'T WE PUT UP OUR SPIRIT POSTER HERE ?

OKAY! THIS LOOKS LIKE A PRETTY GOOD SPOT !

OKAY, THAT DOES IT ! LET'S GET BACK TO THE ART ROOM !
4-1
BATIUK

YEA TEAM!
IS IT ME, OR DOES THERE SEEM TO BE LESS RESPECT FOR AUTHORITY THESE DAYS ?
© Field Enterprises, Inc., 1973

I REALLY DON'T FEEL I'M WANTED AROUND HERE, DEREK!

THIS MORNING I FOUND SOMEONE SCRIBBLING, 'GO BACK TO THE SCHOOL YOU CAME FROM', ON MY LOCKER!

© Field Enterprises, Inc. 1973

I CAN'T BELIEVE ANY KID AROUND HERE WOULD DO THAT, 'CRAZY'!

4-2

IT WASN'T! IT WAS THE PRINCIPAL!
BATIUK

WELL, HAROLD, DO YOU KNOW WHY I HAD YOU COME IN AFTER SCHOOL TONIGHT?
© Field Enterprises, Inc. 1973

BECAUSE YOU'VE GOT A MAD CRUSH ON ME AND YOU WANTED US TO BE ALONE WHEN YOU TOLD ME!
4-3

PRINCIPAL
WRONG AGAIN!
BATIUK

CRAZY HARRY, THIS IS YOUR FIRST YEAR AT OUR SCHOOL AND ALREADY YOU'VE BEEN SENT TO MY OFFICE A RECORD NUMBER OF TIMES!

DO YOU REALIZE WHAT THIS KIND OF RECORD COULD LEAD TO?

ROOKIE OF THE YEAR?
BATIUK
4-4
© Field Enterprises, Inc. 1973

WHY HAVE YOU BEEN SULKING IN YOUR LOCKER ALL DAY, 'CRAZY'?

BECAUSE THE PRINCIPAL WON'T GET OFF MY BACK, THAT'S WHY!

WHAT ARE YOU DOING NOW?
4-5

TYPING UP MY RESIGNATION!
BATIUK
© Field Enterprises, Inc., 1973

STRANGE ...!?

I COULD'VE SWORN I SMELLED PIZZA!

OH WELL ...

PASS THE PEPPERONI!
4-6
© Field Enterprises, Inc., 1973

I THINK MY
GOOD AND BAD POINTS OF WOMEN'S LIB REALLY LAYS IT ON THE LINE!
© Field Enterprises, Inc., 1973

I WONDER WHAT SORT OF REACTION
LOCAL LIBBYS?

SMASH!
4-7
BATIUK

A POSTCARD WOULD HAVE

FUNKY WINKERBEAN
CUB REPORTER

MR. FAIRGOOD, I'M INTERVIEWING FOR THE SCHOOL PAPER AND I'D LIKE TO KNOW HOW YOU VIEW YOUR ROLE AS A COUNSELOR!

I FEEL THAT I REPRESENT SOMEONE TO WHOM A STUDENT CAN RELATE, LES!

SOMEONE WHO IS SYMPATHETIC TO STUDENT PROBLEMS AND IS WILLING TO SIT DOWN AND RAP WITH THEM!
© Field Enterprises, Inc., 1973
BATIUK
4-8

I TRY TO APPROACH EACH STUDENT ON A ONE-TO-ONE BASIS, AND, IN HELPING THEM I MAKE USE OF ALL THE PROFESSIONAL AND MODERN DIAGNOSTIC COUNSELING TOOLS AT MY DISPOSAL!

I TRY TO BE OPEN AND FAIR SO THAT A STUDENT WILL FEEL FREE TO BRING ANY PROBLEM TO ME!

JUST A SEC... MR. FAIRGOOD... SAID HE... FELT...

I DON'T KNOW WHAT IT IS, FUNKY, BUT MY LUCK WITH GIRLS SEEMS MORE DISMAL THAN USUAL LATELY!

LOOK, LES, PRETEND I'M A GIRL AND YOU'RE ASKING ME OUT! MAYBE I CAN SPOT SOME THINGS THAT YOU'RE DOING WRONG!
BATIUK
4-9

THIS IS GOING TO WORK! I'M NOTICING THINGS ALREADY!

SIGH!

I'M SURE THE REASON MARY SUE WON'T GO OUT WITH ME IS BECAUSE HER SIGN IS AQUARIUS!

IF I WERE A SAGITTARIUS, I MIGHT STAND A CHANCE ···
4-10

···BUT TO HER, I'M ONLY ANOTHER PISCES IN THE POND!
BATIUK

MR. BURCH, I THINK WE SHOULD CONSIDER
OUR AMERICAN HISTORY COURSE!

IT DEALS QUITE EXTENSIVELY WITH THE HISTORY OF INDIANS,
BLACKS, AND OTHER OPPRESSED

TERRIFIC! LET ME SEE THE CHAPTERS ON PRINCIPALS!
BATIUK
4-11

YOU KNOW, DAD, MAYBE WE COULD GET ALONG BETTER IF WE'D JUST ADMIT THAT WE BOTH HAVE DIFFERENT LIFE-STYLES!

YOU CALL THAT STYLE ?
BATIUK

CUT IT OUT, MOM!
4-12

I'M GOING TO CONQUER MY FEARS!

NOW THAT NO ONE IS AROUND, I'M GOING TO PROVE TO MYSELF THAT I'M NOT TOO CHICKEN TO CLIMB UP AND DOWN THAT STUPID ROPE!

HERE I GO UP!
BATIUK
4-13

BOY! IT SURE GETS DARK ENOUGH IN THIS GYM AT NIGHT!

AND NOW FOR OUR SATURDAY ADVENTURE MOVIE ...

WE PROUDLY PRESENT ALFONSO RAMANDO IN 'JUNGLE DRUMS'!
FAR OUT!

DUB DUBBA
DUB DUB
DUBBA...
4-14

I HATE MOVIES THAT ARE DUBBED!
BATIUK

FUNKY WINKERBEAN
I GUESS I'LL WATCH THIS TILL THE GAME COMES ON!

THIS IS DICK CLARK AND AMERICAN BANDSTAND CHECKING BACK WITH OUR TWO TEEN JUDGES TO GET THEIR REACTION TO SONG NUMBER TWO!

WHAT DID YOU THINK OF IT, CHERYL?

IT'S NOT YOUR BASIC ROCK! IT'S ACCESSIBLE ONLY ON A HIGHER LEVEL WHERE YOU CAN GET INTO THE ARTIST'S PRIVATE CRUCIBLE OF PAIN!
BATIUK

YOU CAN TELL THE ARTIST HAS STRUGGLED AND THE SONG IS HIS PERSONAL REFLECTION OF THE ULTIMATE AMERICAN CLAUSTROPHOBIA!
4-15

I MEAN IT'S ALL THERE! I'D GIVE IT AN EIGHTY!

WHAT ABOUT YOU, BOB?
© Field Enterprises, Inc., 1973

WELL…I WAS GOING TO SAY IT HAS A GOOD BEAT AND IS FUN TO DANCE TO, BUT I THINK I'LL JUST SIT DOWN!

WELL, FRED, I FINALLY CALLED IN CRAZY HARRY'S PARENTS TO DISCUSS HIS CHRONIC PROBLEM WITH UNEXCUSED TARDINESS!

HOW DID IT GO?
4-16

THEY WERE LATE!
BATIUK

I HEARD THAT THE GOVERNMENT THINKS THE TV NEWS MEDIA PRESENTS A SLANTED VIEW OF THE NEWS AND SAYS THEY ENGAGE IN ELITIST GOSSIP!
4-17

WHERE DID YOU HEAR ALL THIS, LES?
BATIUK

IT WAS JUST ON THE NEWS HERE A WHILE AGO!

SOMETIMES TIME REALLY SEEMS TO DRAG WHEN I'M AT MY HALL MONITOR'S STATION!

LIKE TODAY! IT SEEMS SO LONG SINCE THE BELL HAS RUNG THAT I'VE GOT THIS FUNNY FEELING THAT SCHOOL IS OVER AND I'M THE ONLY ONE HERE!
BATIUK
4-18

AND IT'S GOTTEN A LOT WORSE SINCE THE SUN WENT DOWN!

TELL ME, LES, HOW DID A TURKEY LIKE YOU EVER GET TO BE EDITOR OF THE SCHOOL PAPER?

WELL ACTUALLY, DEREK, I WAS PICKED BY THE PRINCIPAL!

I'M NOT REALLY SURE WHY MYSELF!
4-19
I WAS JUST SITTING AT MY HALL MONITOR'S STATION ONE DAY HUMMING THE SCHOOL FIGHT SONG AND ...

THIS IS YOUR STUDENT COUNCIL PRESIDENT, REMINDING YOU THAT WE NEED YOUR SUPPORT!

HELP MAKE YOUR STUDENT COUNCIL RELEVANT AND MEANINGFUL BECAUSE IT REPRESENTS YOU!
4-20
BATIUK

AND DON'T FORGET THAT FRIDAY, DURING LUNCH, WE'LL HAVE OUR TURTLE RACE BETWEEN HOMEROOMS!

NOW HERE'S THE STUPID NEWS ...

SO PAY ATTENTION, BECAUSE I'M ONLY READING IT ONCE!

...AND BEFORE I START I WANT YOU TO KNOW THAT I HATE YOU, I HATE THIS JOB AND I ONLY STICK AROUND BECAUSE THERE'S MUCHO BUCKS INVOLVED!
BATIUK
4-21

NOW THERE'S A NEWS PROGRAM WITH A REFRESHING FORMAT!

FUNKY WINKERBEAN

BOY! THAT FULL MOON IS REALLY SOMETHING TO SEE, ISN'T IT, HARRY?

EVERY TIME I SEE THE MOON LIKE THAT...

IT MAKES ME REALIZE HOW TINY MAN IS COMPARED TO THE UNIVERSE! IT GIVES ME A TREMENDOUS FEELING OF INSIGNIFICANCE!
© Field Enterprises, Inc., 1973
4-22

NOT ME, FUNKY! I GET A DIFFERENT FEELING!

LIKE WHAT?
BATIUK

I DON'T KNOW... JUST DIFFERENT!

I ASSUME YOU'VE ALL READ THE SUPERINTENDENT'S MESSAGE!

I FOUND MANY ENCOURAGING POINTS AND A FEW DISCOURAGING ONES!

I THINK THE FACT THAT SCHOOL WILL BE CLOSED NEXT YEAR DUE TO LACK OF FUNDS, WOULD HAVE TO RANK AS THE MAJOR DISAPPOINTMENT!
BATIUK
4-23

RRRING
RUMBLE RUM

DON'T YOU HAVE A CLASS NEXT PERIOD?
BATIUK

YES, BUT I NEVER GO OUT IN THE HALL DURING CLASS CHANGE!
4-24

THE LAST TIME I DID I WAS SWEPT ALL THE WAY DOWN PAST THE CAFETERIA BEFORE I MANAGED TO GRAB A LOCKER AND STOP MYSELF!

RRRING!
BATIUK
4-25

DARN IT! I MISSED MY ROOM!
RUMBLE RUMBLE

NOW I'VE GOT TO GO ALL THE WAY AROUND AGAIN!
RUMBLE RUMBLE RUMBL

OH, OH! THIS IS MY ROOM COMING UP!
RUMBLERUMBL

OKAY, GET READY TO BAIL OUT! ONE ··· TWO ··· THREE·· GO!
RUMBLERUM
BATIUK
© Field Enterprises, Inc., 1973
4-26

BLAM!

TOO BAD! HIS TIMING WAS OFF AND HE TURNED RIGHT INTO THE WALL!
RUMBLERU

THE P.T.A. WILL REALLY BE PLEASED WITH THESE COOKIES I MADE FOR THE BAKE SALE!
BATIUK

RRRING!
4-27

SHRIEK!!
RUMBLERU

IS IT MY IMAGINATION, OR DOES IT SEEM LIKE WE'RE WALKING ON CHOCOLATE CHIP COOKIES?
RUMBLERUMBL

PETER SMOOTH'S MAKE-OUT MANUAL!
4-28

RULE NO. 1: DON'T BE AFRAID TO APPROACH A GIRL! JUST WALK RIGHT UP TO HER AND SAY ANYTHING! PRACTICE THIS!
BATIUK

ANYTHING, ANYTHING ANYTHING ····

FUNKY WINKERBEAN

THAT'LL BE TWENTY-FIVE CENTS!

BOY! INFLATION REALLY HITS HOME WHEN THE PRICE OF SUNFLOWER SEEDS GOES UP!

WHAT'S THAT YOU'VE GOT THERE, HARRY?
BATIUK
4-29

I JUST GOT SOME SUNFLOWER SEEDS DOWN AT THE SACRED MUSHROOM ORGANIC SHOP! DO YOU WANT A FEW?

YEAH! THANKS A LOT!

SAY... HOW DEEP ARE YOU SUPPOSED TO PLANT THESE?
©Field Enterprises, Inc., 1973

FUNKY, DO YOU REALIZE THAT YOUR DAD'S COMPANY IS DUMPING INDUSTRIAL WASTES INTO WATER WE EVENTUALLY USE FOR DRINKING?

I KNOW, BUT THEY'RE DOING SOMETHING ABOUT IT, LIVINIA!
LIKE WHAT?
© Field Enterprises, Inc. 1973
BATIUK
4-30

THEY'RE ADDING VITAMINS TO THEIR INDUSTRIAL WASTE!

I HATE SITTING HERE WAITING TO SEE THE PRINCIPAL!

THIS IS GETTING TO BE MORE BORING THAN SOME OF MY CLASSES!
© Field Enterprises, Inc. 1973
BATIUK
5-1

I WONDER WHAT THE CHANCES WOULD BE OF GETTING STUDENT COUNCIL TO PUT A MAGAZINE RACK OUT HERE?

FUNKY, WE'VE JUST DISCOVERED AN OVERDUE BOOK THAT YOU'VE HAD OUT FOR SOME TIME!
© Field Enterprises, Inc. 1973
5-2

DO I OWE A BIG FINE?

WELL, WE'RE NAMING THE NEW WING AFTER YOU!
BATIUK

YOU KNOW, FUNKY, SINCE YOU'VE BEEN HELPING ME, I REALLY LIKE SCIENCE NOW!

IN FACT WHEN I DIE, I'M GOING TO DONATE MY BRAIN TO SCIENCE!
© Field Enterprises, Inc., 1973
5-3

OH, WELL ... IT'S THE THOUGHT THAT COUNTS!
BATIUK

OUR STUDENT COUNCIL 'WAYS AND MEANS' COMMITTEE HAS SUBMITTED THE FOLLOWING REPORT!
5-4

IT SAYS: 'WE'VE RUN OUT OF WAYS, SO YOU KNOW WHAT THAT MEANS'!
BATIUK

I AGREE THAT WOMEN'S LIB IS IMPORTANT, LIVINIA ...

BUT WHY CAN'T WE GET RID OF ALL THESE SEPARATE GROUPS AND JUST WORK FOR HUMAN LIBERATION?
© Field Enterprises, Inc., 1973
BATIUK
5-5

WHAT ARE YOU, SOME KIND OF ANARCHIST?

FUNKY WINKERBEAN
OLDIES

AND THAT'S NOT ALL...

IF YOU ORDER THESE TWO COLLECTORS-ITEM ALBUMS **RIGHT NOW**...

YOU GET NOT ONE, NOT TWO, BUT **THREE** EXTRA ALBUMS CONTAINING AN ADDITIONAL **THREE THOUSAND** HITS FROM THE PAST!

ALSO, IF YOU ORDER **RIGHT AWAY**, YOU'LL GET OUR COMBINATION RECORD RACK, VEGATABLE SLICER, GLASS CUTTER, AND TIRE CHANGER... **ABSOLUTELY FREE**!
5-6

IF THEY'D HAVE THROWN IN A FROG THAT HUMS YANKEE DOODLE, THEY'D HAVE SOLD ME!
BATIUK

PLUS! YOU GET A **FROG** THAT HUMS **YANKEE DOODLE**!

ARE YOU STILL BOYCOTTING MEAT, MARCIA?
5-7

YOU'RE DARN RIGHT I AM, JAN! I'M HAVING MEATLESS MEALS EVERY NIGHT THIS WEEK!

TONIGHT WE'RE HAVING HOT DOGS!
BATIUK

BOY! HAVE I GOT SPRING FEVER!

NOT ONLY THAT, BUT JUST LIKE THEY SAY ... SPRING IS THE TIME OF YEAR ...
BATIUK

... WHEN YOUNG MEN'S THOUGHTS TURN ...
5-8

TO WHAT I HAVEN'T BEEN ABLE TO STOP THINKING ABOUT SINCE LAST SPRING!

WHEN I GOT BACK FROM SPRING BREAK THERE WAS ONLY AN INCH OF WATER IN MY AQUARIUM!

HOW WERE THE FISH?

EXTREMELY NERVOUS!
BATIUK
5-9
© Field Enterprises, Inc., 1973

THAT LITTLE CORAL JOB IN THE CORNER IS WHERE MY FISH GO TO WORSHIP!

OH YEAH? WHO DO THEY WORSHIP?
© Field Enterprises, Inc., 1973

ME, OF COURSE! I'M THE BENEVOLENT PROVIDER OF FOOD!

SORT OF GOT YOUR OWN LITTLE EGO TRIP GOING HERE DON'T YOU?
BATIUK
5-10

ARISE, FISH! THE GREAT PROVIDER OF **FOOD** IS HERE!

AMAZING!
© Field Enterprises, Inc., 1973

I'VE NEVER SEEN A FISH GENUFLECT BEFORE!
BATIUK
5-11

TONIGHT WILL BE A VICTORY FOR WILLPOWER!

I'M GOING TO SAVE MY MONEY BY RESISTING THE TEMPTATION TO ORDER A SMALL PIZZA!

ON TONIGHT'S PROGRAM WE'LL STUDY, IN DETAIL, THE OVER-KILL CAPABILITIES OF THE UNITED STATES' AND SOVIET UNION'S NUCLEAR ARSENALS!
BATIUK
© Field Enterprises, Inc., 1973
5-12

HELLO! I'D LIKE TO ORDER ONE OF YOUR LARGE DELUXE PIZZAS!

FUNKY WINKERBEAN

THE BAND SOUNDED PRETTY GOOD TONIGHT, AL!

PRETTY GOOD!?
BATIUK

PRETTY GOOD!?
eld Enterprises, Inc., 1973

YOU'RE CALLING THE BAND THAT WON THE **FUCHSIA RIBBON** FOR BEST OVER-ALL SEATING AND POSTURE IN THE TRI-COUNTY CONTEST FOR MEDIUM-SIZED SENIOR HIGH BANDS PRETTY GOOD!?

A TIN EAR! THAT'S WHAT YOU'VE GOT!
5-13

I DON'T UNDERSTAND THIS! HOW COULD BULL BUSHKA, THE SCHOOL'S STAR ATHLETE, HAVE A NEGATIVE I.Q.?

WELL ... NOT ONLY DIDN'T HE KNOW ANY ANSWERS ON HIS I.Q. TEST ...
BATIUK

... BUT HE LOWERED THE SCORE OF THE TWO PEOPLE SITTING NEXT TO HIM!
5-14

ROLAND, IF YOU'LL THINK OF ME AS A FRIEND AND NOT A COUNSELOR, MAYBE WE COULD RAP AWHILE AND FIND OUT WHAT BOTHERS YOU ABOUT SCHOOL!
BATIUK 5-15

I HATE THIS PLACE!
COULD YOU ELABORATE ON THAT?

I HATE THIS PLACE A LOT!

ROLAND, WE'D LIKE TO HELP YOU AS MUCH AS WE CAN ...
BATIUK 5-16

...BUT YOU'RE ALSO GOING TO HAVE TO MEET US HALF-WAY!
NO DEAL!

IF THE BUS DOESN'T PICK ME UP AT MY HOUSE, I'M NOT COMING!

DON'T GIVE ME THAT!

CHECK THE DRESS CODE YOURSELF IF YOU DON'T BELIEVE ME!
5-17
BATIUK

ALL IT SAYS IS THAT A GUY'S HAIR SHOULDN'T EXTEND OVER HIS COLLAR!

OKAY, MEN! LINE UP FOR THE SIX-STEP RUNNING BROAD-JUMP!

NOW ON THIS YOU JUST RUN SIX STEPS AND JUMP! THEN WE'LL MEASURE AND RECORD THE DISTANCE! LET'S GO!
BATIUK

CLOP
CLOP
CLOP
CLOP
SMASH!
5-18

OKAY, BEFORE THE NEXT GUY GOES... LET'S MOVE THE STARTING LINE BACK FROM THE WALL A LITTLE!

WHY AM I STUCK COACHING THESE RUM-DUMS WHO CAN'T TELL A BASEBALL BAT FROM A GOAL POST?

I COULD BE A COACH IN THE MAJORS! I CAN SEE ME BEING CARRIED OFF THE FIELD ON THE SHOULDERS OF MY VICTORIOUS WORLD SERIES TEAM!
BATIUK

AND THEN THE GREATEST ACCOLADE OF ALL!
5-19

MY PICTURE ON A BOX OF WHEATIES!

FUNKY WINKERBEAN
THIS ISN'T SO BAD!

THIS IS MY FIRST TIME AT THIS HALL MONITOR'S POST!

THEY SAY THE KID THAT HAD THIS POST BEFORE ME CRACKED-UP ON THE JOB!

I WONDER WHAT GOT TO HIM? ... THIS SEEMS TO BE A LESS TRAVELED AREA OF THE BUILDING!
© Field Enterprises, Inc., 1973
BATIUK

HE PROBABLY WASN'T ABLE TO COPE WITH THE LONG STRETCHES OF LONELY SILENCE!
5-20

RRRING!

ON THE OTHER HAND!

HI YA, FATTY!

SQUIRT
SQUIRT
SQUIRT

SOMETHING TELLS ME RALPH HAS BEEN OFFERED A CONTRACT WITH ANOTHER SCHOOL SYSTEM!

From the preceding paragraph we can conclude that:

(A.) All the tin in the world comes from Bolivia.

(B.) None of the tin in the world comes from Bolivia.

(C.) Both of the above.

I CAN TELL THIS NEW ALBUM I BOUGHT IS REALLY GOING TO BE SOMETHING, FUNKY!

HOW CAN YOU TELL?

WHEN I OPENED THE JACKET IT CRAWLED OUT AND PUT ITSELF ON!

WHAT DOES AN OVEN THAT COOKS THINGS WITH SOUND WAVES HAVE TO DO WITH CRAZY HARRY'S BEING ABSENT TODAY, FUNKY?

WELL, MISS WRIGHTON, YOU KNOW HOW HE LIKES TO LISTEN TO HARD ROCK ON HIS STEREO EARPHONES AT FULL VOLUME?
YOU MEAN...!?

THAT'S RIGHT! HE COOKED HIS BRAIN!
BATIUK
© Field Enterprises, Inc., 1973
5-24

I WAS SENT OVER TO BE INTERVIEWED FOR AN OPENING IN YOUR ENGLISH DEPARTMENT!
5-25

FINE, WHERE DID YOU STUDY?

OH, USUALLY IN MY DORM ROOM!
BATIUK
© Field Enterprises, Inc., 1973

THE LAB BOOK SAYS WE HAVE TO DETERMINE IF A WORM IS A MALE, FEMALE, OR BOTH!

MALE OR FEMALE?
BATIUK

I DON'T EVEN KNOW WHERE TO LOOK!
© Field Enterprises, Inc., 1973
5-26

FUNKY WINKERBEAN

THAT 'TUFF' LOOKING NEW GIRL FROM MY STUDY HALL IS HERE AT THE LIBRARY!

I'VE GOT TO GET HER TO NOTICE ME SOMEHOW! I KNOW...
5-27

I'LL JUST GRAB A BOOK!

CASUALLY SIT NEXT TO HER...

...AND BROWSE THROUGH MY THREE LITTLE PIGS POP-UP BOOK!

TELL ME, LES, DOES THAT MACHINE GUN FIRE BLANKS OR REAL BULLETS?
© Field Enterprises, Inc. 1973

ACTUALLY, FUNKY, NEITHER!
BATIUK
5-28

YOU TURN THIS LITTLE CRANK HERE AND IT PLAYS THE SCHOOL FIGHT SONG!

I'M GOING TO WALK OVER TO MARY SUE SWEETWATER ... TAKE HER IN MY ARMS AND TELL HER HOW MADLY I LOVE HER!
© Field Enterprises, Inc. 1973

NAW, I CAN'T DO THAT! SHE'LL THINK I'M CRAZY!

WELL, SO WHAT? YOU ONLY LIVE ONCE! AND BESIDES, SCHOOL IS ALMOST OVER! THIS IS MY LAST CHANCE! I'M GOING TO DO IT!
5-29

TOO BAD THIS IS THE LAST PANEL, FOLKS! YOU'RE GOING TO MISS THE WHOLE THING!
BATIUK

HOW DID YOUR EVALUATION BY THE PRINCIPAL GO, RITA?

I WAS LUCKY! HE CAUGHT MY CLASS ON ONE OF ITS BETTER DAYS!
© Field Enterprises, Inc. 1973
BATIUK
5-30

SO I'LL BE GIVEN AN OPTION TO RESIGN INSTEAD OF JUST BEING FIRED!

I THINK THE PRINCIPAL WAS UPSET BY THE FACT A STUDENT THREW A CHAIR OUT THE WINDOW DURING MY EVALUATION!

WELL, I CAN SORT OF SEE HIS POINT!
5-31
© Field Enterprises, Inc., 1973

WELL, I DON'T SEE WHAT **HE'S** SO UPSET ABOUT! **I'M** THE ONE WHO WAS TIED IN IT!
BATIUK

MISS WRIGHTON, I'D LIKE TO KNOW IF I CAN STILL DO SOMETHING TO PULL UP MY GRADE?

WHAT DID YOU HAVE IN MIND?

BEGGING!
6-1

AND NOW WE'LL HAVE A
REPRESENTATIVE TO THE COMMITTEE FOR CURRICULUM DEVELOPMENT!

UH... NEXT YEAR WE PLAN TO STUDY MANY
6-2
BATIUK

AS YOU CAN SEE, THINGS STILL APPEAR TO BE IN THE FORMATIVE STAGES!
© Field Enterprises, Inc., 1973

FUNKY WINKERBEAN

WOW! IS IT NICE OUT TODAY!

WHAT IS SO RARE AS A DAY IN JUNE ?!

I THINK SUMMER JUST HAS TO BE THE GREATEST SEASON OF ALL!
6-3

IT REALLY MAKES YOU FEEL GLAD TO BE ALIVE!
BATIUK

IN FACT THERE'S JUST NO ...
© Field Enterprises, Inc., 1973

SOMEONE MUST HAVE BEEN MESSING AROUND WITH MOTHER NATURE'S BUTTER AGAIN!

SAYINGS FROM THE
I CHONG
ANCIENT BOOK OF CHINESE PHILOSOPHY
6-4

THE MASTER SAYS: FEW PEOPLE EVER TAKE ADVANTAGE OF THE GIFTS MOTHER NATURE OFFERS!

IF YOU WOULD LIKE TO, FILL OUT THE ATTACHED COUPON AND MAIL IT TODAY!

SAYINGS FROM THE
I CHONG
ANCIENT BOOK OF CHINESE PHILOSOPHY

IT IS BEST NOT TO GO OUT INTO LIFE WITH A YEN FOR PLEASURES OF THE FLESH!
I CHONG

FOR A GOOD TIME THESE DAYS YOU SHOULD FIGURE ON SIX YEN AND UP!
I CHONG
6-5

SAYINGS FROM THE
I CHONG
ANCIENT BOOK OF CHINESE PHILOSOPHY

THE MASTER SAYS: THE GOOD THAT WE DO IS FOREVER
IN OUR FAVOR! THE BAD THAT WE DO IS FOREVER ASSESSED AGAINST US!
6-6

THE LIST IS THEN PASSED ON TO SANTA CLAUS AND VARIOUS CREDIT ORGANIZATIONS!

FUNKY! YOU'VE GOT TO TELL ME!

IS TODAY THE LAST DAY OF SCHOOL?

NO, HARRY! IT'S STILL A WEEK AWAY!
© Field Enterprises, Inc., 1973
BATIUK
6-7

(WHEW!) I'M SCARED TO DEATH I WON'T KNOW WHEN IT IS AND ACCIDENTALLY SHOW UP HERE AN EXTRA DAY!

I HEARD THAT NEW STUDENT WE GOT REALLY PICKS THINGS UP FAST!

HE MUST REALLY BE BRIGHT!

NO, HE'S A KLEPTOMANIAC!
© Field Enterprises, Inc., 1973
BATIUK
6-8

YOU'VE BEEN PRETTY BUSY LATELY, HAVEN'T YOU?

YES, FRED! I'M CHAIRING A PROFESSIONAL DEVELOPMENT SEMINAR AT OUR SCHOOL THIS WEEKEND ...
BATIUK
6-9

AND I STILL NEED TO LOCATE ABOUT TWENTY-FIVE MORE CHAIRS!
© Field Enterprises, Inc., 1973

FUNKY WINKERBEAN
AAHHHHHH

AAHHHHHH

AAAUUGH
6-10

YOU KIND OF HAVE TO ADMIRE HIS INDEPENDENCE!

WHILE THE REST OF US ARE LEADING LIVES OF QUIET DESPERATION...

BATIUK
HE'S LEADING ONE OF NOISY DESPERATION!

RAH!
RAH!
SISS!
BOOM!
BAH!
BATIUK

GOOD GRIEF! WHAT WAS THAT?

THAT'S THE OLD SCHOOL SPIRIT!
6-11

I CAN'T GET TO SLEEP THINKING ABOUT MY FINAL EXAMS!

I CAN'T LET THIS GET TO ME! I'VE GOT TO GET MY MIND ON SOMETHING ELSE! I'LL THINK ABOUT MARY SUE SWEETWATER!
BATIUK
6-12

I'M WIDER AWAKE THAN I WAS BEFORE!

DID YOU FINISH YOUR FINAL ALREADY, FUNKY?

NOT REALLY, MISS WRIGHTON!
BATIUK
6-13

MY FINAL FINISHED ME!

WELL, SCHOOL IS ALMOST OVER AND AT THIS POINT MARY SUE SWEETWATER HARDLY EVEN KNOWS I EXIST!

WHAT COULD BE MORE TRAGIC THAN UNREQUITED LOVE?
BATIUK
© Field Enterprises, Inc., 1973
6-14

HAVING TO PAY A BOOK FINE FOR SCRIBBLING HER NAME ON EVERY STUPID PAGE, THAT'S WHAT!

WELL, IT'S THE LAST DAY OF SCHOOL AND I'M THE ONLY ONE LEFT IN THE BUILDING!

THIS IS MY LAST CHANCE TO PROVE TO MYSELF THAT I CAN CLIMB THAT STUPID ROPE, WITHOUT GETTING TOO SCARED TO CLIMB BACK DOWN!
© Field Enterprises, Inc., 1973
6-15

IT'S GOING TO BE A LONG SUMMER!
BATIUK

BOY! THE LAST DAY OF SCHOOL WAS REALLY SOMETHING, DEREK!

ALL OF THAT SCREAMING, HOLLERING AND CELEBRATING!

YEAH, AND THE KIDS WERE PRETTY NOISY, TOO!
© Field Enterprises, Inc., 1973
6-16
BATIUK

FUNKY WINKERBEAN
TILT!
ON OFF

THIS LITTLE POCKET CALCULATOR IS A REAL BEAUTY!

IT'S NICE AND LIGHT SO YOU CAN TAKE IT ANYWHERE!

AND IT HAS AN EIGHT DIGITAL READ-OUT WITH AUTOMATIC ROUND-OFF!

NOT ONLY THAT, BUT IT HAS A FLOATING DECIMAL WHICH ENABLES YOU TO SOLVE **ANY** TYPE OF PROBLEM WITH IT!
BATIUK
6-17

AMAZING! MAY I TRY IT OUT!

HELLO, POCKET CALCULATOR? WHY DO I HAVE SO MUCH TROUBLE GETTING GIRLS TO LIKE ME?

WELL, YOUR APPLICATION FOR A PLAYGROUND SUPERVISOR SEEMS IN ORDER, FUNKY!

CONCERNING THIS PART ABOUT HONORS RECEIVED OR POSITIONS OF RESPONSIBILITY YOU'VE HELD...

WERE YOU EVER ANYTHING ELSE BESIDES A GYM-LEADER IN THE SEVENTH GRADE?

HI! I'M GOING TO BE YOUR PLAYGROUND SUPERVISOR THIS SUMMER!

MY NAME IS FUNKY WINKERBEAN!

HA! HA! HA! HA! HA!

AS YOUR PLAYGROUND SUPERVISOR, I'LL BE AROUND AT ALL TIMES IF YOU NEED ME!

ARE THERE ANY QUESTIONS?

OKAY, THEN ...

WOULD YOU HELP ME WITH MY JACKET, MR. WINKERBEAN?
BATIUK

SURE! I'D BE GLAD TO!

YOU'RE NEW AT THIS, AREN'T YOU?
6-21

SAYINGS FROM THE
I CHONG
ANCIENT BOOK OF CHINESE PHILOSOPHY
BATIUK

THE MASTER SAYS: A WATCHED POT NEVER BOILS!

HOWEVER, PUT SOME WATER IN IT AND PLACE IT OVER A FIRE, AND YOU'VE GOT A WHOLE NEW BALLGAME!

WE'LL TAKE A BREAK AND BE RIGHT BACK, OKAY?

OKAY!
BATIUK 6-23

AAUUGH!

FUNKY WINKERBEAN

BOY! I'D GIVE ANYTHING FOR A DATE WITH THAT CUTE BLOND LIFEGUARD!

YOU'VE REALLY FALLEN FOR HER, HUH?

DON'T SAY **FALL**... LOVE DOESN'T BRING YOU DOWN! IT'S AN UPLIFTING FEELING!
BATIUK

YOU REACH JOYOUS NEW **HEIGHTS**, SO INSTEAD YOU SHOULD SAY YOU'VE **CLIMBED** INTO LOVE!
6/24

WHAT DO YOU THINK?
© Field Enterprises, Inc.

I THINK YOU SHOULD WEAR A HAT WHEN YOU'RE OUT IN THE HOT SUN!

DO YOU REALIZE, 'CRAZY,' THAT THIS IS OUR FIRST SUMMER OF PEACE?

EVER SINCE I'VE BEEN IN SCHOOL, THERE'S BEEN A WAR, PROTESTING THE DRAFT... AT LAST WE'RE FREE OF ALL THAT TENSION AND ANXIETY!

SO WHAT DO YOU PLAN TO DO?

SIT AROUND THE POOL AND WATCH GIRLS LIKE I DO EVERY SUMMER!
BATIUK

WOW! THAT CUTE BLOND LIFEGUARD IS TAKING A DIP IN THE POOL ON HER BREAK!

JUST THINK... THE WATER THAT SURROUNDS HER BODY IS THE SAME WATER THAT SURROUNDS MINE!

OF COURSE, IT ALSO SURROUNDS THAT BALD-HEADED FAT GUY, TOO!
BATIUK

THE BAD THING ABOUT BEING IN A POOL LIKE THIS IS THAT ONLY THE UPPER HALF OF YOUR BODY GETS A TAN!
BATIUK

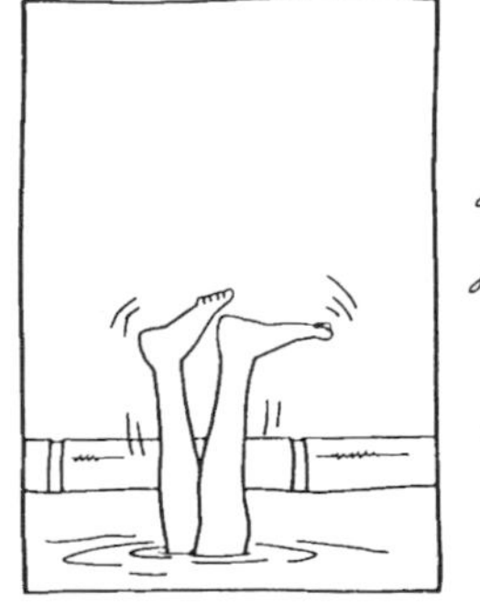

GASP!

OBVIOUSLY THAT'S THE WAY NATURE INTENDED IT!

IF I JUMP OFF THIS HIGH DIVE ... I COULD REALLY MAKE A BIG IMPRESSION WITH THAT CUTE BLOND LIFEGUARD!
6-28

OF COURSE, I COULD ALSO MAKE A BIG IMPRESSION ON THE BOTTOM OF THE POOL!

LUCKY I THOUGHT OF THAT!
BATIUK
© Field Enterprises, Inc., 1973

SAYINGS FROM THE
I CHONG
ANCIENT BOOK OF CHINESE PHILOSOPHY

MANY WISH TO KNOW THE ANSWER TO THE MYSTERY OF LIFE! LET IT NOW BE REVEALED ...
BATIUK
6-29

THE BUTLER DID IT!
© Field Enterprises, Inc., 1973

DAD, I WAS WONDERING IF ...

DAD ...!?
© Field Enterprises, Inc., 1973
BATIUK

JUST WHAT I WAS AFRAID OF, BASEBALL HYPNOSIS!
6-30

BATIUK © Field Enterprises, Inc., 1973

I DIDN'T HAVE ANY FISH FOOD SO I GAVE MY FISH SOME PARAKEET FOOD!

IS IT OKAY TO DO THAT, LES?
I DON'T SEE WHY NOT!
© Field Enterprises, Inc., 1973
BATIUK
7-2

JUST TO BE SAFE THOUGH, I DID PUT SOME NEWSPAPER ON THE BOTTOM OF THEIR AQUARIUM!

MY BROTHER WON'T BE HERE TODAY! HE'S SICK!

WELL, LITTLE KIDS ALWAYS SEEM TO GO THROUGH A LOT OF CHILDHOOD ILLNESSES!
BATIUK
7-3

HE'S GOT MONO!
© Field Enterprises, Inc., 1973

MR WINKERBEAN,
SO GOOD!
7-4

WELL, WHICH HAND SEEMS
GIVING YOU THE MOST TROUBLE?
BATIUK

TERRIFIC! I NEED A
GET A STAND-UP COMIC!
© Field Enterprises, Inc., 1973

+

WHAT'S UP?
BATIUK
7-5

OH, I'VE JUST BEEN DOING A LITTLE POSITIVE THINKING!

SAYINGS FROM THE
I CHONG
ANCIENT BOOK OF CHINESE PHILOSOPHY

AS YOU GO THROUGH LIFE, BE GUIDED BY THE FACT THAT THE RAIN IS ALWAYS FOLLOWED BY THE SUN!
BATIUK

OF COURSE THE SUN IS ALWAYS FOLLOWED BY THE RAIN, SO USE YOUR OWN JUDGEMENT!

I WONDER WHAT IT IS THAT COMPELS US TO GO OUT AND GAZE AT THE STARS, 'CRAZY'?

UNION RULES!
BATIUK
7-7

ALL COMIC STRIP CHARACTERS HAVE TO GAZE AT THE STARS AT LEAST TWICE A YEAR!

FUNKY WINKERBEAN
I DON'T FEEL SO HOT! YOU'D BETTER CALL A PAWN SHOP!

BATIUK

CHECKMATE!

DARN!
© Field Enterprises, Inc., 1973

I CAN'T WAIT TO HEAR WHAT MY NEW AMPLIFIERS AND SPEAKERS SOUND LIKE!

I'LL GIVE IT THE ACID TEST AND PLAY MY NUCLEAR NOODLE ALBUM!
BATIUK
7-9

I DIG IT!
© Field Enterprises, Inc., 1973

IS YOUR NEW AMPLIFIER REALLY THAT GOOD, 'CRAZY'?
7-10

WELL YOU KNOW HOW THE PROPER SOUND CAN SHATTER GLASS?
YEAH!

WELL THIS MORNING IT SHATTERED MY BED!
© Field Enterprises, Inc., 1973
BATIUK

I'LL BET YOUR NEW AMP REALLY DRAWS A LOT OF POWER, 'CRAZY'!
7-11

YOU'RE NOT KIDDING, FUNKY!
© Field Enterprises, Inc., 1973
BATIUK

WHEN I TURN IT ON, NIAGARA FALLS RUNS BACKWARDS!

DON'T WORRY! YOUR PARENTS WON'T LEAVE HOME WHILE YOU'RE HERE AT THE PLAYGROUND!

SO JUST GO PLAY AND HAVE A GOOD TIME!

I WISH SHE HADN'T BROUGHT THAT UP! NOW I'M WORRYING ABOUT IT!

SAYINGS FROM THE
I CHONG
ANCIENT BOOK OF CHINESE PHILOSOPHY

THE MASTER SAYS: HE WHO GOES AROUND WITH A SONG IN HIS HEART SHOULD SEE A DOCTOR…

HIS VOCAL CHORDS HAVE SLIPPED INTO HIS AORTA!

NOW THAT I'VE CLIMBED UP ON THIS HIGH DIVE I'M NOT GOING TO BACK DOWN!

I'M GOING TO JUMP OFF HERE
ALL DAY!

OR ALL NIGHT!

FUNKY WINKERBEAN
AMAZING!

YOU KNOW, 'CRAZY', GAZING AT THE STARS REALLY MAKES YOU THINK!

WE ALWAYS TALK ABOUT STARS BEING SO SMALL...
BATIUK

...WHEN ACTUALLY STARS ARE ENORMOUS COSMIC FURNACES!

I WONDER WHY WE NEVER THINK OF THEM THAT WAY!
7-15

I SUPPOSE BECAUSE IT'S SO AWKWARD TO SAY 'TWINKLE, TWINKLE ENORMOUS COSMIC FURNACE'!

THERE'S A SEVERE THUNDERSTORM WATCH UNTIL ELEVEN O'CLOCK TONIGHT!

RESIDENTS ARE ADVISED TO TAKE THE PROPER PRECAUTIONS!
BATIUK

RAIN, RAIN, GO AWAY... COME AGAIN ANOTHER DAY!

SO YOU'RE THE SUPERVISOR AT THIS PLAYGROUND, HUH, FUNKY?

YEOOW!
BATIUK

WHAT WAS THAT?

THAT WAS SOMEBODY ON THE SLIDE! IT USUALLY GETS PRETTY HOT AROUND NOON!

ARE YOU GOING TO HELP OUR TEAM WIN THE CITY PLAYGROUND TROPHY, MR. WINKERBEAN?

WELL I'LL TRY, BUT REMEMBER... THE MAIN REASON WE PLAY BASEBALL IS TO HAVE FUN!
BATIUK

CAN I BE TRADED TO ANOTHER PLAYGROUND?
WE'RE DOOMED!
OH NO!

WELL, DON'T FEEL TOO BAD ABOUT GETTING CLOBBERED, GUYS!

WINNING IS FINE, BUT YOU CAN LEARN A LOT FROM DEFEAT!
© Field Enterprises, Inc., 1973
BATIUK
7-19

BY THE END OF THE SUMMER WE'LL BE THE SMARTEST TEAM IN THE WORLD!

WHO'S ON THE LATE NIGHT ROCK SPECIAL, VICKI?

LET'S SEE, THE FERMENTED CABBAGE, NUCLEAR NOODLE, BROOKSKI, THRASHER, AND PITTS AND THE YUGOSLAVIAN ELECTRIC TAMBOURITZAN BAND!
© Field Enterprises, Inc., 1973
BATIUK
7-20

THAT REALLY BURNS ME WHEN THEY GET A CLASS LINE-UP, AND THEN STICK IN A TEENYBOP GROUP LIKE THE NUCLEAR NOODLE!

WHEN I SIT OUTSIDE ON A WARM, MOONLIT SUMMER NIGHT, FUNKY, I JUST FEEL TINGLY ALL OVER!

I WONDER WHAT CAUSES THAT?
© Field Enterprises, Inc., 1973

MOSQUITOES!
BATIUK
7-21

OF ALL THE NERVE! THAT STUPID DISC JOCKEY HUNG UP ON ME JUST WHEN I WAS GOING TO PICK PRIZE NUMBER SIX!

7-11

THIS NATURAL SCENIC MARSHLAND DOESN'T LOOK LIKE A PLACE FOR AN OIL WELL, DOES IT?

IT'S HARD TO BELIEVE THAT WE'VE HAD AN OIL WELL HERE FOR OVER THREE YEARS!
7-13

AND YET THE NATURAL BEAUTY AND ECOLOGY OF THE AREA HAS REMAINED UNCHANGED!

YES, THAT LITTLE TAX WRITE-OFF TURNED OUT TO BE DRY AS A BONE!

SAYINGS FROM THE
I CHONG
ANCIENT BOOK OF CHINESE PHILOSOPHY

THE MASTER REVEALS: HE WHO SPENDS HIS LIFE PURSUING WOMEN IS A FOOL!
BATIUK
7-24

I THINK!

WHAT WAS YOUR DAD SO UPSET ABOUT THIS MORNING, FUNKY?

OH, WE GOT A NASTY CALL FROM THE POWER COMPANY!
BATIUK

APPARENTLY, WHEN WE TURNED ON OUR AIR CONDITIONER, WE KNOCKED OUT CINCINNATI!
7-25

DON'T STAND THERE LIKE A BUNCH OF STATUES!

LET'S HEAR A LITTLE CHATTER OUT THERE!
BATIUK
7-26

HELP! GET ME OUTTA HERE! I WANT MY MOMMY!

BOY! AM I GLAD TODAY IS FRIDAY!
BATIUK

THIS PLAYGROUND JOB KIND OF GETS TO YOU, DOESN'T IT, MR. WINKERBEAN?

WHY DON'T YOU WISE-UP AND BLOW THIS POP STAND?
7-27

WHAT'S THIS YOU'RE WATCHING?

A SENATOR IS MAKING A SPEECH FROM THE FLOOR OF THE SENATE!
BATIUK

THEY COULD PROBABLY HEAR HIM BETTER IF HE'D STAND UP!

FUNKY WINKERBEAN
ZZZZZZ
0700
AM
FM

CLICK! AT THE TOP OF THE SEVEN O'CLOCK NEWS THIS MORNING ··· THERE'S BEEN A NEW OUTBREAK OF VIOLENCE IN THE MID-EAST!
7-29

NEW REVELATIONS IN THE WATERGATE SCANDAL HAVE IMPLICATED ONE-THIRD OF THE PEOPLE IN THE COUNTRY!

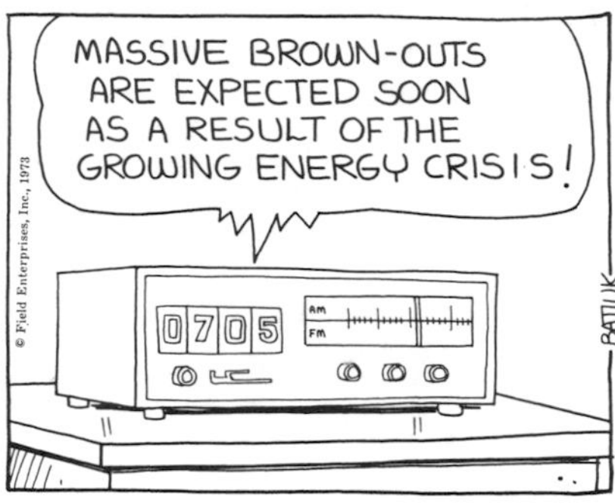
MASSIVE BROWN-OUTS ARE EXPECTED SOON AS A RESULT OF THE GROWING ENERGY CRISIS!
0705
AM
FM
© Field Enterprises, Inc., 1973
BATIUK

FINALLY ··· A RECORD NUMBER OF AUTO ACCIDENTS ARE PREDICTED FOR STATE HIGHWAYS THIS WEEKEND!

YA KNOW, HAVING A CLOCK RADIO ISN'T AS NEAT AS I THOUGHT IT WOULD BE!

REMEMBER THAT THEME ON 'WHAT AMERICA MEANS TO ME' THAT WE WROTE IN SCHOOL LAST SPRING?

I WROTE ABOUT HOW AMERICA MEANT INTEGRITY, HONESTY, AND FAIR PLAY!

WELL, MY THEME WAS PICKED AS ONE OF THE WINNERS AND I GET TO GO TO WASHINGTON TO MEET OUR NATION'S LEADERS AND HAVE DINNER AT THE WHITE HOUSE!
7-30

I DON'T GET THE CONNECTION!

IMAGINE, FUNKY... A TRIP TO WASHINGTON!

AND ALL THE CONTEST WINNERS WILL BE GIVEN FRAMED CERTIFICATES OF COMMENDATION!
BATIUK
7-31

PLUS THE TOP FIVE WINNERS GET THEIR THEMES RUN THROUGH A SHREDDER!

BEFORE YOU HAVE DINNER AT THE WHITE HOUSE, WE'VE PLANNED A TOUR OF OUR NATION'S CAPITAL!
CLAIM

I HOPE WE GO TO THE ZOO!
BATIUK
8-1

MY DAD WANTED ME TO GET A PICTURE OF THE PRESIDENTIAL SEAL!
CLAIM

I CAN'T BELIEVE IT! HERE I AM IN OUR NATION'S CAPITAL BECAUSE THE THEME I WROTE ON 'WHAT AMERICA MEANS TO ME'!
BATIUK
8-2

VISITING THE WHITE HOUSE WILL BE NICE ...

... BUT I REALLY CAN'T WAIT TO VISIT PARLIAMENT!

THIS IS REALLY IT! I'M ACTUALLY HAVING DINNER IN THE WHITE HOUSE!
8-3

SOMEHOW I EXPECTED MORE THAN SWISS STEAK!
BATIUK

WHAT'S THIS?
THE PRESIDENT IS SPEAKING TO ME?!
8-4

UHH, YES, SIR!
BATIUK

I KNOW WHAT YOU MEAN!

MY SUMMER HAS KIND OF BEEN LIKE THAT, TOO!

FUNKY WINKERBEAN
PLAYGROUND

SO THIS IS THE PLAYGROUND YOU'VE BEEN SUPERVISING, HUH, FUNKY?

THAT'S RIGHT, CRAZY!

YOU KNOW, LITTLE KIDS ARE REALLY OKAY!
© Field Enterprises, Inc., 1973
BATIUK

THEY'RE ALL SO HAPPY AND CAREFREE!

AND THEY'RE COMPLETELY UNSPOILED BY ANY PRECONCEIVED NOTIONS OR PREJUDICES!

HI, MR. WINKERBEAN! WHO'S THE FREAK?
8-5

HOW DID YOU FIND WASHINGTON, LES?
BATIUK

IT WASN'T HARD! THE PILOT OF OUR PLANE KNEW WHERE IT WAS!

DID YOU MEET HENNY YOUNGMAN WHILE YOU WERE THERE?

I'M GOING TO COMPLAIN ABOUT THAT GIRL YOU'VE GOT PLAYING ON YOUR TEAM, MARY ELLEN!
CITY RECREATION

WHY? DOES IT BRUISE YOUR MALE EGO?
NO! I JUST DON'T LIKE THE WAY SHE SPIKED MY SECOND BASEMAN!
CITY
8-7

YEAH, SHE REALLY STAPLED HIM INTO THE GROUND, DIDN'T SHE?
BATIUK

DON'T YOU SEE WHAT YOU'RE DOING, MARY ELLEN?

YOU'RE PROJECTING ALL OF YOUR AGGRESSIVE AND COMPETITIVE TENDENCIES ONTO THOSE KIDS ON YOUR TEAM!
8-8

IF YOU DON'T SHUT UP, I'M GOING TO PROJECT AN AGGRESSIVE TENDENCY RIGHT ON YOUR NOSE!
CITY RECREATION

I DON'T THINK YOU UNDERSTAND THE MEANING OF THE TERM, 'PROJECT'!

SURE, AS YOUR PLAYGROUND DIRECTOR I FEEL BAD THAT WE HAVEN'T WON ANY GAMES!
BATIUK
8-9

BUT YOU CAN'T WIN ALL THE TIME, SO WHAT ARE YOU SUPPOSED TO DO WHEN YOU LOSE?

KICK! KICK! KICK!
© Field Enterprises, Inc., 1973

I'LL HAVE TWO SCOOPS OF THE PINK DAIQUIRI, BUTTER-SCOTCH, FUDGE RIPPLE, NUT SHERBERT!

YOU'VE ADDED A NEW FLAVOR, HUH?
© Field Enterprises, Inc., 1973
BATIUK
8-10

NO! WE JUST CLEANED THE PLACE YESTERDAY!

WE HAVE TWO FULL HOURS OF GOLF ENJOYMENT FOR YOU NUTS ... ER, FANS THIS AFTERNOON ...
8-11
© Field Enterprises, Inc., 1973

AND OF COURSE WE'LL HAVE OUR FINE EXPERT ANALYSIS FROM OUR TOP GOLF PRO!
BATIUK

WHO'LL BE WITH US ALL DAY BECAUSE HE FAILED TO MAKE THE CUT AGAIN!

FUNKY WINKERBEAN
F.W. + V.E.

SUMMER NIGHTS ARE REALLY NICE AREN'T THEY, FUNKY?
8-12

HAVE YOU EVER BEEN ALONE WITH SOMEONE YOU REALLY LIKE AND SUDDENLY YOU GET THAT MAGIC FEELING?
BATIUK
YEAH!
IN FACT I'VE GOT THAT MAGIC FEELING RIGHT NOW!

GOOD! PICK A CARD... ANY CARD AT ALL!

OKAY, GANG, WHILE WE'RE ON OUR HIKE, DON'T EAT ANY BERRIES OR ANYTHING!
© Field Enterprises, Inc., 1973
8-13

SOME OF THE THINGS YOU FIND GROWING WILD CAN BE POISONOUS!
BATIUK

DOES THE FOOD AND DRUG ADMINISTRATION KNOW ABOUT THIS?

SEE THESE PLANTS? THESE ARE BEANS!

THE FARMER WILL LATER PICK THESE AND THEY'LL END UP IN CANS IN YOUR LOCAL SUPERMARKET!
BATIUK
8-14

HE HAS A PRETTY WILD IMAGINATION, DOESN'T HE?
© Field Enterprises, Inc., 1973

LOOK, 'CRAZY', THEY'RE ADDING CHLORINE TO THE WATER!
8-15

I USED TO THINK THAT TOO, LES!
© Field Enterprises, Inc., 1973
BATIUK

ACTUALLY, THEY'RE ADDING WATER TO THE CHLORINE!

HOW CAN YOU JUSTIFY BUYING THESE SUPER-POWERFUL AMPS, 'CRAZY'?

WHEN OUR PLANET IS FACING AN ENERGY AND POWER CRISIS?
8-16
BATIUK

I'M DOING MY BIT, DEREK! I'M FOLLOWING GOVERNMENT RECOMMENDATIONS BY PLAYING ALL MY 45'S AT 33⅓!

BUMP!
8-17

BAM!
BATIUK

WHOEVER OKAYED AIR-BAGS FOR BICYCLES WAS OUT OF HIS MIND!

DO YOU PLAN TO GO TO COLLEGE, MARY ELLEN?

YEAH... I WAS THINKING OF U.C.L.A.!

...BUT THEY WANTED TO USE ME AS A DEFENSIVE BACK!
BATIUK
8-18

FUNKY WINKERBEAN
GO DIRECTLY TO JAIL!
DO NOT PASS GO AND DO NOT COLLECT 200 DOLLARS!

OKAY, LES ... HERES YOUR HOUSE AND AN EXTRA MARKER!

HEY! WHAT'S THE EXTRA MARKER NEXT TO MINE FOR?
BATIUK

THAT'S A NEW WRINKLE THEY'VE ADDED TO THE MONOPOLY GAME!
8-19

AS SOON AS YOU OWN A HOUSE ...

... A LIFE INSURANCE SALESMAN STARTS TO FOLLOW YOU AROUND!

HI! JOHN DARLING HERE, GETTING THE OPINIONS OF TODAY'S YOUTH ON THE TOPICAL ISSUES OF THE DAY!
BATIUK
8-20

EXCUSE ME, TYPICAL YOUNG PERSON, WHAT DO YOU THINK ABOUT THE RECENT TENNIS EXPLOSION?
© Field Enterprises, Inc., 1973

I THINK THERE'S NO DOUBT THAT IT WAS POLITICALLY MOTIVATED!

HI, JOHN DARLING HERE! WE'RE OUT ON A TYPICAL CITY PLAYGROUND TO SEE HOW THE KIDS ARE ENJOYING THEIR SUMMER!

HOW DO YOU LIKE IT HERE TODAY, LITTLE GIRL?
© Field Enterprises, Inc., 1973
8-21

IT'S HOTTER THAN ████ OUT HERE!
BATIUK

AND NOW BACK TO YOU, DAVE!

SAY, WHERE DID LES DISAPPEAR TO, FUNKY?
© Field Enterprises, Inc., 1973

HE WENT HOME TO GET SOME OF HIS SWIMMING GEAR, DEREK! HE THOUGHT IT MIGHT HELP HIM IMPRESS THAT GIRL LIFE-GUARD HE'S GOT A CRUSH ON!

I SEE IT, BUT I DON'T BELIEVE IT!
BATIUK
8-22

I PROMISED TO TAKE YOU GUYS OUT FOR A CONE IF YOU LOST...
© Field Enterprises, Inc., 1973
BATIUK
8-23

SO GO EASY ON THE LICKS, IT HAS A LONG WAY TO GO!
COOL CONE

YOUR HOROSCOPE
by CLAIR VOYANT
8-24

TOMORROW IS GOING TO BE A GREAT DAY FOR YOU!
© Field Enterprises, Inc., 1973
BATIUK

YOUR LUCKY PLANET IS IN THE SAME HOUSE WITH SKYLAB!

HOW DO YOU EXPECT TO UNDERSTAND ME WHEN YOU NEVER SAY TWO WORDS TO ME, DAD?

BEAT IT!
BATIUK

HOW DO YOU EXPECT TO UNDERSTAND ME WHEN YOU NEVER SAY THREE WORDS TO ME?
© Field Enterprises, Inc., 1973
8-25

FUNKY
WINKERBEAN

CHOP!
CHOP!
CHOP!

© Field Enterprises, Inc., 1973
8-26

BATIUKS

WHACK!
WHACK!
WHACK

WOW! I JUST DREAMED
I WAS BUSHWHACKED!

WHY DOES YOUR DAD CALL HIS PUTTER EXCALIBUR, FUNKY?

IS IT BECAUSE HE FEELS INVINCIBLE WHEN HE PUTTS WITH IT?
BATIUK

NO, BECAUSE IT'S STUCK IN A ROCK ON A PAR-FIVE AT WILDBROOK!
© Field Enterprises, Inc., 1973
8-27

DON'T GIVE ME THAT, MARY ELLEN!
© Field Enterprises, Inc., 1973
CITY RECREAT

YOU'RE JUST TRYING TO GAIN AN UNFAIR ADVANTAGE FOR YOUR TEAM!

I CAN TELL A WATERED-DOWN BASEPATH WHEN I SEE ONE!
HELP!
8-28

AFTER OUR LAST GAME WITH YOUR TEAM, MARY ELLEN, I WORKED WITH MY PITCHER ALL WEEK!
CITY RECREAT
© Field Enterprises, Inc., 1973

ON HIS SLIDER?

BATIUK
NO, ON HIS DUCKING!
CITY RECREAT
8-29

AND NOW ···

IT'S TIME ONCE AGAIN FOR ····
BATIUK

AS THE WATERGATE TURNS ···
8-30

I'M ONLY A PLAY-GROUND SUPERVISOR NOW ···
© Field Enterprises, Inc., 1973

··· BUT SOMEDAY (TA-DAA!) I'LL BE THE FIRST WOMAN TO MANAGE A MAJOR LEAGUE BASEBALL TEAM!
BATIUK

A LOT OF PEOPLE THINK IT'S JUST BECAUSE I'M A PUSHY FEMALE!
8-31

IT'S JUST THAT IT'S THE ONLY JOB WHERE IT'S ACCEPTABLE TO GO AROUND PATTING GUYS ON THE FANNY!

JUST THINK, VICKI! WHEN YOU WERE UPSTATE VISITING YOUR COUSIN ···
© Field Enterprises, Inc., 1973

EVEN THOUGH WE WERE SEPARATED BY HUNDREDS OF MILES, WE COULD BOTH LOOK UP AND SEE THE SAME MOON!
BATIUK

OH, REALLY?

OH BOY!
9-1

FUNKY WINKERBEAN

SOMETIMES WHEN I'M IN BED I START TO WONDER ABOUT THINGS...
I WONDER WHAT THE FUTURE HOLDS FOR ME?

I WONDER HOW THEY GET THE JELLY IN JELLY DONUTS?
BATIUK

I WONDER IF SUPERMAN WILL EVER MARRY LOIS LANE?

9-2

I WONDER IF MARY SUE WEARS ANYTHING UNDER THAT RED SWEATSHIRT OF HERS!

I WONDER WHAT I'M DOING IN BED AT 7:30 ON A SATURDAY NIGHT?

I CAN'T BELIEVE THAT YOU'VE ALREADY BEEN SENT TO MY OFFICE, 'CRAZY'!

WHAT REALLY BOTHERS ME THOUGH ...
© Field Enterprises, Inc., 1973
BATIUK
9-3

... IS THAT SCHOOL DOESN'T START UNTIL TOMORROW!
PRINCIPAL

SCHEDULE CHANGES
I KNOW YOU HATE CAFETERIA DUTY, GEORGE, BUT THIS SCHEDULE CHANGE IS ONLY FOR STUDENTS!
© Field Enterprises, Inc., 1973
BATIUK
9-4

WAIT A MINUTE HERE!
© Field Enterprises, Inc., 1973

WELL, NO WONDER YOU'VE BEEN HAVING TROUBLE, FUNKY!
BATIUK

YOU'VE BEEN TRYING TO OPEN YOUR LOCKER COMBINATION WITH YOUR STUDENT IDENTIFICATION NUMBER!
9-5

I'D LIKE TO TELL YOU STUDENTS THERE WILL BE NO MORE CORPORAL PUNISHMENT THIS YEAR!

SINCE CORPORAL LANCE HAS RETIRED...
BATIUK

...SERGEANT STONE WILL BE TAKING OVER IN THE SWAT DEPARTMENT!
9-6

I MUST REMIND YOU STUDENTS THAT YOU ARE NOT ALLOWED TO SMOKE IN SCHOOL!
BATIUK

IF YOU SHOULD FIND YOURSELF SMOKING...

GO TO THE NEAREST FIRE EXTINGUISHER AND PUT YOURSELF OUT!
9-7

WE'RE HAVING SOME TROUBLE WITH THE MEDIA SPECIALIST!

WHAT SEEMS TO BE THE PROBLEM?
BATIUK

SHE REFUSES TO RELEASE ANY OF THE MEDIA CENTER'S TAPES WITHOUT A SUBPOENA!
9-8

FUNKY WINKERBEAN
WELCOME BACK STUDENTS

ON BEHALF OF THE FACULTY AND MYSELF, I'D LIKE TO WELCOME YOU STUDENTS BACK TO SCHOOL!

WE'VE WORKED HARD TO PROVIDE YOU WITH AN OPEN AND CHALLANGING LEARNING ENVIRONMENT!
BATIUK

WE HOPE THAT WE CAN HELP YOU GROW AS AN INDIVIDUAL AND THAT WITH THAT GROWTH WILL COME THE MATURITY THAT WILL HELP YOU DECIDE WHAT YOU WANT TO DO WITH YOUR LIFE!
9-9

WE'D LIKE TO HAVE YOU DO THIS BY NEXT TUESDAY SO THAT WE CAN BEGIN STUDENT SCHEDULING!

MAY I GO TO THE RESTROOM ?
9/10

IN SPANISH CLASS WE ASK ALL OUR QUESTIONS IN SPANISH, SENOR !

MAY I GO TO THE JUAN ?
© Field Enterprises, Inc., 1973
BATIUK

YOU KNOW, AL, SOME-TIMES I THINK BULL BUSHKA, THE SCHOOL'S STAR ATHLETE, IS RETARDED !

IMPOSSIBLE, FRED !
OFFICE
BATIUK
9/11

ACCORDING TO OUR RECORDS, HE WAS NEVER TARDED TO BEGIN WITH !
© Field Enterprises, Inc., 1973

BULL, I ASKED YOU HERE SO WE COULD RAP AND TOUCH BASES !

I FEEL THAT IT'S GOOD FOR A STUDENT TO SIT DOWN WITH HIS COUNSELOR AT THE BEGINNING OF THE YEAR AND REVIEW HIS PROGRAM !
BATIUK
9/12

LET'S SEE ... YOU'RE ON THE SEVEN-YEAR PLAN, RIGHT ?
© Field Enterprises, Inc., 1973

THE COACH IS TRYING OUT THE WISHBONE-T AT FOOTBALL PRACTICE TODAY, RITA!

NO KIDDING... WISHBONE TEA?

IS THAT BETTER THAN GATORADE?
© Field Enterprises, Inc., 1973
BATIUK
9/13

COULD I HEAR WHAT ONE OF MY RECORDS SOUNDS LIKE ON YOUR STEREO, 'CRAZY'?
9/14

SURE, LES, PUT IT ON!
© Field Enterprises, Inc., 1973

WITH A QUACK QUACK HERE AND A QUACK QUACK THERE...
BATIUK

WELL, THAT WAS QUITE A FOOTBALL GAME!
© Field Enterprises, Inc., 1973

AND NOW WE GO TO AL RAGATTO FOR OUR POST-GAME ANALYSIS...
BATIUK

...WELL, CURT, ACCORDING TO THE DOCTOR, EVERY-BODY TURNED UP CLEAN!
9/15

FUNKY WINKERBEAN
I THINK YOU SHOULD DO IT!

LOOK AT IT THIS WAY, FUNKY, IF YOU DON'T BREAK UP WITH VICKI YOU MIGHT MARRY HER SOME DAY!

THE MARRIAGE MIGHT BE UNHAPPY AND YOU'D HAVE UNHAPPY KIDS!

AND ONE OF THOSE KIDS MIGHT GROW UP TO BE AN ASTRONAUT WHO IN HIS UNHAPPINESS MIGHT PRESS THE WRONG BUTTON AND MAKE A PERFECT LANDING ON THE SUN!

YOU WOULDN'T WANT THAT, WOULD YOU?
© Field Enterprises, Inc., 1973

YOU'RE RIGHT, LES!
BATIUK
9-16

BREAKING UP IS THE ONLY SENSIBLE THING TO DO!

LES, HOW DO YOU TELL A GIRL THAT IT'S OVER?

YOU'VE GOT ME!

I'M STILL WORKING ON HOW YOU TELL A GIRL IT'S STARTING!
BATIUK

YOU KNOW, 'CRAZY'... BREAKING UP WITH A GIRL HAS TO BE THE HARDEST THING IN THE WORLD TO DO!

I WOULDN'T AGREE WITH THAT, FUNKY!
BATIUK
9/18

THE HARDEST THING IN THE WORLD TO DO IS TOUCH YOUR NOSE WITH YOUR TONGUE!

I'VE GOT A PROBLEM, DEREK! HOW DO I TELL A GIRL I DON'T WANT TO SEE HER ANYMORE?

SIMPLE! JUST TELL HER IT'S OVER!
BATIUK
9/19

DON'T YOU THINK I SHOULD SUGAR-COAT IT A LITTLE?

OKAY, JUST SAY... SUGAR, IT'S OVER!

I'VE BEEN LOOKING FORWARD TO TONIGHT ALL WEEK, LIVINIA!

RIGGS AND KING ARE GOING TO PLAY ON T.V.!
BATIUK
9/20

ARE THEY THAT NEW BRITISH ROCK GROUP?

VICKI, I'M AFRAID IT'S ALL OVER BETWEEN US!

I KNOW, FUNKY! IT'S MY FAULT!
BATIUK
9/21

I MUST HAVE SPILLED IT WHEN I WAS GETTING THE LID OFF MY DRINK!

I'VE REALLY BEEN DEPRESSED SINCE I BROKE UP WITH VICKI!

EVERYONE I SEE IS SO HAPPY! AND EVERY SONG I HEAR REMINDS ME OF HER!

WITH A QUACK QUACK HERE AND A QUACK QUACK THERE...

WELL... ALMOST EVERY SONG!
BATIUK
9/22

FUNKY WINKERBEAN
MAYBE OUR TEAM PLAYS FRIZZY 'CAUSE WE HAVE SO MANY SPLIT-ENDS!

OKAY, MEN ... LISTEN UP!
THIS GAME IS THE **BIG** ONE!

WE'RE PLAYING OUR ARCH-RIVALS, BIG WALNUT TECH!

NOW, I DON'T HAVE TO TELL YOU WHAT THAT MEANS!
9-23
BATIUK

YEAH, QUESTION IN THE BACK THERE ...
© Field Enterprises, Inc., 1973

OKAY ... I GUESS I **DO** HAVE TO TELL YOU WHAT THAT MEANS!

MR. FAIRGOOD, UNDER THIS NEW PROGRAM, WILL OUR COMPUTERIZED REPORT CARD HAVE BUMPS INSTEAD OF HOLES?

WHAT ON EARTH DOES THAT HAVE TO DO WITH MODULAR PROGRAMMING?

MODULAR? ... OH, I THOUGHT IT WAS **NODULAR** PROGRAMMING!
BATIUK
9-24

I GOT A NOTE TELLING ME TO REPORT TO THE SCHOOL COMPUTER!

I WONDER IF THIS IS THE RIGHT PLACE?
BATIUK

what does this look like, chopped liver?
9/25

what is your student number?

MY STUDENT NUMBER? I DON'T KNOW WHAT MY STUDENT NUMBER IS!
BATIUK

you're joking of course!
9/26

you are being changed from algebra class 121 to 122.

BUT I LIKE THE CLASS I'M IN! I DON'T WANT TO CHANGE!
BATIUK

one more word and all record of your existence will be systematically destroyed!
9/27

IF YOU DON'T MIND MY SAYING SO, FOR A SCHOOL COMPUTER, YOU SURE ARE TOUCHY!

i'm only here to serve you.
BATIUK

but you can't be too careful! there's no telling who may be out to get me.
9/28

NOW REMEMBER, MEN... WHEN YOU STEP OUT OF THE SHOWERS ALWAYS USE THE FOOTBATH!

THE SOLUTION IN THERE WILL KILL ANY TYPE OF GERM OR FUNGUS ON CONTACT! YOU MAY RECOGNIZE IT!
BATIUK

IT'S THE CHICKEN NOODLE SOUP FROM THE CAFETERIA!
9/29

FUNKY WINKERBEAN

WHAT DO YOU THINK OF BIG BUCK BILLINGSLY, THE CHARGERS' TIGHT-END, AL?

WELL, CURT, HE DOESN'T HAVE BLAZING SPEED, BUT HE'S BIG AND STRONG WITH LOTS OF MOBILITY FOR A GUY HIS SIZE!

HE STILL MAKES SOME MENTAL ERRORS, BUT HE'S A REAL STUDENT OF THE GAME!
BATIUK

LATELY HE'S HAD SOME TROUBLE FINDING THE HANDLE ON THE BALL, BUT HE'S GOT A GREAT PAIR OF HANDS IN THE CLUTCH!
9-30

HE HAS THE POTENTIAL TO BE A GREAT ONE!

WHAT ABOUT THEIR FULLBACK, RHINO WILSON?

WELL, CURT, HE DOESN'T HAVE BLAZING SPEED, BUT...

'CRAZY,' YOU'VE BEEN SENT HERE FOR VIOLATING THE STUDENT CODE OF CONDUCT!

DO YOU KNOW WHY WE HAVE A STUDENT CODE?
BATIUK
10-1

SO WE CAN SEND SECRET MESSAGES?
© Field Enterprises, Inc., 1973

i think the school is planning to replace me.

it's not my fault things got messed up. i've just had faulty programmers.
BATIUK

i take the responsibility but not the blame.
© Field Enterprises, Inc., 1973
10-2

i've got to stop being so paranoid about them replacing me!

i've got to get on with the business of running this school.
© Field Enterprises, Inc., 1973
BATIUK

let's see now, what did i do with that list of students whose schedules i plan to mess up?
10-3

so they're really going to replace me.

let them. i don't care.
BATIUK

they won't have the 300 series to kick around anymore!
10-4

THIS NEW SPECIALLY PREPARED DRINK VIRTUALLY GUARANTEES A VICTORY TO THE TEAM THAT USES IT!

DO YOU DRINK IT BEFORE OR DURING THE GAME?
BATIUK
10-5

NEITHER! YOU SLIP IT IN THE OTHER TEAM'S WATERBUCKET AT HALFTIME!

YOU GUYS ARE ALWAYS BELLYACHING ABOUT YOUR LITTLE BRUISES!

YOU DON'T KNOW WHAT IT MEANS TO PLAY WITH PAIN! LOOK AT OUR STAR FULLBACK, BULL BUSHKA! HE'S BEEN PLAYING HURT ALL YEAR, BUT HE KNOWS HOW TO PLAY WITH PAIN! RIGHT, BULL?

AUUGGH!

HE SAID, 'RIGHT!'
BATIUK
10-6

FUNKY WINKERBEAN
RAP CELLAR

WOULD ANYONE LIKE TO KICK OFF OUR 'RAP CELLAR' DISCUSSION ON CHANGING SOCIAL ATTITUDES?
10-7

YES! HOW DO YOU FEEL ABOUT THE CONCEPT OF OPEN MARRIAGE, MARCIA?

I'M GLAD YOU ASKED ME ABOUT THAT, LIVINIA!

I'M VERY OPEN-MINDED AND LIBERAL ABOUT THAT!
BATIUK

I FEEL THAT REGARDLESS OF SEX, RACE, OR CREED, EVERYONE HAS THE RIGHT TO GET MARRIED!

Please respond to the questions in section B with the following:

JOHN-BOY, COME HERE!

TELL ME SOMETHING, JOHN-BOY!
BATIUK

HOW'D YOU EVER GET A STUPID NAME LIKE JOHN-BOY?

OKAY, NOW ON THE WEAK SIDE FORMATION OUR BACK HITS THIS HOLE!
81
11
14

WHAT HAPPENS THEN?
BATIUK

HE GETS RACKED UP!

SO YOUR UNDERGROUND PAPER HAS REALLY BEEN LOSING MONEY, HUH, ROLAND?

ARE YOU GOING TO CALL IT QUITS?

NO, DEREK! I'VE TORN THE WORD QUIT OUT OF MY DICTIONARY!

ALONG WITH QUITE, QUIVER, QUIXOTIC, QUIZ ...

FUNKY WINKERBEAN
ARE YOU A FOOTBALL FAN?

YAHOO!

AT LAST I'M FINALLY GOING TO WIN A FOOTBALL BET!
© Field Enterprises, Inc., 1973

THAT RECEIVER FOR MY TEAM WAS WIDE OPEN! HE'S GOING ALL THE WAY!

NOTHING CAN STOP HIM NOW!
BATIUK

OH NO...

I **KNEW** THAT STUPID BLIMP WAS GOING TO FALL ON SOMEONE SOONER OR LATER!
10-14

FRED, YOU DIDN'T GET YOUR SICK LEAVE FORM FILED SOON ENOUGH!

OH, NO! DOES THAT MEAN I'M GOING TO GET DOCKED?
I'M AFRAID SO!

DOCK!
BATIUK
10-15

IT'S GOOD TO HAVE THAT FIRST YEAR OF TEACHING BEHIND YOU, ISN'T IT, RITA?

OF COURSE, I'M SURE IT WAS REALLY A GROWING EXPERIENCE FOR YOU!
BATIUK E.M.
10-16

OH, IT WAS ... I GREW BITTER!

YOU TRIMMED YOUR MOUSTACHE, DIDN'T YOU, GEORGE?

YEAH, I HAD TO, RITA!
BATIUK
10-17

I WAS GETTING FUR-BALLS!

RRRING!

WE HIGH SCHOOL STUDENTS ARE BULLISH ON AMERICA!
RUMBLERUMBLERUMBLERUMBLERUMB

I'VE PLOTTED THE RESULTS OF YOUR APTITUDE TEST ON THIS GRAPH, FUNKY!

THIS SHOWS YOUR STRONG AND WEAK POINTS AND WILL HELP US DETERMINE WHAT CAREER YOU'RE BEST SUITED FOR!
YOU'LL NOTICE THIS LOOKS LIKE A BUNCH OF MOUNTAINS!
SO PERHAPS YOU SHOULD BECOME A SKI INSTRUCTOR!

'FOOTBALL BUILDS CHARACTER'!

THAT'S REALLY TRUE, COACH!

I KNOW! YOU SHOULD SEE SOME OF THE CHARACTERS WE'VE GOT ON THE TEAM THIS YEAR!

FUNKY WINKERBEAN
TEACHING TEAM

YOU WANTED TO SEE ME, MISS WRIGHTON?

YES, HAROLD, I WANTED TO TALK TO YOU ABOUT YOUR GRADES!

YOU'VE MISSED SO MANY ASSIGNMENTS, THAT RIGHT NOW YOU'RE ON THE BORDERLINE OF FAILING!
BATIUK

DOESN'T THAT WORRY YOU AT ALL?

WELL, YOU KNOW WHAT THEY SAY... ALL THINGS MUST PASS!

THAT'S CUTE, HAROLD!
10-21

SAYINGS FROM THE
I CHONG
ANCIENT BOOK OF CHINESE PHILOSOPHY
10-22

THE MASTER SAYS: THERE IS MUCH TO BE LEARNED BY SITTING NEXT TO A RUSHING STREAM AND LISTENING TO WHAT IT TELLS YOU!

UNLESS, OF COURSE, YOU'RE SITTING NEXT TO A BABBLING BROOK!

THIS IS A LEARNING CONTRACT, HAROLD!

IN IT, YOU AGREE TO ACCOMPLISH A CERTAIN AMOUNT OF WORK WITHIN A SET AMOUNT OF TIME!
BATIUK
10-23

IF YOU DON'T, WE SEND A HIT MAN AFTER YOU!

MISS WRIGHTON SENT ME TO THE OFFICE BECAUSE SHE DOESN'T KNOW WHAT TO DO WITH ME ANYMORE!
BATIUK

GO HOME
10-24

YOUR HOROSCOPE
by CLAIR VOYANT

THURSDAY WILL BE A FAVORABLE DAY FOR A PISCES TO SETTLE HIS ROMANTIC AFFAIRS!
BATIUK

RENEW YOUR SUBSCRIPTION TO PLAYBOY!
© Field Enterprises, Inc., 1973
10-25

WOW!

I COULD GO FOR A DATE WITH ANY ONE OF THAT OTHER SCHOOL'S MAJORETTES!
© Field Enterprises, Inc., 1973
BATIUK
10-26

I'D SETTLE FOR A DATE WITH ONE OF THEIR MINORETTES!

HAVE YOU HEARD THE LATEST, AL?

THERE'S A RUMOR GOING AROUND THAT THE POLICE ARE PLANNING A DOPE RAID AT OUR SCHOOL!
10-27

YOU'D THINK BY NOW, THEY'D HAVE LEARNED TO SEND IN THEIR BEST MEN!
© Field Enterprises, Inc., 1973
BATIUK

FUNKY
WINKERBEAN

DON'T ACT SO DOWN, LES!

YOU'VE GOT TO CHEER UP AND BE PROUD OF YOURSELF!

REMEMBER THAT YOU'RE A UNIQUE CREATION!

THERE'S NO ONE ELSE EXACTLY LIKE YOU IN THE WHOLE UNIVERSE!
10/28

THAT'S TRUE, FUNKY!
BATIUK

NOW I FEEL ALIENATED!

AT TONIGHT'S STAFF MEETING, I FELT IT WOULD BE GOOD TO DISCUSS THE DOCTRINE OF 'IN LOCO PARENTIS'!

LET ME PREFACE THIS BY SAYING...
© Field Enterprises, Inc., 1973
BATIUK

...THAT IT'S ONLY A SMALL MINORITY OF THE PARENTS WE DEAL WITH WHO ARE REALLY LOCO!
10-29

TRICK OR TREAT, MARY SUE, AND I'M THE TREAT!

10-30
BATIUK

WHAT'S THE TRICK?
© Field Enterprises, Inc., 1973

DAD, THIS IS MY FRIEND, CRAZY HARRY!

HE'S GOING WITH ME TO FUNKY'S HALLOWEEN PARTY!
© Field Enterprises, Inc., 1973
BATIUK
10-31

HE'LL WIN FIRST PRIZE!

KIDS HAVE IT TOO EASY THESE DAYS!
© Field Enterprises, Inc., 1973
11-1

EVERYTHING IS HANDED TO THEM ON A SILVER PLATTER!
BATIUK

I WISH I WERE A KID!

A PUNT RETURN MAN HAS TO BE READY TO GO INTO A GAME AT ANY MOMENT!
© Field Enterprises, Inc., 1973

HE HAS TO BE BOTH PHYSICALLY AND MENTALLY TOUGH!

WHEN HE GOES IN, EVERYONE'S ATTENTION IS FOCUSED ON HIM, AND THE ENTIRE OPPOSING TEAM WANTS TO MANGLE HIM!
BATIUK
11-2

THAT'S WHY I'M GLAD I'M NOT A PUNT RETURN MAN!

HE'S DOWN TO THE THIRTY...

THEY MARK IT THE TWELVE...
© Field Enterprises, Inc., 1973

WE'LL CALL IT THE THREE!
BATIUK
11-3

FUNKY WINKERBEAN

OUR SCHOOL COMPUTER HAS REALLY BEEN MAKING A LOT OF ERRORS LATELY, AL!

WHAT DO YOU THINK WE SHOULD DO?
© Field Enterprises, Inc., 1973
BATIUK

SIMPLE, FRED! WE'LL HANDLE IT THE WAY WE WOULD ANY PROBLEM!

GIVE IT THREE SWATS!
1/4

HI THERE! MY NAME'S ...

DOPEY!

DOPEY! THAT'S THE NAME OF THE DWARF WE COULDN'T THINK OF!

ARE YOU COMING TO THE BAND SHOW FRIDAY, FRED?

BAND SHOW? I THOUGHT YOU WERE PLAYING AT THE GAME THIS WEEKEND!

OH, WELL, THE FOOTBALL TEAM WILL BE PLAYING BEFORE AND AFTER THE BAND SHOW!

WE'RE GOING TO KEEP PRACTICING IF IT TAKES ALL NIGHT!

WHEN WE GET TO THAT BAND CONTEST WE'RE GOING TO BE THE BEST BAND THERE!

THAT'S THE PURPOSE OF GOOD MUSIC ...

..TO WIN!

ACHTUNG!

ER ···

AH ··· I MEAN, UH ONE AND UH TWO ···
11-8

WHY IS SOMETHING USED TO COVER A CUT LIKE A KID WHO HELPS THE BAND DIRECTOR?

BECAUSE THEY'RE BOTH BAND-AIDS!

GET IT? BAND-AID AND BAND-AIDE! HAR! HAR! HAR!
BATIUK

SNIFF! THOSE BAND JOKES JUST TEAR ME UP!
11-9

DR. JOYCE, MY HUSBAND JUST RAN AWAY WITH MY SON'S GIRLFRIEND ···

THE BANK IS FORECLOSING ON THE MORTGAGE, MY DAUGHTER ELOPED WITH HER GURU, AND I CAN'T SLEEP BECAUSE OUR ST. BERNARD HAS WHOOPING COUGH!
BATIUK
11-10

WHAT SHOULD I DO, DR. JOYCE?

STAY AWAY FROM OPEN WINDOWS!

FUNKY WINKERBEAN
I'M SO HUNGRY I COULD EAT A SEA-HORSE

OKAY, GANG! CHOW TIME!
STAT

LINE UP IN ALPHABETICAL ORDER!

LOOK, IF YOU GUYS DON'T LINE UP WHEN THE 'GREAT PROVIDER' FEEDS YOU, HE'LL BRING DOWN THE DARKNESS UPON YOU!
BATIUK
11-11

THAT **DOES** IT! YOU HAVE INCURRED MY **WRATH**!
© Field Enterprises, Inc., 1973

CLICK!

CLICK!

THAT ALWAYS SHAKES 'EM UP!
STAT

JOHN DARLING HERE, TRYING TO FIND OUT IF SCANDALS LIKE WATERGATE HAVE AFFECTED THE MORAL FIBER OF OUR YOUTH!

COACH, HOW WOULD YOU ASSESS THE MORAL FIBER?

PERSONALLY, I PREFER ASTRO-TURF!
BATIUK
11-12

HI! J. DARLING HERE, BRINGING YOU THE ATTITUDES OF TODAY'S YOUTH!
11-13

I'M SPEAKING HERE TO A ···

BATIUK
CLOMP!

COMPLETE WEIRDO!
© Field Enterprises, Inc., 1973

THE COMPUTER ACCIDENTALLY USED THE STAFF PAYROLL TO ORDER EXTRA FOOD FOR THE CAFETERIA!

NOW WHAT ARE WE GOING TO DO?
© Field Enterprises, Inc., 1973

would you consider taking your payment in hotdogs?
BATIUK
11-14

many people are amazed at the complex mathematical ability of a computer.

actually though, the concept is quite simple!
BATIUK

inside we're just filled with thousands of toes that we count on!
11-15

WHEN YOU GO OUT ON THAT FIELD, MEN, BE PROUD!
11
14

BE PROUD OF YOURSELF, BE PROUD OF YOUR TEAM, BE PROUD OF YOUR SCHOOL···
BATIUK
11-16

···BE PROUD THAT YOU GOT OUT OF LAST WEEK'S GAME ALIVE!

SAYINGS FROM THE
I CHONG
ANCIENT BOOK OF CHINESE PHILOSOPHY

THE MASTER SAYS: HE WHO SPIT-SHINES HIS BUST OF PLATO···
BATIUK
11-17

···IS WAXING PHILOSOPHIC!

FUNKY WINKERBEAN

THE LAST LEAF OF SUMMER!
DESPERATELY CLINGING TO ITS FINAL HOURS OF GLORY!

KNOWING THAT, TRY AS IT MIGHT, IT CAN'T PREVAIL AGAINST THE INEVITABLE WILL OF MOTHER NATURE!
BATIUK
11-18

KA-POW

LET'S HEAR IT FOR MOTHER NATURE!

SAYINGS FROM THE
I CHONG
ANCIENT BOOK OF CHINESE PHILOSOPHY
11-19

THE MASTER SAYS: IF YOU WISH TO KNOW TRUE BEAUTY, SEEK OUT A BEEKEEPER WITH A BEE IN HIS LEFT HAND ...

FOR BEAUTY IS IN THE EYE OF THE BEE-HOLDER!
BATIUK
© Field Enterprises, Inc. 1973

YOU SEEM KINDA DISCOURAGED, LES! WHAT'S WRONG?

WHEN I WAS IN MR. FAIRGOOD'S OFFICE I TOOK A LOOK AT MY STUDENT PERSONALITY PROFILE!

WHAT DID IT SAY?
BATIUK
11-20

© Field Enterprises, Inc. 1973
NOTHING ...

I'VE BEEN LOOKING FORWARD TO TOMORROW ALL MONTH, LIVINIA!

AT LAST IT'S TURKEY DAY!

OH? ... IT'S YOUR BIRTHDAY?
BATIUK
11-21
© Field Enterprises, Inc. 1973

STATE COMES INTO TODAY'S FOOTBALL GAME A HEAVY FAVORITE!

AND THEIR FULLBACK IS A REAL WORKHORSE!
BATIUK
11-22

FRANKLY, I'M SURPRISED THEY ALLOW A REAL WORK-HORSE TO PLAY FOOTBALL!

I'M THROUGH ORDERING SO MANY PIZZAS!

IT'S GOING TO TAKE ALL OF MY WILL POWER ...

BUT THIS TIME I'M GOING TO MAKE IT STICK!
BATIUK
11-23

STARTING TODAY, I'M GOING **COLD TURKEY**!

WHERE'S MY BOX OF VAMPIRE FRUITTIES?

IT'S ALL GONE!

TRY SOME OF YOUR FATHER'S CEREAL!
BATIUK

ORGANIZATIONAL CRUNCH?
11-24

FUNKY WINKERBEAN
I CAN'T WAIT TILL THREE O'CLOCK!

OH, OH! I WAS GOING TO ASK OUT MARY SUE AFTER SCHOOL TODAY...

...BUT SHE'S WITH SOME GUY!

WELL, SO WHAT? WHY SHOULD I LET THAT STOP ME? I DON'T KNOW IF SHE LIKES HIM OR NOT!
© Field Enterprises, Inc., 1973
BATIUK

IT MAY BE A PURELY PLATONIC RELATIONSHIP!

YEAH! I'M GOING OVER AND ASK HER OUT!
11-25

UH... EXCUSE ME, MARY SUE...

i wonder what the purpose of life really is?

the office copier had a good point the other day.
BATIUK

he said there must be more to life than just reproduction.
© Field Enterprises, Inc., 1973
11-26

ANOTHER WEEKEND AND I HAVEN'T GOT A DATE!

WELL, LIKE THEY SAY, 'UNLUCKY AT LOVE, LUCKY AT CARDS'!
BATIUK

I THINK I'LL GO HOME AND WIN A FEW GAMES OF SOLITAIRE!
© Field Enterprises, Inc., 1973
11-27

DAD, I WANT YOU TO KNOW SOMETHING!

'CRAZY' HARRY, HERE, REALLY LIKES YOU!
© Field Enterprises, Inc., 1973
BATIUK
11-28

PRAY FOR ME!

WHY DO THEY CALL YOU 'CRAZY' HARRY?

COCK-A-DOODLE-DOO!
BATIUK
© Field Enterprises, Inc., 1973

ASK A SILLY QUESTION...
11-29

WHY DON'T YOU WIPE THAT SILLY SMILE OFF YOUR FACE?

BATIUK

© Field Enterprises, Inc., 1973
11-30

© Field Enterprises, Inc., 1973
BATIUK

WHY DON'T YOU GO OUT AND THROW SOME BODY-BLOCKS ON TRUCKS FOR AWHILE?
12-1

FUNKY WINKERBEAN

LIBRARY
MEDIA CENTER

NEXT ON OUR STAFF MEETING AGENDA IS A WORD FROM MISS RUDOLPH, OUR MEDIA SPECIALIST!
12-2

THIS YEAR WE PLANNED MANY NEW CHANGES FOR THE MEDIA CENTER!

OUR BASIC GOAL WAS TO **MOTIVATE** THE STUDENTS!
© Field Enterprises, Inc., 1973

AND WE FEEL WE'VE SUCCEEDED IN MAKING THE MEDIA CENTER AN EXCITING PLACE!
BATIUK

IN THE MEDIA CENTER THE STUDENTS **WANT** TO LEARN!

BRUNO **MAKES** THEM WANT TO LEARN!

BUZZZZZ

UP UP AND AWAY!!
12-3

SUPERFLY?
BATIUK

I'M JUST FINISHING MY FICTIONALIZED STORY OF THE WATERGATE TAPES FOR ENGLISH CLASS!

After listening to three hours of the White House tapes, Senator Baker turned to Senator Ervin and said: "Play it again, Sam!"
12-4
BATIUK

I'M THINKING OF CALLING IT CASSETTE BLANKA!

WE REALLY LIVE IN TROUBLED TIMES DEREK!

IT'S HARD TO BELIEVE THERE WAS TALK OF IMPEACHING THE MOST POWERFUL MAN IN THE COUNTRY!

YOU MEAN THEY WERE GOING TO GET RID OF PETE ROZELLE?
12-5

I'VE REALLY PUT IN SOME LONG, HARD AND DEDICATED HOURS AS A HALL MONITOR!

AND WHAT DO I GET FOR IT?

A LAMINATED, LIFETIME RESTROOM PASS!

THESE LONG GRUELING HOURS AT MY HALL-MONITOR'S STATION ARE STARTING TO GET TO ME!

I THINK I'M STARTING TO DEVELOP

...A NERVOUS TWITCH!

YOUR HOROSCOPE
by CLAIR VOYANT

THIS IS A BLACK DAY FOR PISCES!

YOUR LUCKY PLANET TURNED OUT TO BE A UFO!

FUNKY WINKERBEAN

DO YOU HAVE ANY OF YOUR TERM PAPERS FROM MISS WRIGHTON'S CLASS, FUNKY?

NO, I THREW ALL MINE AWAY, LES!

'CRAZY,' DO YOU STILL HAVE ANY OF YOUR OLD TERM PAPERS?
TOO LATE! I GAVE MINE TO ROLAND!
BATIUK

NOPE!

SORRY!

NO!

I'LL TELL YA, THE HARDEST THING ABOUT A TERM PAPER IS DOING THE RESEARCH!
12-9

I HOPE THESE KUNG FU LESSONS I'M GOING TO TAKE DO ME SOME GOOD!

I CAN'T WAIT TILL I'VE MASTERED THE ART OF KUNG FU COMPLETELY!
12-10

THEN I CAN DRAW INNER PEACE AND CALM FROM THE QUIET KNOWLEDGE..
BATIUK

THAT I CAN KILL OR MAIM ANYTHING IN SIGHT!

WHY DO I WANT TO LEARN KUNG FU, JUAN?

SO I CAN HAVE THE CONFIDENCE AND PEACE OF MIND TO KNOW THAT I CAN DEFEND MYSELF IN ANY KIND OF SITUATION!

ROTSA RUCK!
BATIUK

HI-YAA!
12-12

SAY, JUAN, WHAT DOES 'HI-YAA' MEAN ANYWAY?
BATIUK

HI-YAA IS CHINESE FOR 'HELLO'!

OKAY, PUSSYWILLOW, LET'S TRY OUT WHAT YOU HAVE LEARNED AGAINST A REAL OPPONENT!
BATIUK

HI-YAAA!

KA-BLAM!
12-13

YOUR KUNG WASN'T BAD BUT YOUR FU NEEDS WORK!

HI-YAAA!

YII!

REMEMBER TO KEEP YOUR HEAD DOWN AND FOLLOW THROUGH!
12-14

FISH ARE REALLY LUCKY!

THEY LEAD SIMPLE UNCOMPLICATED WORRY-FREE LIVES!

OF COURSE THEY'LL NEVER GET A CHANCE TO GO OUT WITH RAQUEL WELCH!
BATIUK

BUT THEN I'LL NEVER GET A CHANCE TO GO OUT WITH RAQUEL WELCH EITHER!
12-15

FUNKY WINKERBEAN
PRINCIPAL

WHEN I'M SITTING BEHIND MY PRINCIPAL'S DESK ...

I KNOW IT'S WHERE I REALLY BELONG!

I'VE ALWAYS DREAMED OF BEING A PRINCIPAL AND LENDING MY GUIDANCE TO A HIGHLY MOTIVATED AND INTELLIGENT STAFF!
BATIUK
12-16

MR. BURCH, TELL MISS WRIGHTON TO STOP TAKING THE ERASERS FROM MY ROOM ...

... OR I'LL START TAKING THE CHALK FROM HERS!

I STILL DREAM ABOUT IT A LOT!
© Field Enterprises, Inc., 1973

HI!
12-17

I'D LIKE SOME OF THOSE FREE CHRISTMAS EVER-GREEN SPRIGS THAT YOUR BANK IS GIVING AWAY!
BATIUK

OH, IN THAT CASE YOU WANT OUR BRANCH OFFICE!

MERRY CHRISTMAS! HO! HO! HO!

OH, NO!
BATIUK

IT'S THE GHOST OF CHRISTMAS PAST!
12-18

TO THE STAFF: AS WE NEAR THE HOLIDAY SEASON WE PAUSE TO REFLECT ON THE PASSING YEAR!

IT IS A TIME TO REDEDICATE OURSELVES TO OUR GOALS! WE FACE A MASSIVE CHALLENGE, BUT WITH OUR COMBINED EFFORT WE SHALL REAP THE REWARDS!
BATIUK
12-19

YOUR NEGOTIATING COMMITTEE!

they think that just because i'm a computer they can work me silly!

they'll be sorry one day, won't they, igor?
BATIUK

YES, MASTER!
12-20

I CAN'T BELIEVE WE HAVE TO WRITE A THEME OVER CHRISTMAS VACATION!
12-21

WHAT'S YOURS GOING TO BE ABOUT, FUNKY?
BATIUK

ABOUT TWO PAGES!

I WONDER WHAT IT WAS THAT THE THREE WISE MEN SAW IN THE SKY ON THAT FIRST CHRISTMAS?

SOME SCIENTISTS SPECULATE THAT THE BRIGHT LIGHT MAY HAVE BEEN A SUPERNOVA!
BATIUK

PERSONALLY I THINK IT WAS THE GOODYEAR BLIMP!

FUNKY WINKERBEAN
GOD REST YE MERRY GENTLEPERSONS

HI THERE! WHO ARE YOU, THE CHRISTMAS SPIRIT?

VERY FUNNY!
BATIUK
© Field Enterprises, Inc., 1973

ACTUALLY, I WAS TOLD THAT AT CHRISTMAS YOU'RE SUPPOSED TO GO OUT AND TRICK OR TREAT LIKE YOU DO ON HALLOWEEN!

I HAVEN'T GOTTEN ANYTHING SO FAR!
12-23

FRANKLY, I THINK I'VE BEEN HAD!
HOW ABOUT SOME HOT CHOCOLATE AT MY HOUSE?
BEST OFFER I'VE HAD ALL NIGHT!

AHH! CHRISTMAS EVE!

I ALWAYS DROP OFF TO SLEEP WITH VISIONS OF SUGAR PLUMS DANCING IN MY HEAD!
BATIUK
12-24

AND I ALWAYS WAKE UP CHRISTMAS MORNING WITH A SPLITTING HEADACHE!

here i sit lonely and ignored on christmas day.
BATIUK

MERRY CHRISTMAS!

how nice! cookie and punch cards!
MERRY CHRISTMAS, MASTER!
12-25

IS THIS THE CHEAPEST POCKET CALCULATOR YOU HAVE?

WELL, WE DO HAVE A THREE-DOLLAR MODEL!
BATIUK
12-26

YOU PRESS THIS BUTTON, A PIECE OF PAPER POPS OUT, AND YOU FIGURE OUT YOUR PROBLEM ON THAT!

WHAT DO YOU THINK OF ALL THIS TALK ABOUT THE METRIC SYSTEM, MARCIA?

I'M NOT SURE, JAN!
BATIUK
12-27

IS THAT ANYTHING LIKE THE ADKINS DIET?

I'M GLAD YOU COULD ALL MAKE IT TO OUR RAP CELLAR MEETING!

TONIGHT I THOUGHT WE'D DO SOMETHING TO RAISE OUR SOCIAL CONSCIOUSNESS!
BATIUK

IS THAT ANYTHING LIKE TRANSCENDENTAL LEVITATION?

NOW TO TYPE UP MY THEME THAT I WROTE OVER CHRISTMAS VACATION!
BATIUK

I REALLY DON'T HAVE TOO MUCH HERE ...

... BUT LUCKILY I'M VERY DEFT AT THE ART OF USING FOUR-INCH MARGINS!

FUNKY WINKERBEAN

MR. SMITH MADE A REALLY GOOD POINT IN SCIENCE CLASS, LIVINIA!
WHAT DID HE SAY, FUNKY?
12-30
BATIUK

HE SAID IT WAS STUPID TO WORRY ABOUT GETTING OIL FROM THE MID-EAST FOR ENERY, WHEN WE CAN USE THE SUN!

OH, THAT'S EASY TO SAY...

BUT THERE ARE A LOT OF DIFFICULT TECHNOLOGICAL PROBLEMS IN USING THE SUN!

LIKE HOW DO THEY PLAN TO GET THE OIL WELLS UP THERE?

THREE ... TWO ... ONE ...
HAPPY NEW YEAR!
IT'S 1974!!

¡BLEEP!
BATIUK

WHOOPEE!

1974

I WONDER WHAT THE COMING YEAR HAS IN STORE FOR ME?

IT'S OFTEN BEEN SAID THAT LIFE IS LIKE A PLAY AND WE ARE THE ACTORS!
© Field Enterprises, Inc., 1974
1-1

I LIKE SOME OF THE CHARACTERS, BUT THE PLOT'S CONFUSING!

THAT'S COMET KOHOUTEK UP THERE!

IT'S A BALL OF ICE ABOUT TEN MILES IN DIAMETER AND WEIGHS AN ESTIMATED THREE TRILLION TONS! NOT ONLY THAT BUT THE TAIL IS FIFTY MILLION MILES LONG!
© Field Enterprises, Inc., 1974
BATIUK

YEAH! SURE, FELLA!
1-2

I THINK IT WOULD REALLY BE NEAT TO BE AN ASTRONOMER SO I COULD DISCOVER A COMET AND HAVE IT NAMED AFTER ME!

WINKERBEAN'S COMET?
BATIUK

YOU'D BE THE LAUGHING-STOCK OF THE UNIVERSE!
1-3

COMET KOHOUTEK IS REALLY SOMETHING, 'CRAZY'!

I WONDER HOW IT CAME TO BE CALLED COMET KOHOUTEK?
BATIUK

KOHOUTEK WON IT IN A RAFFLE AT THE OBSERVATORY!
1-4

WHERE DID COMET KOHOUTEK COME FROM, FUNKY?
1-5

WELL, LIVINIA, SOME SCIENTISTS THEORIZE THAT IT IS CHUNKS OF MATTER THAT WERE CREATED AT THE SAME TIME AS THE SUN AND THE PLANETS!
BATIUK

OTHERS SUGGEST IT WAS CREATED BY THE PRESIDENT TO DIVERT ATTENTION FROM WATERGATE!

FUNKY WINKERBEAN

WHAT CAN I DO FOR YOU, DEREK ?

WE'RE BEING TREATED LIKE LITTLE KIDS AT THIS SCHOOL, MR. BURCH!

THE TEACHERS DON'T HAVE HALF AS MANY RULES TO FOLLOW AS THE STUDENTS DO!
BATIUK
1-6

I KNOW!

THAT'S THE OLD DOUBLE STANDARD!

WE MAKE UP OUR RULES AND THEN DOUBLE THEM FOR YOU!

IF THERE'S ONE THING I HATE, IT'S WHEN THEY WAX THE FLOORS OVER THE CHRISTMAS BREAK!
BATIUK

BOY! IS THIS EVER A BEAUTIFUL NIGHT FOR LOOKING AT THE COMET!

BATIUK

AND WHATEVER!

LOOK, LES, IF YOU HAVE A FEAR OF CLIMBING THAT ROPE, THE ONLY WAY TO OVERCOME IT IS TO DO IT!

JUST LIKE WHEN YOU FALL OFF A HORSE, THE FIRST THING YOU SHOULD DO IS GET BACK ON!
BATIUK

I THINK I'D RATHER FALL OFF A HORSE!

TAKE IT EASY AS YOU'RE CLIMBING THE ROPE, LES!

YOU'VE GOT TO LEARN TO RELAX!
1-10

YOU'RE TOO TENSE!
BATIUK

MISS WRIGHTON, I...

DEREK, FROM NOW ON I PREFER MS. WRIGHTON!
BATIUK
1-11

SHO-NUFF, MS. WRIGHTON!

SOMETIMES THE THOUGHT OF AN ATOMIC WAR REALLY WORRIES ME, FUNKY!

YOU GET SCARED BY THE THOUGHT OF ALL THE CHAOS AND DESTRUCTION, HUH?
BATIUK

NO! I WONDER HOW IT WOULD AFFECT MY CHANCES FOR ACHIEVING GROWTH AND SELF-ACTUALIZATION!
1-12

FUNKY WINKERBEAN

BANG!
BLAM!
BAM!

WHAT ARE YOU WATCHING, 'CRAZY'?

THIS IS A SEQUEL THEY MADE TO THE MOVIE, 'THE GUN'!
BATIUK
1-13

WHAT'S IT CALLED?

'SON OF A GUN'!

WELL, RITA ...

HOW DID YOUR FIRST DAY IN TEAM TEACHING GO?
BATIUK
1-14

THEIR TEAM WON!

SEEMS LIKE YOU HAD A LOT OF KIDS OUT FOR BASKETBALL, COACH!

DID YOU HAVE MANY SQUAD-CUTS?
1-15

NO, FRED, SO FAR WE'VE BEEN PRETTY INJURY-FREE!
BATIUK

JOHN DARLING HERE, BRINGING YOU A LOOK AT AREA ROUNDBALLERS!

COACH, HAVE YOU SEEN ANYTHING HERE IN THESE EARLY GAMES THAT FILLS YOU WITH HOPE?

YEAH, THE CHEERLEADERS!
BATIUK
1-16

WE'D LIKE TO SEE YOUR OCTOBER 15TH TAPE TO SEE IF WE CAN LOCATE THE ERROR WE'RE LOOKING FOR !

october 15th?
BATIUK
© Field Enterprises, Inc., 1974
1-17

i'm sorry, there was no october 15th this year!

we computers are powerful enough to rule the world!

of course, all someone has to do is pull out our plug and we've had it.
© Field Enterprises, Inc., 1974
BATIUK

that's always been our achilles' socket.
1-18

SAYINGS FROM THE
I CHONG
ANCIENT BOOK OF CHINESE PHILOSOPHY

THE MASTER SAYS: IF YOU CAN WALK WITH YOUR HEAD IN THE CLOUDS AND YOUR FEET ON THE GROUND ···
1-19
© Field Enterprises, Inc., 1974

AN NBA CONTRACT WILL BE YOURS!

FUNKY WINKERBEAN

SIGH!

WELL, IT HAD TO HAPPEN!

THE SUNDAY I DREAD MORE THAN ANY OTHER IS FINALLY HERE!

THAT VAGUE, LOST, EMPTY FEELING INSIDE!

LET'S FACE IT...
BATIUK

I'VE GOT A CLASSIC CASE OF POST-SUPER-BOWL LET-DOWN!
© Field Enterprises, Inc., 1974
1-20

I'D LIKE A JAR OF HAIR REMOVER!

THE **EXTRA LARGE** SIZE!
BATIUK
1-21

BLAST THAT STUPID SPINACH ANYWAY!

WELL, LES, HOW DID IT GO? DID NANCY SAY SHE'D GO OUT WITH YOU?
BATIUK

NO! SHE TOOK THE FIFTH AMENDMENT!
1-22

ARE THEY ALLOWED TO DO THAT?

WOW! THAT GIRL IN THE RED SWEATER IS REALLY TUFF, FUNKY!

YEAH, BUT YOU KNOW WHAT THEY SAY, LES, BEAUTY IS ONLY SKIN DEEP!
BATIUK

BOY! SHE MUST HAVE REALLY THICK SKIN!
1-23

IN TAKING THIS COMPUTERIZED TEST ··· BE SURE AND USE A # 2 PENCIL ONLY!

ONE ··· TWO!
BATIUK

THAT WASN'T SO HARD!
1-24

WHAT A GREAT DAY I HAD TODAY!
RUMBLERUMBLE

I GOT AN 'A' ON MY THEME ··· WE DON'T HAVE ANY HOMEWORK FOR OVER THE WEEKEND ···
UMBLERUMBLER
1-25

··· AND I MADE IT ALL THE WAY DOWN THE HALL WITHOUT STEPPING ON A CRACK!
BLERUMBLERU

WHAT'S THAT YOU'RE READING, LES?

IT'S A NEW BOOK WRITTEN BY A FAMOUS PSYCHOLOGIST, DEREK!
BATIUK

IT'S CALLED: 'I'M A MESS AND HEAVEN ONLY KNOWS WHAT SHAPE YOU'RE IN'!
1-26

FUNKY WINKERBEAN
ARE YOU A NEWS-BEET ?

HI, JOHN DARLING HERE!

TALKING TO A TYPICAL HIGH SCHOOL COACH ABOUT ATTITUDES IN TODAY'S SPORTS!
COACH

TELL ME, COACH...
COACH

DO YOU FEEL THAT TOO MUCH EMPHASIS IS PLACED ON WINNING THESE DAYS?
1-27

YES, DEFINITELY!

IN FACT, I WAS JUST TELLING THAT TO THE SCHOOL BOARD THE OTHER DAY!
COACH
© Field Enterprises, Inc., 1974

© Field Enterprises, Inc., 1974

A LIGHT BULB?

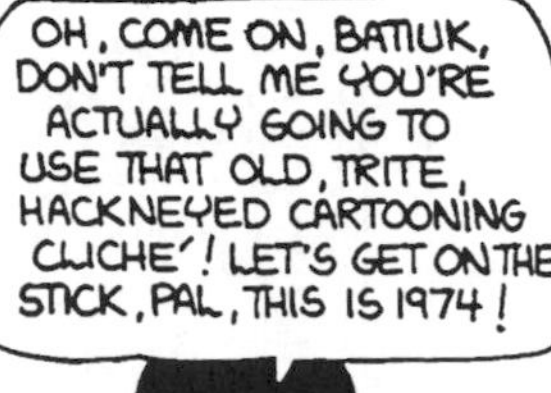
OH, COME ON, BATIUK, DON'T TELL ME YOU'RE ACTUALLY GOING TO USE THAT OLD, TRITE, HACKNEYED CARTOONING CLICHE'! LET'S GET ON THE STICK, PAL, THIS IS 1974!

1-28
BATIUK

CUTE!

WHAT'S WITH THE CANDLE?

THAT SIGNIFIES THAT I'VE JUST COME UP WITH A KEEN IDEA OF SOME KIND!
WHAT HAPPENED TO THE OLD LIGHT BULB?
BATIUK
1-29

WE'RE CUTTING BACK TO CONSERVE ENERGY!

BOOM! BOOM! BOOM!

NO! NO! YOU'RE NOT GETTING THE PROPER SOUND!

THAT'S NO WAY TO PLAY A FLUTE!

MUSIC HAS ALWAYS BEEN GOOD TO ME!

FROM MY VERY FIRST FLUTAPHONE TO MY ESTEEMED POSITION AS BAND DIRECTOR I'VE ENJOYED EVERY MINUTE OF IT!
BATIUK
1-31

OH IT'S HAD IT'S ANDANTES AND ALLEGROS ··· BUT BASICALLY IT'S BEEN A GOOD LIFE!

SAYINGS FROM THE
I CHONG
ANCIENT BOOK OF CHINESE PHILOSOPHY

THE MASTER SAYS: OF ALL OF NATURE'S VEGETABLES ···
BATIUK
2-1

··· ONLY THE BEET GOES ON!

WELL, PIONEER 10 HAS LONG SINCE COMPLETED IT'S HISTORIC FLYBY OF JUPITER ···

··· AND AFTER SIFTING THROUGH THE DATA, SCIENTISTS HAVE FINALLY BEEN ABLE TO FIGURE OUT WHAT THAT MYSTERIOUS RED SPOT IS ···
BATIUK

RINGWORM!
2-2

FUNKY WINKERBEAN
MEMO
FROM THE DESK OF:
TO THE WASTEBASKET OF:

SIGH!

ANOTHER STAFF BULLETIN TO WRITE!

FEW PEOPLE REALIZE HOW DIFFICULT IT IS TO WRITE A STAFF BULLETIN!
2-3

IT TAKES YEARS OF INTENSIVE STUDY!

WHY, I EVEN MINORED IN BULLETIN WRITING WHEN I WAS GETTING MY MASTERS!
BATIUK

I'LL NEVER FORGET HOW PROUD I WAS THE DAY I PASSED MY BULLETIN BOARDS!
© Field Enterprises, Inc., 1974

WHAT WAS ALL THE COMMOTION ABOUT THIS MORNING?
BATIUK

THERE WAS A FREAK ACCIDENT IN THE CHEMISTRY LAB!

WAS IT A FREAK WE KNOW?
© Field Enterprises, Inc., 1974
2-4

I'M BEAT!

MY SEAT IS KILLING ME AND MY LEGS ARE REALLY SORE!
© Field Enterprises, Inc., 1974

I SURE HOPE THAT FAT GIRL WHO SITS HERE SEVENTH PERIOD IS ABSENT TODAY!
BATIUK
2-5

NUTS!

HERE COMES THAT FAT GIRL!

I CAN'T STAND HER!
© Field Enterprises, Inc., 1974
2-6

I THINK I'LL SNAG HER HOSE TODAY!
BATIUK

ONE MORE PERIOD TO GO!

I HOPE I DON'T GET ONE OF THOSE GUM-CHEWERS THIS PERIOD!
BATIUK

I HATE IT WHEN THEY STICK GUM IN MY ARMPITS!
© Field Enterprises, Inc., 1974
2-7

OH, OH!

HERE COMES ONE OF THE FOOTBALL PLAYERS!
BATIUK

I HOPE HE ISN'T PLANNING TO WORK ON MATH PROBLEMS!
© Field Enterprises, Inc., 1974
2-8

IT'S ALWAYS SO OBNOXIOUS WHEN THEY TAKE THEIR SHOES AND SOCKS OFF!

MY FATHER WAS A BIG OVERSTUFFED CHAIR ...

... AND MY MOTHER WAS AN EARLY AMERICAN ROCKER!

MY BROTHERS AND SISTERS ARE ALL PATIO FURNITURE NOW!
© Field Enterprises, Inc., 1974
2-9

ACTUALLY, I'M THE FIRST ONE IN OUR FAMILY TO GO INTO EDUCATION!

FUNKY WINKERBEAN
CHECKPOINT CHARLIE

WELL, HERE I AM AT MY HALL MONITOR'S POST AGAIN!

ANOTHER DAY, ANOTHER HALL PASS!

HALL MONITORING IS A PECULIAR BUSINESS!

SOMETIMES YOU WON'T SEE ANYONE FOR HOURS...
© Field Enterprises, Inc., 1974
2-10
BATIUK

AND THEN YOU'RE REAL BUSY
RUMBLERUMBLERUMBLERUMB

BATIUK

BAM!

I'M NOT SURE, BUT I THINK I BLEW A WOOFER!
2-11

DON'T YOU PLAY FROZEN PIZZAS ON YOUR STEREO ANYMORE, 'CRAZY'?
2-12

NO, I HAD TO QUIT, FUNKY!
BATIUK

I COULDN'T AFFORD THE REPAIR BILLS FOR GETTING MOZZARELLA OUT OF MY WOOFER!

YA KNOW, I THINK I'D LIKE TO BE A FISH!
BATIUK
2-13

ALL THEY DO IS SWIM AROUND ALL DAY WITHOUT A CARE IN THE WORLD!

OF COURSE, IT'S ROUGH IF YOU HAVE SINUS TROUBLE!

YOUR HOROSCOPE
by CLAIR VOYANT

YOUR SHIP CAME IN WHILE YOU WERE ASLEEP!
BATIUK

YOU MISSED THE BOAT AGAIN!
2-14

2-15

BATIUK

IT SURE GETS DIRTY FAST, DOESN'T IT?

THERE'S ONE FINAL IMPORTANT RULE IN CHESS, 'CRAZY'!

IF ONE OF MY PAWNS MAKES IT TO THE LAST ROW ON YOUR SIDE, DO YOU KNOW WHAT HAPPENS THEN?

YEAH, YOU GET TO BUILD A HOTEL, RIGHT?
2-16

FUNKY
WINKERBEAN

NOTHING CAN COMPARE WITH LOOKING UP AT THE SKY AT NIGHT!

THERE'S ALWAYS SOMETHING NEW TO SEE!

© Field Enterprises, Inc., 1974

HEY, FUNKY, I THINK I JUST SAW A UFO!
BATIUK
2-17

OH YEAH? WHAT DID IT LOOK LIKE, 'CRAZY'?

IT WAS KIND OF CIGAR-SHAPED!

FINALLY IN THE NEWS TODAY WE HAVE ...
BATIUK

CRASH!
2-18

WAIT A MINUTE! WE HAVE SOME LATE-BREAKING NEWS HERE!

THIS COMPUTER IS REALLY FOULING THINGS UP! WE OUGHT TO CONSIDER REPLACING IT!

ZZiiP!
WHAT WAS THAT?
© Field Enterprises, Inc., 1974

I THINK IT JUST SHREDDED YOUR PAYCHECK!
BATIUK
2-19

CLACK! CLACK!
CLACK!

oops! i made a mistake and punched too many holes in that card.
2-20

i wonder how you erase a hole?
BATIUK

a computer can solve problems thousands of times faster than a man.

but it is said we lack real intelligence.
BATIUK
2-21

however, no computer ever started a war.

IT'S TWO O'CLOCK IN THE MORNING AND I STILL HAVEN'T FALLEN ASLEEP!

IF I'D KNOWN THIS WAS GOING TO HAPPEN ...
BATIUK
2-22

I'D HAVE STAYED UP AND WATCHED JOHNNY CARSON!

I'VE GOT TO KEEP REPEATING TO MYSELF... I'M NOT GOING TO ORDER ANY MORE PIZZAS!

I'M NOT GOING TO ORDER ANY MORE PIZZAS ... I'M NOT GOING TO ORDER ANY MORE PIZZAS ...

BATIUK
2-23

THAT WAS THE LAST PIZZA I'M GOING TO ORDER ... THAT WAS THE LAST ...

FUNKY
WINKERBEAN

I'M NOT GOING TO ORDER A PIZZA!

I'VE GOT TO LEARN TO EXERCISE MY WILL POWER!

WHEN I START THINKING ABOUT A PIZZA, I HAVE TO REMEMBER THE ANSWER IS, NO!
2-24

NO! NO! NO! NO!
BATIUK

AM I GOING TO SIT HERE AND DEPRIVE MYSELF OF A LARGE JUICY PIZZA, THE FOOD OF THE GODS? ... NO!

THE TRICK IS IN ASKING THE RIGHT QUESTION!
© Field Enterprises, Inc., 1974

TELL YOU WHAT, BULL ···

YOU CAN BE THE SCHOOL PAPER'S ACE REPORTER! JUST GO OUT IN THE HALL ···
2-25
BATIUK

AND AS SOON AS YOU SEE AN ACE ··· REPORT ON IT!

NOW WE'LL HAVE OUR FIRST REPORT FROM THE CURRICULUM STUDY COMMITTEE!

THE GOALS OF OUR COMMITTEE ARE AS FOLLOWS: ITEM 'A'-- IDENTIFICATION OF CRITERIA USED IN EXAMINATION OF THE INTEGRAL OBJECTIVES AND GOALS OF THE CURRENT PROGRAM!
2-26
BATIUK

ITEM 'B'- FIGURING OUT WHAT ITEM 'A' REALLY MEANS!

HERE'S THE FEATHER FOR THE FROG!

KITCHY, KITCHY!
HEE! HEE! HEE!
BATIUK

YUP! THAT'S THE FUNNYBONE ALRIGHT!
2-27

SCHOOL IS A PLACE WHERE THE YOUNG HUMANS GO TO BE EDUCATED BY THE OLDER HUMANS ...

SO THEY CAN BECOME CONTRIBUTING MEMBERS OF SOCIETY AND THUS ENABLE SOCIETY TO CONTINUE JUST THE WAY IT IS!
© Field Enterprises, Inc., 1974
BATIUK

I THINK I'VE FIGURED OUT WHERE THEY'RE GOING WRONG!
2-28

WE HAVE A SPECIAL TREAT PLANNED FOR TONIGHT'S RAP CELLAR MEETING!

WE'RE GOING TO HAVE A JAM SESSION!
© Field Enterprises, Inc., 1974
BATIUK
3-1

HOW MANY WOULD LIKE TO START WITH THE STRAWBERRY?
NO! NO!

SAYINGS FROM THE
I CHONG
ANCIENT BOOK OF CHINESE PHILOSOPHY
BATIUK

THE MASTER IS OFTEN ASKED: HOW DOES ONE BECOME A MASTER ANYHOW?
3-2

FIRST ... YOU HAVE TO GET YOUR MASTER'S DEGREE!
© Field Enterprises, Inc., 1974

FUNKY WINKERBEAN
PERIOD
HOME
VISITOR

JOHN DARLING HERE, TAKING A LOOK AT THE LOCAL SPORTS SCENE ...

... AND ASKING THE QUESTION OF THE DAY!

COACH, DO YOU AGREE WITH THE SAYING THAT A TIE IS LIKE KISSING YOUR SISTER?
COACH
3-3

SMOOCH!
COACH

BATIUK
COACH
© Field Enterprises, Inc., 1974

YEAH, I'D SAY SO!
COACH

THERE WILL BE A PEP RALLY AT THREE O'CLOCK TODAY!
3-4

ALL THOSE WISHING TO PARTICIPATE...
BATIUK

SHOULD GO TO ROOM 121 TO REGISTER THEIR PEPS!

WHEN I STARTED AS A HALL MONITOR, THEY TOLD ME TO KEEP AN EYE ON THE HALL!
3-5

...AND I'VE DONE THAT!

BUT IN ALL THE TIME I'VE BEEN HERE IT HASN'T MOVED ONCE!
BATIUK

DO YOU FIND YOURSELF A LITTLE SHORT OF CASH FOR ALL OF THOSE MONTHLY BILLS?

NEED A LITTLE MONEY FOR THOSE HOUSE REPAIRS YOU'VE BEEN PUTTING OFF?
BATIUK
3-6

WE WANT TO HELP!

ME AND ARNIE AND DA BOYS HAVE A NEAT LITTLE OPERATION HERE THAT COULD REALLY HELP YOU OUT!

HMM ··· THEY'RE BRINGING IN SOME EXTRA CHAIRS FROM THE CAFETERIA!
3-7

SAY!
BATIUK

THAT LITTLE LIGHT BROWN ONE HASN'T GOT A BAD SET OF LEGS!
© Field Enterprises, Inc., 1974

SAYINGS FROM THE
I CHONG
ANCIENT BOOK OF CHINESE PHILOSOPHY
3-8

THE MASTER SAYS: TO THE MAN WHO GALLOPS THROUGH LIFE ···
BATIUK

WHOA UNTO HIM!
© Field Enterprises, Inc., 1974

DR. JOYCE, DO YOU BELIEVE THAT MARRIAGE IS ON THE WAY OUT?

OH, NO! I FEEL THAT MARRIAGE IS MORE POPULAR THAN EVER!
© Field Enterprises, Inc. 1974
BATIUK
3-9

WHY SOME OF MY FRIENDS HAVE BEEN MARRIED THREE OR FOUR TIMES!

FUNKY WINKERBEAN

I WANT TO WORK ON THE SCHOOL PAPER!

WELL GEE, I DON'T KNOW ...

WE'D LIKE TO HAVE YOU HELP ON THE SCHOOL PAPER, BULL ...
© Field Enterprises, Inc., 1974

BUT RIGHT NOW WE'RE LOOKING FOR SOMEONE WHO CAN WRITE BROAD SATIRE!
3-10

I CAN DO THAT!
BATIUK

I KNOW LOTS OF JOKES ABOUT GIRLS!

FUNKY, DO YOU RESPECT ME FOR MY MIND?
BATIUK

I DON'T KNOW!

I HAVEN'T FIGURED OUT WHETHER YOU MIND OR NOT!
3-11

HERE WE ARE IN THE WOODS WITH OUR WORLD FAMOUS EXPERT ON NATURAL FOODS!

HE'S EATING HIS FAVORITE FOOD ... A MONTONI'S PIZZA!

YES, IT REMINDS ME OF THE TASTE OF WILD HICKORY NUTS!

UH ... YOU'RE EATING THE BOX!
BATIUK
3-12

MR. FAIRGOOD, DO YOU VIEW YOUR JOB AS ONE THAT GUIDES STUDENTS INTO CAREERS OR ONE THAT HELPS THEM TO BECOME FULFILLED AND HAPPY HUMAN BEINGS?

3-13

YES!
BATIUK

I'M DOING A PROFILE ON YOU FOR THE SCHOOL PAPER, MR. DINKLE!

WERE YOU A CHILD PRODIGY?

NO! WE WERE PRESBYTERIANS!
BATIUK
3-14

AS WE ANNOUNCED EARLIER IN THE WEEK, THE STATUS OF THE BAND ASSEMBLY WAS TO DEPEND ON STUDENT BEHAVIOR AT OTHER ASSEMBLIES!

UNFORTUNATELY, STUDENT BEHAVIOR WAS EXTREMELY POOR...
BATIUK

SO WE **WILL** BE HAVING THE BAND ASSEMBLY THIS AFTERNOON!
3-15

ON ST. PATRICK'S DAY I ALWAYS FEEL A LITTLE BIT LIKE A...

...UH, LIKE A... OH WHAT DO THEY CALL THOSE LITTLE PEOPLE IN IRELAND?

MIDGETS!
BATIUK
3-16

FUNKY WINKERBEAN
193 9648

what seems to be the problem?

I WAS TOLD TO SEE THE COMPUTER ABOUT MY REPORT CARD!

I GOT AN 'A' IN HOME ECONOMICS AND I DIDN'T EVEN TAKE THE COURSE!
© Field Enterprises, Inc., 1974
3-17
BATIUK

no kidding!

perhaps you should be placed in the advanced group!

THERE ARE MANY INSTANCES IN OUR LANGUAGE WHEN MAN IS REFERRED TO AS IF HE WERE WOOD!

HE'S A CHIP OFF THE OLD BLOCK! HE'S PRESIDENTIAL TIMBER! IT GOES AGAINST MY GRAIN!
BATIUK

ALL OF THIS TENDS TO LEND CREDENCE TO THE OLD THEORY THAT MAN DESCENDED FROM A MAPLE TREE!
3-18

WHEN I WAKE UP IN THE MORNING AFTER MARY SUE HAS TURNED ME DOWN FOR A DATE, I FEEL SO LOW I DON'T EVEN WANT TO GET OUT OF BED!

WELL, THE ONLY THING TO DO IS TAKE THE ONE LOGICAL COURSE OPEN TO ME!
BATIUK
I'M NEVER GETTING OUT OF BED AGAIN!
3-19

SO WHAT IF MARY SUE DOESN'T LOVE ME?

BIG DEAL! LOVE ISN'T EVERYTHING!
BATIUK

OF COURSE, WITHOUT LOVE ... EVERYTHING ISN'T EVERYTHING EITHER!
3-20

YOU'RE MAKING A MISTAKE, LES! YOU CAN'T STAY HERE AND HIDE FROM LIFE!

I GUESS YOU'RE RIGHT, FUNKY!
BATIUK

WHERE DO I GO TO SURRENDER?
3-21

sometimes my programmers really put my circuits on edge.

that's why it was so good to learn about watergate.
BATIUK

it's nice to know humans bug each other too.
3-22

IT SAYS HERE THAT DUE TO THE ENERGY CRISIS, MANY PEOPLE ARE USING NEWSPAPERS AS FUEL IN THEIR FIREPLACES!

COMIC PAGES TOO?
YEAH!

THAT REALLY BURNS ME UP!
BATIUK
3-23

FUNKY WINKERBEAN

DON'T ASK ME HOW TODAY WENT! IT WAS JUST UNREEL ALL DAY!

AHH, GOOD! MY FILM ON THE LIFE CYCLE OF THE MEALWORM CAME IN!

I WAS TOLD THAT ONLY ONE OF THE PROJECTORS RUNS OKAY!
3-24

I WONDER IF I'VE GOT THE GOOD ONE OR THE BAD ONE!

SPROING!

© Field Enterprises, Inc., 1974
BATIUK
I'M IN LUCK! I'VE GOT THE GOOD ONE!

CRAZY! HEY, CRAZY!
KNOCK! KNOCK!

DON'T FORGET YOU HAVE A TEST NEXT PERIOD!

OKAY! THANKS A LOT!

WHY DOES SOMEONE ALWAYS COME TO THE DOOR WHEN YOU'RE IN THE SHOWER?
BATIUK
3-25

OH, OH! THIS IS TUESDAY MORNING!

I ALMOST FORGOT!
BATIUK

3-26

THESE HIBACHIS AREN'T ALL THEY'RE CRACKED UP TO BE!
BATIUK
3-27

I THOUGHT THAT AT TONIGHT'S RAP CELLAR MEETING WE'D TALK ABOUT THE NUCLEAR FAMILY!

WHY DO WE CALL TODAY'S FAMILY THE NUCLEAR FAMILY?
3-28

BECAUSE IT'S BASICALLY UNSTABLE!
BATIUK

I JUST PICKED UP THIS ISSUE OF COSMOPOLITAN YESTERDAY!
3-29

BATIUK

WHEN DID IT CHANGE?

SAYINGS FROM THE
I CHONG
ANCIENT BOOK OF CHINESE PHILOSOPHY

THE MASTER ADVISES: EARLY TO BED AND EARLY TO RISE MAKES A MAN HEALTHY, WEALTHY, AND WISE!
BATIUK
3-30

IF YOU BELIEVE THAT, YOU'LL BELIEVE ANYTHING!

FUNKY WINKERBEAN
MISS WRIGHTON, WOULD YOU COME TO THE OFFICE!

YOU WANTED TO SEE ME, MR. BURCH ?

YES, I DID!

RITA, I'M TAKING AWAY YOUR FREE PERIOD AND GIVING YOU THE CAFETERIA STUDY HALL!

AAAAAA

© Field Enterprises, Inc., 1974
AAAAAAAA
APRIL FOOL! HEH! HEH!
BATIUK
3-31

AAAAAAA
OH, BOY!

WHEN I READ A BOOK I REALLY LIKE TO SAVOR IT!

SOMETIMES IT HELPS MY APPRECIATION TO READ AN ESPECIALLY MOVING PASSAGE ALOUD!
BATIUK

'SEE JIP! SEE JIP RUN! RUN, JIP, RUN!'
4-1

HI!

I'LL BET YOU DON'T REMEMBER ME!

YOU WIN!
BATIUK
4-2

WHEN A FIRE DRILL OCCURS, STUDENTS ARE TO MOVE QUICKLY AND QUIETLY TO THE NEAREST EXIT!

SHOULD A REAL FIRE OCCUR ...
4-3

STUDENTS ARE ASKED NOT TO FAN THE FLAMES AS THEY LEAVE THE BUILDING!
BATIUK

I HATE ALL-NIGHTERS!
BATIUK
4-4
© Field Enterprises, Inc., 1974

I SEE IN THIS ISSUE OF SPITVALUE MAGAZINE THAT YOU CAN BUY ELECTRIC BATONS!

YEAH, ACTUALLY THOSE ARE SURPLUS CATTLE PRODS!
BATIUK
4-5

THEY REALLY KEEP THE CLARINETS ON THEIR TOES!

I'M GOING OUT, DAD!

I'LL BE BACK LATER!

SPOILED A PERFECT EVENING!
BATIUK
4-6

FUNKY WINKERBEAN
WHAT ARE YOU STARING AT? HAVEN'T YOU EVER SEEN A HAMBURGER-STAND BEFORE?

SOMETHING BOTHERING YOU, FUNKY?

YEAH, I NEED SOME ADVICE!

I DON'T KNOW WHAT TO DO, LES! YOU SEE I HAVE THIS GIRLFRIEND I LIKE A LOT, BUT I ALSO WANT TO SEE OTHER GIRLS AND I DON'T KNOW HOW TO TELL HER WITHOUT HURTING HER FEELINGS!

I'VE GOT A **GREAT** IDEA! WHY DON'T YOU FIX HER UP WITH **ME**?
BATIUK

© Field Enterprises, Inc., 1974
4-7

I DON'T KNOW WHAT TO DO! YOU SEE I HAVE THIS FRIEND AND I LIKE HIM A LOT...
76

I TAKE IT MONDAY NIGHT BASEBALL STARTS TONIGHT!

AND NOW WE'LL CLOSE OUR STAFF MEETING WITH A REPORT FROM THE CURRICULUM STUDY COMMITTEE!

AT THREE THIRTY-TWO, A MOTION WAS MADE THAT WE END THE MEETING AND GO HOME, TO WHICH THE CHAIRMAN REPLIED: "OVER MY DEAD BODY!"

AT THREE FORTY-FIVE THE AMBULANCE ARRIVED!

I'M JIM WATSON FROM THE LOCAL PAPER AND I'D LIKE TO DO A PROFILE INTERVIEW ON YOU, MR. BURCH!

WAS YOUR FIRST POSITION AS A PRINCIPAL ON THE SECONDARY LEVEL?

NO, IT WAS ELEMENTARY, MY DEAR WATSON!

SAYINGS FROM THE
I CHONG
ANCIENT BOOK OF CHINESE PHILOSOPHY

THE MASTER REVEALS: LIFE IS A STAGE AND WE ARE THE ACTORS!
© Field Enterprises, Inc., 1974

ALTHOUGH SOME WOMEN PAD THEIR PARTS!
BATIUK
4-11

I HATE INFLATING THESE STUPID VOLLEYBALLS!
© Field Enterprises, Inc., 1974

IT'S A LOT OF WORK, HUH?
YEAH!

THE HARD PART IS TRYING TO PUCKER YOUR LIPS OVER THAT LITTLE HOLE!
BATIUK
4-12

STUDENT PROGRESS REPORT
CHECK ONE:
☐ HAS SATISFACTORY STUDY HABITS.

☐ HAS POOR STUDY HABITS.
BATIUK
4-13

☐ HAS SEVERAL OBNOXIOUS HABITS!

FUNKY WINKERBEAN

SON OF A GUN!

I'M CURED!

LOOK AT THIS, DEREK! I HAD A WART ON MY HAND, SO I SAID, 'WART, WART GO AWAY, COME AGAIN ANOTHER DAY!'

AND A WEEK LATER, IT'S GONE!
BATIUK

YEAH, WARTS OFTEN COME AND GO THAT WAY NORMALLY!

WELL, THAT BLOWS MY SHOT AT THE NOBEL PRIZE IN MEDICINE!
4-14
© Field Enterprises, Inc., 1974

SPRING, AND THE TIME OF THE BACCHANALIA ...

... WHEN THE ANCIENT ROMANS USED TO CELEBRATE WITH A WEEK-LONG DRUNKEN ORGY!
BATIUK

A CUSTOM CARRIED ON TO THIS DAY, EACH SPRING IN FT. LAUDERDALE, FLORIDA!
4-15

OKAY, READY FOR A GREAT GAME OF PING PONG, LES?

YEAH, JUST A SEC!

BATIUK
4-16

I HATE IT WHEN HE HAS TO PLAY THE NATIONAL ANTHEM!

YOUR HOROSCOPE
BY CLAIR VOYANT

TODAY IS A RED LETTER DAY FOR YOU!
BATIUK

YOU GOT AN 'F' ON YOUR TERM PAPER!
4-17

FUNKY, YOU SCORED VERY WELL ON THIS STANDARDIZED APTITUDE TEST!

SO WHAT DOES THAT MEAN, MR. FAIRGOOD?
4-18
BATIUK

IT MEANS YOU'RE VERY GOOD AT TAKING STANDARDIZED TESTS!

NEITHER BIG BUSINESS NOR THE GOVERNMENT SEEMS TO HAVE ANY KIND OF MORAL RESPONSIBILITY!

THERE MUST BE SOMETHING WE CAN DO IN THE SCHOOLS TO HELP CHANGE THIS!
BATIUK
4-19

WE CAN'T! THEY'VE OUTLAWED PRAYING IN SCHOOL!

IS IT DIFFICULT TO BECOME A COUNSELOR, FRED?

OH YES, RITA, YOU HAVE TO MEET RIGID REQUIREMENTS! I HAD FOUR YEARS OF COLLEGE AND TWO YEARS OF POST-GRADUATE WORK ...
BATIUK
4-20

...AND TWO LOSING SEASONS AS A BASKETBALL COACH!

FUNKY WINKERBEAN
SPRINGS FOR SPRING CONCERT

I'VE GOT TO COME UP WITH SOMETHING ...

THE SPRING CONCERT IS ONLY TWO WEEKS AWAY!

WHAT I NEED FOR OUR SPRING CONCERT IS A COMPLETELY UNIQUE OPENING NUMBER!
4-21

I'VE GOT IT!

BATIUK
WE'LL PLAY THE THEME FROM 2001 ...

© Field Enterprises, Inc., 1974
BACKWARDS!

OVER THE SPRING BREAKS I USUALLY HAVE A LOT OF TIME ON MY LEGS!

I SOMETIMES START TO PONDER SOME OF THE GREAT PHILOSOPHICAL QUESTIONS!
BATIUK
4-22

LIKE, IS THERE LIFE AFTER RECYCLING?

I'VE NOTICED LATELY THAT A LOT OF PEOPLE ARE REALLY PREOCCUPIED WITH NOSTALGIA FOR THE FIFTIES!

HEY, FUNKY BABY! YOU'VE GOT IT MADE IN THE SHADE!
BIG

INCLUDING SOME PRETTY EXTREME CASES!
4-23

CRAZY, WHAT HAPPENED TO YOUR DUCK-TAIL?

I HAD TO GET RID OF IT BECAUSE I COULDN'T GET ANY SLEEP!

MY HEAD KEPT SLIDING OFF MY PILLOW!
BATIUK
4-24

SIGH!

NOTHING IS MORE SOOTHING THAN LISTENING TO SAP RUN!
BATIUK
4-25
© Field Enterprises, Inc. 1974

WELL, DEREK, I'M AFRAID THAT THE HALCYON DAYS OF THE UNDERGROUND PAPER ARE GONE FOREVER!

IN FACT I HAD TO FOLD MINE THIS MORNING!

SEE, WHEN I FOLD IT LIKE THIS I ONLY HAVE TO USE ONE SHEET!
BATIUK
4-26
© Field Enterprises, Inc. 1974

IF YOU'VE BEEN RELUCTANT TO ABANDON ELEGANCE AND LUXURY TO SAVE ON GAS, YOU'LL BE HAPPY TO HEAR THIS!

I JUST DROVE THIS BEAUTIFUL PANTHER X-R SEDAN ACROSS THE COUNTRY, AND I ENDED UP WITH MORE GAS IN MY TANK THAN WHEN I LEFT!
© Field Enterprises, Inc. 1974
4-27

NOW, OF COURSE, NO TWO DRIVERS ARE EXACTLY ALIKE AND YOU MAY NOT GET THE SAME RESULTS IN YOUR CAR BUT---
BATIUK

FUNKY WINKERBEAN

RRRING!

HAROLD!

I WANT TO SPEAK WITH YOU FOR A MINUTE!

HAROLD, I'M GETTING FED UP WITH YOUR ATTITUDE!
© Field Enterprises, Inc., 1974

FROM NOW ON I WANT YOU TO SHOW ME MORE RESPECT!

PRINCIPAL
APPARENTLY SHOUTING SIEG HEIL AND CLICKING MY SNEAKERS TOGETHER WASN'T WHAT SHE HAD IN MIND!
BATIUK
4-28

what seems to be the problem?

WELL, MY NAME'S FUNKY WINKERBEAN AND...
BATIUK

hmm. that is a problem!
4-29

I THINK WE'LL CALL OUR ENGLISH LITERATURE PROGRAM FOR THE AVERAGE STUDENT, THE BASIC CORE!

AND THEN WE'LL CALL OUR ADVANCED PROGRAM, THE HARD CORE!

THAT SHOULD BLOW A FEW PARENTS' MINDS!
BATIUK
4-30

HI-HO SILVER!

5-1

WHO WAS THAT MASKED MAN?
BATIUK

WHAT'S THIS NOTICE ABOUT, FRED?

IT SAYS THEY'RE PLANNING TO HAVE A CARPOOL HERE AT SCHOOL!
BATIUK

OH, THAT'S GOOD! MINE COULD REALLY STAND A GOOD WASHING!
5-2

STUDENT PROGRESS REPORT. CHECK ONE:
☐ OUTSTANDING PROGRESS

☐ ADEQUATE PROGRESS

☐ NEEDS TO IMPROVE
BATIUK

☐ LEARNING TO RECOGNIZE THE BUILDING!
5-3

DURING THIS ENERGY CRISIS, WE IN THE OIL INDUSTRY URGE AMERICANS TO WORK TOGETHER!

A GREAT DEAL CAN BE ACCOMPLISHED AND WE CAN ALL PROFIT IF WE JUST UNITE TOWARDS A COMMON GOAL!

AFTER ALL, WE IN THE OIL INDUSTRY HAVE BEEN DOING THIS FOR YEARS!
BATIUK
5-4

FUNKY WINKERBEAN
C. HARRY

'CRAZY', I'M SURE YOU'LL BE GLAD TO HEAR THAT I'VE GOT THE SCORES FROM YOUR BASIC SKILLS TEST!
YIPPEEE ...

'CRAZY', ACCORDING TO THIS BASIC SKILLS TEST, YOU SCORED IN THE NINETY-FIFTH PERCENTILE IN READING ...

... BUT ZERO IN VOCABULARY!
BATIUK

HOW CAN YOU READ SO WELL IF YOU DON'T KNOW ANY WORDS ?
5-5

I READ BETWEEN THE LINES!

TODAY WAS REALLY A GOOD DAY!

GUIDANCE COUNSELING HAS BEEN A LOT LESS HECTIC SINCE I INSTITUTED THE OREGON PLAN!
BATIUK

I ONLY SEE THE ODD KIDS EVERY OTHER DAY!

MISS WRIGHTON, THE COMPUTER MADE A MISTAKE AND GAVE ME YOUR PAYCHECK INSTEAD OF MY REPORT CARD!

THAT WAS VERY HONEST OF YOU TO RETURN IT, FUNKY!

HONEST NOTHING, I MAKE MORE THAN THAT IF I GET STRAIGHT A'S!
BATIUK

HOMEROOM ATTENDANCE!

THIRTY-SIX ··· GIVE OR TAKE A COUPLE!
BATIUK

I'M GOING TO HAVE TO HAVE A LITTLE CHAT WITH MS. WRIGHTON!

WE AT THE SLICKO OIL COMPANY ARE DOING EVERYTHING IN OUR POWER TO BRING THE PRESENT ENERGY CRISES TO AN END!

OF COURSE, THIS WILL COST MONEY AND IT MAY NECESSITATE HIGHER PRICES AT YOUR LOCAL GAS STATION!
BATIUK

BUT OUR GOAL IS TO PROVIDE BETTER SERVICE FOR YOU, AND AT SLICKO WE'VE ALWAYS BELIEVED IN GIVING YOU THE GAS!

AND NOW, LIVINIA WILL READ THE MINUTES FROM THE LAST STUDENT COUNCIL MEETING!

THANK YOU!
BATIUK
5-10

THREE: TWENTY-ONE, THREE: TWENTY-TWO, THREE: TWENTY THREE...

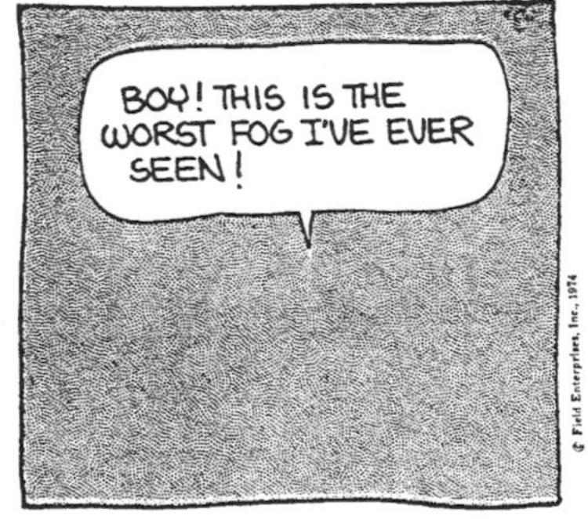
BOY! THIS IS THE WORST FOG I'VE EVER SEEN!

YOU CAN'T EVEN SEE YOUR HAND IN FRONT OF YOUR FACE!
BATIUK

I WONDER WHAT IT'S LIKE OUTSIDE?

FUNKY WINKERBEAN

OKAY, MEN! IT'S TIME FOR A LITTLE JUMP-ROPE!

YOU'RE FIRST, LES! LET'S SEE HOW YOU DO JUMPING ROPE!
BATIUK

WHAT?!
© Field Enterprises, Inc., 1974

YOU WANT ME TO JUMP IT RIGHT HERE?! LIKE THIS?!

WITHOUT A SAFETY-NET?!

THE ANGLE IN PROBLEM TWELVE IS:

(A.) OBTUSE
(B.) RIGHT
(C.) ACUTE
© Field Enterprises, Inc., 1974
5-13

(C.) acute
SCRITCH SCRITCH

I THINK IT'S A CUTE ONE!
BATIUK

I'M DOING A SURVEY OF THE STUDENTS FOR THE SCHOOL PAPER, BULL!

ARE YOU A LIBERAL?
© Field Enterprises, Inc., 1974
BATIUK

NO, LIVINIA! I'M A TAURUS!
5-14

BOY, THE WFL REALLY SEEMS TO BE COMING ON STRONG!

I'M REALLY GLAD TO SEE THAT, FUNKY!
BATIUK

IT'S ABOUT TIME WE HAD A WOMEN'S FOOTBALL LEAGUE!
© Field Enterprises, Inc., 1974
5-15

BEFORE WE WORK OUT NEXT YEAR'S SCHEDULE, CRAZY, LET'S REVIEW YOUR CREDITS!

SO FAR YOU'VE TAKEN ENGLISH, HISTORY, AND FORTY-TWO MINI-COURSES

FOR A TOTAL OF TWO AND SEVEN-SIXTEENTHS CREDITS!

HAVE YOU CONSIDERED TAKING GENERAL MATH, CRAZY?

WHY SHOULD I, MR. FAIRGOOD?

I DON'T EVEN PLAN TO GO INTO THE ARMY!

I REALLY ENJOY LISTENING TO SOUSA MARCHES ON MY STEREO!

ESPECIALLY WHEN I PLAY THEM AT SEVENTY-EIGHT!

FUNKY WINKERBEAN

ONE THOUSAND, THREE HUNDRED AND THIRTY-SEVEN ...

ONE THOUSAND, THREE HUNDRED AND THIRTY-EIGHT ...

ONE THOUSAND, THREE HUNDRED AND THIRTY-NINE! THERE!
© Field Enterprises, Inc., 1974
5-19

I FINALLY MANAGED TO GET EVERY PIN OUT OF MY NEW FLANNEL SHIRT!

BATIUK

AHHHGG!

AS EDUCATORS WE HAVE TO BREAK DOWN THE BARRIERS OF TRADITIONAL AND CONDITIONED THINKING...

...AND REPLACE THEM WITH NEW CONCEPTS BASED ON FLEXIBILITY AND IMAGINATION!
BATIUK

DOES THIS MEAN WE CAN PARK ALONG THE SIDE OF THE BUILDING INSTEAD OF IN THE REGULAR LOTS?

I'M STUCK!

I'M LOOKING FOR AN OPENING FOR THE SPRING CONCERT THAT WILL BE TOTALLY DIFFERENT THAN ANYTHING WE'VE EVER DONE BEFORE!
BATIUK
5-21

WHY NOT HAVE EVERYONE START IN THE SAME KEY?

many people are afraid that computers are going to take over the world and dominate man.

let me assure you that you have nothing to fear...
BATIUK

...as long as you cooperate!
5-22

I WAS JUST TALKING WITH THE PRINCIPAL ABOUT THE PROBLEM OF RAISING STUDENT CONSCIOUSNESS!

I COULD USE SOME HELP THERE!
5-23

I'VE GOT TWO STUDENTS WHO'VE BEEN UNCONSCIOUS SINCE CHRISTMAS VACATION!
BATIUK

HOW ABOUT A LITTLE TENNIS AFTER SCHOOL, COACH?

WHAT!? YOU MEAN TAKE OUT MY CAT-GUT, HAND-STRUNG, LACQUER-FINISHED RACKET ON A CLOUDY DAY?
BATIUK

ARE YOU NUTS?
5-24

WOW! ISN'T THAT EXCITING? OUR BASEBALL TEAM FINALLY DID IT!

ALL OF THE PLAYERS JUMPING UP AND DOWN AND CARRYING THE COACH AROUND THE FIELD ON THEIR SHOULDERS!
BATIUK

DO THEY DO THIS EVERY INNING?
5-25

FUNKY WINKERBEAN

WHY CAN'T I MAKE IT WITH GIRLS, FUNKY?

SIMPLE! YOU LACK CONFIDENCE!
.99¢

CONFIDENCE IS REALLY IMPORTANT IN DEALING WITH GIRLS, LES!

IT'S A LOT LIKE MEETING A STRANGE DOG! IF HE SENSES THAT YOU'RE AFRAID, HE'S MORE LIKELY TO BITE YOU!
BATIUK
5-26

© Field Enterprises, Inc., 1974
THAT HAPPENED TO ME ONCE!

I ASKED A GIRL OUT AND SHE BIT ME!

AND NOW WE'LL HAVE OUR FINAL REPORT OF THE YEAR FROM THE CURRICULUM STUDY COMMITTEE!
BATIUK
5-27

AT OUR LAST MEETING THE COMMITTEE DIVIDED INTO TWO GROUPS ··· GROUP A AND GROUP B!

GROUP B WON ON A DISPUTED CALL AT HOME PLATE!
© Field Enterprises, Inc., 1974

AND REMEMBER, WHILE YOU'RE TAKING THIS TEST KEEP YOUR EYES ON YOUR OWN PAPER ···

···AND DON'T LOOK AT YOUR NEIGHBOR'S PAPER!
© Field Enterprises, Inc., 1974
BATIUK
5-28

LUCKILY MY NEIGHBOR IS A LITTLE OLD LADY AND SHE DOESN'T EVEN GO TO SCHOOL!

Fill in the following:

George Washington was ___ _____ of our country.
BATIUK
5-29

George Washington was very fond of our country.
© Field Enterprises, Inc., 1974

WELCOME TO THE AWARDS ASSEMBLY!

AS YOU KNOW, THIS ASSEMBLY MARKS THE APPROACHING END OF ANOTHER SCHOOL YEAR!
© Field Enterprises, Inc., 1974
BATIUK

PRAISE THE LORD!
5-30

SAYINGS FROM THE
I CHONG
ANCIENT BOOK OF CHINESE PHILOSOPHY
© Field Enterprises, Inc., 1974
BATIUK

THE MASTER SAYS: WHEN YOU SERVE BOTH BALLS INTO THE NET ...

IT'S NOBODY'S FAULT BUT YOUR OWN!
5-31

ISN'T IT FUNNY, LES, HOW LOVE MEANS ONE THING IN LIFE AND SOMETHING ELSE ENTIRELY IN TENNIS?

NOT FOR ME IT DOESN'T!
BATIUK
6-1

EITHER WAY IT MEANS 'NO SCORE'!

FUNKY WINKERBEAN
ZZZZZ

PRINCIPAL
SEND IN THE NEXT ONE!

'CRAZY' HARRY, LAST WEEK YOU WERE RESPONSIBLE FOR A FAKE FIRE ALARM! THIS WEEK YOU'RE RESPONSIBLE FOR THE BROKEN WINDOW IN THE BOYS' LOCKER-ROOM!

IN FACT YOU'RE ALWAYS IN MY OFFICE BECAUSE YOU'RE RESPONSIBLE FOR MOST OF THE TROUBLE AROUND HERE!
© Field Enterprises, Inc., 1974
BATIUK

HAVE YOU LEARNED ANYTHING FROM ALL OF THIS?
6-2

YEAH, RESPONSIBILITY!

I WANT TO REMIND THE STAFF THAT THIS FRIDAY IS RECORDS DAY!

I HAVE A QUESTION ABOUT THAT!

IS ANYONE ELSE GOING TO BE BRINGING IN CAROLE KING RECORDS?
BATIUK

OUR EXAM IS GOING TO BE OPEN BOOK, SO I COULD WRITE SOME OF THE ANSWERS IN THE MARGIN!

BUT THAT WOULD BE CHEATING, AND BY CHEATING I'D ONLY BE HURTING MYSELF!

OH WELL, I'VE GOT TO LEARN TO LIVE WITH PAIN SOONER OR LATER!
BATIUK

I CAN'T TAKE ANYMORE OF THIS ALL-NIGHTER, FUNKY!

I'VE GOT TO QUIT! I JUST HAVEN'T GOT THE WILL POWER TO GO ON ANY LONGER!
BATIUK

HANG IN THERE, LES, THE FIRST FIVE MINUTES ARE ALWAYS THE ROUGHEST!

A GOOD MANY OF THE TERMS WE USE IN LIFE ARE MISNOMERS!

LIKE THE TERM, 'FINAL EXAM'! IT REALLY ISN'T FINAL, BUT MERELY ONE OF AN ENDLESS STREAM OF EXAMS THAT WE MUST FACE IN LIFE!
BATIUK

HOWEVER, WHEN YOU HAVEN'T CRACKED A BOOK IN THREE MONTHS, THE TERM 'FINAL EXAM' TAKES ON NEW MEANING!
6-6

SIGH!
CLICK!

I'VE NEVER KNOWN IT TO FAIL!

JUST WHEN I GET MY LOCKER COMBINATION MEMORIZED ... SCHOOL ENDS!
BATIUK
6-7

'CRAZY', WE CAN'T ALLOW YOU TO STAY IN YOUR LOCKER OVER THE SUMMER!

BUT WE WILL ALLOW YOU TO LEAVE YOUR THINGS THERE!
BATIUK

WILL YOU WATER MY FERN?
6-8

FUNKY WINKERBEAN

BEFORE I HAND OUT YOUR DIPLOMAS AND YOU PEEL OUT OF THE SCHOOL FOR THE LAST TIME, I HAVE A FEW BRIEF WORDS!

THE CLASS OF '74 FACES MANY DIFFICULT CHALLENGES!
BATIUK

AS YOU VENTURE FORTH INTO THE REAL WORLD...

YOU'RE GOING TO FIND THAT THINGS ARE QUITE DIFFERENT FROM WHAT YOU'VE KNOWN IN SCHOOL!
© Field Enterprises, Inc., 1974

FOR ONE THING, YOU CAN SMOKE IN THE RESTROOMS!

AS I LOOK UPON THIS GRADUATING CLASS ...
6-10

... ONE THOUGHT COMES TO MY MIND!
BATIUK

BUT I'LL IGNORE IT AND LET BYGONES BE BYGONES!

THE SCHOOL IS VERY GRATEFUL FOR THIS YEAR'S SENIOR CLASS GIFT!

I MUST ADMIT THAT I'M DEEPLY TOUCHED!
BATIUK

FRANKLY, I NEVER EXPECTED THE DOORS TO THE RESTROOMS TO BE RETURNED!
6-11

IT'S SAID THE CONSTELLATIONS WERE PROBABLY GIVEN THEIR NAMES BY EARLY SHEPHERDS!
BATIUK
© Field Enterprises, Inc., 1974

THEY MUST HAVE BEEN VERY COORDINATED TO LOOK AT THE SKY AND WATCH WHERE THEY STEPPED AT THE SAME TIME!
6-12

HI! I'M YOUR PLAYGROUND SUPERVISOR!

SOME OF YOU MAY REMEMBER ME FROM LAST YEAR! MY NAME'S FUNKY WINKERBEAN!
6-13
BATIUK

EVERY YEAR THE SAME OLD JOKES!

SO YOUR NAME IS FUNKY WINKERBEAN, HUH?
THAT'S RIGHT!
BATIUK
6-14

LET'S BOOGIE

ALL KIDDING ASIDE, WHAT IS IT REALLY?

I'M TAKING A POLL FOR MY UNDER-GROUND PAPER, DEREK!

HAS WATERGATE CHANGED YOUR POLITICAL VIEWS?
BATIUK
6-15

YEAH! NOW I FAVOR THE LEFT!
THE FAR LEFT?

NO! WHATEVER'S LEFT!

FUNKY WINKERBEAN

MR. WINKERBEAN! MR. WINKERBEAN!

WHAT SEEMS TO BE THE PROBLEM?

RICHARD IS WINNING ALL OF OUR MARBLES BECAUSE HE'S PLAYING WITH HIS DAD'S LUCKY MARBLE!

WELL, HE MAY THINK IT'S A LUCKY MARBLE, BUT THERE'S NO SUCH THING!
6-16

HE'S JUST WINNING BECAUSE HE'S GOOD!
BATIUK
© Field Enterprises, Inc., 1974

MR. WINKERBEAN SAYS HE CAN USE IT!

I'LL HAVE TO ADMIT, MARY ELLEN ...
BATIUK

FOR THE FIRST GAME OF THE YEAR, THE KIDS FROM YOUR PLAYGROUND LOOK PRETTY SHARP!
6-17

YEAH! WE PLAYED WINTER BALL IN VENEZUELA!

ZOOP!
6-18

QUITE A CURVE BALL YOUR PITCHER'S GOT THERE!
BATIUK

IN THE STOCK NEWS ...

THE MARKET WAS DOWN TODAY!
BATIUK
6-19

EXPERTS FEEL THIS WAS DUE TO THE FACT THAT STOCKS WERE SELLING FOR LOW PRICES!

I JUST DON'T KNOW!
© Field Enterprises, Inc., 1974

ANOTHER FORMER GOVERNMENT OFFICIAL RECEIVED A REDUCED SENTENCE THROUGH PLEA-BARGAINING!
BATIUK

WELL, IT'S NICE TO SEE THERE ARE STILL SOME BARGAINS LEFT IN THIS WORLD!
6-20

Yiiii!
BATIUK
6-21
© Field Enterprises, Inc., 1974

BOY! THE UNDERTOW IN THIS THING IS TERRIFIC!

SAYINGS FROM THE
I CHONG
ANCIENT BOOK OF CHINESE PHILOSOPHY
6-22

THE MASTER SAYS: WHEN YOU LOSE YOUR DOG...
BATIUK

IT'S A DOGGONE SITUATION!
© Field Enterprises, Inc., 1974

FUNKY WINKERBEAN

I CAN'T WAIT TO SEE HOW THIS NEW ALBUM SOUNDS AT FULL VOLUME!

FAR IN!

MANY PEOPLE THINK THAT LISTENING TO ROCK MUSIC AT FULL VOLUME THROUGH A SET OF STEREO EARPHONES CAN BE HARMFUL!

ON THE CONTRARY!

IT CAN BE VERY HEALTHY AND GOOD FOR YOU!
© Field Enterprises, Inc., 1974

FOR ONE THING, IT DISINTEGRATES EARWAX!

ARE YOU MR. WINKERBEAN, OUR PLAYGROUND COUNSELOR?

YES I AM!
BATIUK
6-24

WELL, IT ALL STARTED WHEN I WAS IN KINDERGARTEN!

MY DAD'S UPTOWN GETTING SOME SHOCKS, FUNKY!

WAS YOUR CAR RIDING ROUGH, ROLAND?
BATIUK
6-25

OH NO, I MEANT HE WAS AT THE SUPERMARKET WITH MY MOM!

I THOUGHT I WAS IN LOVE WITH THAT CUTE BLOND LIFEGUARD LAST SUMMER!

BUT NOW I'M TOTALLY IN LOVE WITH THAT BEAUTIFUL BRUNETTE LIFEGUARD!
BATIUK
6-26

I GUESS I'M JUST A SUCKER FOR A GIRL IN A UNIFORM!

BOY! THAT BEAUTIFUL BRUNETTE LIFEGUARD IS REALLY SOMETHING ELSE, ISN'T SHE, LES?

AND LOOK AT THAT POLKA-DOT BIKINI OF HERS! I WONDER HOW MANY DOTS THERE ARE ON IT?
6-27

BATIUK
THIRTY-TWO

I HAVE TO DO WHAT FUNKY SAID ...

AND REMEMBER TO KEEP MY BODY RIGID WHEN I'M DIVING!
BATIUK
6-28

HARD TO DO WHEN YOU'RE PARALYZED WITH FEAR!

SAYINGS FROM THE
ANCIENT BOOK OF CHINESE PHILOSOPHY

THERE ARE MANY DOORS WHICH OPEN UNTO THE UNIVERSE!
6-29
BATIUK

THAT'S WHY IT'S SO DRAFTY OUT THERE IN SPACE!

FUNKY WINKERBEAN

SORRY, I DON'T FEEL LIKE BETTING!

WHAT'S THE MATTER? ARE YOU CHICKEN?

OKAY, ROGER, IF YOU INSIST, THE LOSER OF THIS CHESS GAME WILL TREAT THE WINNER TO AN ICE CREAM CONE!

DON'T YOU KNOW HOW TO START?
BATIUK

NO!

I DON'T KNOW WHETHER TO USE THE SICILIAN DEFENSE VARIATION EMPLOYED BY CAPABLANCA IN BUENOS AIRES IN 1939 OR THE OPENING USED BY FISCHER IN THE SECOND GAME AT REYKJAVIK IN 1972!
6-30

I'M GOING TO START EXERCISING MY WILL POWER...NO MORE PIZZAS!

© Field Enterprises, Inc., 1976

THERE, THAT WAS PRETTY GOOD! I THINK I'LL GET A PIZZA NOW!
BATIUK

WELL, YOU KNOW HOW THEY WARN YOU NOT TO OVER-EXERCISE ON THE FIRST DAY!
7-1

YES, THIS IS MONTONI'S PIZZA!
BATIUK

YEAH, WE DELIVER!
7-2

OKAY, LET'S SEE ---THAT'S ONE SLICE TO 201 FIFTH ST.! TWO SLICES TO 506 MIDDLE AVENUE ...
© Field Enterprises, Inc., 1976

MONTONI'S PIZZA!

NO, THIS ISN'T THE FIRE DEPARTMENT!
BATIUK
7-3

BUT HOW ABOUT A NICE PIZZA FOR AFTER THE FIRE?
© Field Enterprises, Inc., 1976

KA-BLAM!
KA-POW!
7-4
© Field Enterprises, Inc., 1974

IT'S TOO BAD THE CITY HAD TO CUT BACK ON ITS FIREWORKS DISPLAY THIS YEAR, FUNKY!
BATIUK

YEAH, BUT THAT GUY CAN REALLY YELL, CAN'T HE ?

ARE YOU SURE YOU STILL REMEMBER HOW TO PLAY CHESS ?

ARE YOU KIDDING? ONCE I PICK UP A GAME, IT STAYS IN THE OLD MEMORY BANK!
BATIUK
7-5

LET'S SEE NOW, PAWNS ARE TRUMP, RIGHT ?
© Field Enterprises, Inc., 1974

SAYINGS FROM THE
I CHONG
ANCIENT BOOK OF CHINESE PHILOSOPHY
7-6

THE MASTER LAYS ONE ON YOU : HE WHO LAUGHS LAST ...
BATIUK

... USUALLY DOES SO BECAUSE HE DIDN'T GET THE JOKE THE FIRST TIME !
© Field Enterprises, Inc., 1974

FUNKY WINKERBEAN

WELL, THERE'S ONLY ONE WAY TO FIND OUT!

WHERE SHALL I START?

LET'S SEE, I CAN SEE MY FEET... MY LEGS...
AND MY STOMACH...

...AND I CAN SEE MY HANDS AND ARMS!
7-7

WHAT ARE YOU DOING, 'CRAZY'?
© Field Enterprises, Inc., 1974
BATIUK

I'M TRYING TO FIND OUT WHERE MY HEAD'S AT!

HERE I AM ON THE HIGH DIVE, FACING THE MOMENT OF TRUTH!

BATIUK

YA KNOW, I NEVER REALIZED WHAT A PRETTY VIEW IT IS FROM UP HERE!
© Field Enterprises, Inc., 1974
7-8

AS I STAND HERE POISED ON THE HIGH DIVE, I FEEL MY ENTIRE LIFE FLASH BEFORE ME!

BATIUK

THAT'S IT?
© Field Enterprises, Inc., 1974
7-9

WELL, HERE GOES NOTHING!

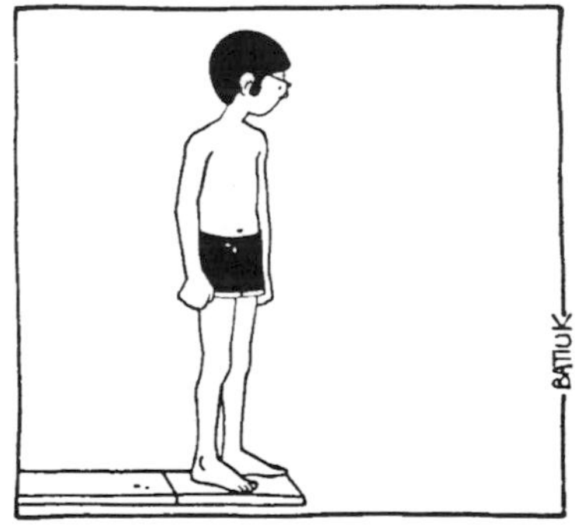
BATIUK

I MEANT EXACTLY WHAT I SAID!
© Field Enterprises, Inc., 1974
7-10

I HATE IT WHEN THAT BEAUTIFUL BRUNETTE LIFEGUARD WEARS SUNGLASSES!

WHEN SHE WEARS THEM I CAN'T TELL IF SHE'S LOOKING AT ME OR NOT ··· AND I NEED TO KNOW THAT
BATIUK
7-11

BECAUSE I CAN'T HOLD MY STOMACH IN MUCH LONGER!
© Field Enterprises, Inc. 1974

I WONDER IF THERE'S INTELLIGENT LIFE OUT THERE IN THE UNIVERSE

YEAH, JUST THINK, HUMAN BEINGS ON SOME OTHER PLANET!
BATIUK
© Field Enterprises, Inc. 1974
7-12

THAT'S NOT WHAT I SAID!

SAYINGS FROM THE
I CHONG
ANCIENT BOOK OF CHINESE PHILOSOPHY
7-13

THE MASTER SAYS: THE SOUNDS OF NATURE ARE THE MUSIC OF THE UNIVERSE!
BATIUK
© Field Enterprises, Inc. 1974

FOR A COMPLETE COLLECTION OF MOTHER NATURE'S GREATEST HITS, RUSH $5.95 TO GREATEST HITS, HOLLYWOOD, CALIFORNIA!

FUNKY WINKERBEAN
SIGH!

BOY! IS THIS BABYSITTING EVER A DRAG!

I WONDER IF THERE'S ANYTHING GOOD ON THE OLD TUBE?

HEY, THESE PEOPLE I'M BABYSITTING FOR HAVE ONE OF THOSE AUTOMATIC TV SELECTORS!

I THINK I'LL TRY IT OUT!
CLICK!
ZIIIP!
7-14

CLICK!
ZIIIP!
© Field Enterprises, Inc., 1974
BATIUK

MY LUCK! IT'S BUSTED!

WITH HIS OWN ORGANIC GARDEN A PERSON CAN GROW ALL HE NEEDS TO SUSTAIN LIFE, FUNKY!

HOW'S IT GOING?
BATIUK

NOT TOO BAD! EVERYTHING IS UP EXCEPT THE PEPPERONIES!
7-15

I WANT YOU TO DO AS I SAY AND NOT AS I DO!

WHAT ARE YOU WORRIED ABOUT?
BATIUK

YOU NEVER DO ANYTHING!
7-16

AND NOW WILD WORLD OF SPORTS TAKES YOU TO THE WORLD RODEO CHAMPIONSHIP!

THE WINNER OF THIS RODEO WILL GET TO CLAIM A ONE THOUSAND DOLLAR PURSE!
BATIUK

DISGUSTING! YOU'D NEVER SEE THE DUKE WITH A PURSE!
7-17

WHAT ARE WE DOING TODAY, MR. WINKERBEAN?

TODAY IS 'CRAFTS DAY', MIKE! WE'RE GOING TO TAKE THESE STRIPS OF PLASTIC AND BRAID THEM INTO ZIPPER-PULLS!
BATIUK

LUCKILY I DON'T HAVE A WEAK HEART OR THE EXCITEMENT MIGHT HAVE FINISHED ME!
7-18

YOU KNOW THOSE ZIPPER-PULLS WE BRAIDED, FUNKY?
YEAH...
BATIUK
7-19

WELL... I THINK I MADE MINE TOO LONG!

SAYINGS FROM THE
I CHONG
ANCIENT BOOK OF CHINESE PHILOSOPHY

THE MASTER SAYS: TIME HEALS ALL WOUNDS!
BATIUK

AND THE **AMA** IS JUST FURIOUS ABOUT IT!
7-20

FUNKY WINKERBEAN

THERE'S JUPITER!

AND THAT MUST BE THE BIG DIPPER!

BOY! THE STARS ARE REALLY CLEAR TONIGHT!
BATIUK

ON A NIGHT LIKE THIS, IT'S POSSIBLE TO FAINTLY SEE THE HAZE OF OUR MILKY WAY GALAXY!

I'VE OFTEN WONDERED ABOUT THAT!
7-21
© Field Enterprises, Inc., 1974

HOW DID A GALAXY EVER GET NAMED AFTER A CANDY BAR?

The rain was falling on the roof ...

My eyes are drawn to gaze upon the lonely railroad track,

I see the wave approach the beach,

I see the shore it wants to reach,

I see the rock on which it slams,

Smashing all the little clams!
7-25

LET'S MOVE TO THE ACTION ON SEVENTEEN WITH BYRON!

THANKS, CHRIS! ARNIE HAD A BEAUTIFUL DRIVE HERE AND HE PLACED HIS IRON SHOT THREE FEET FROM THE PIN! AND NOW HE JUST SANK HIS PUTT!
BATIUK

BIG DEAL! BACK TO YOU, CHRIS!
7-26

SAYINGS FROM THE
I CHONG
ANCIENT BOOK OF CHINESE PHILOSOPHY

THE MASTER ANSWERS THE ETERNAL QUESTION ...
WHY?
7-27

BATIUK
... BECAUSE!

FUNKY WINKERBEAN
HAVEN'T YOU EVER SEEN A GREASEBALL BEFORE?

IT LOOKS LIKE OUR PITCHER IS GETTING TIRED! I'M GOING TO PUT YOU IN, ACE!

REMEMBER, KEEP THE BALL LOW AND OVER THE PLATE!

ARE YOU SURE YOU CAN SEE OKAY WITH THOSE GLASSES, ACE?

YEAH, NO SWEAT!
BATIUK
7-28

GREAT!

THEN HOME PLATE IS BACK HERE!

BATIUK

7-29

SO YOU TWO HAVE BEEN FIGHTING AGAIN, HUH ?
7-30

OKAY, WHO STARTED IT THIS TIME ?

BATIUK
ACTUALLY, MR. WINKERBEAN, I'M NOT YOUR BEST WITNESS ON THAT !

WOW!

BATIUK
I'M REALLY DOING GOOD ON THE SLIDE TODAY !
7-31

IT MUST BE THOSE WAX BEANS I HAD LAST NIGHT!

OH, OH, BULL BUSHKA, PROFESSIONAL BULLY, IS HERE AT THE POOL LOOKING FOR ME!
BATIUK

I'LL HIDE FROM HIM BY DUCKING UNDER THE WATER AND BREATHING THROUGH THIS REED!

FOOP!
8-1

FUNNY, IT ALWAYS WORKS IN THE MOVIES!

BULL BUSHKA DOESN'T KNOW THAT I'M HIDING FROM HIM UNDERWATER BY BREATHING THROUGH THIS REED!

PUFF! PUFF! PUFF! PUFF!
BATIUK
8-2

BURP!

HERE I AM HIDING FROM THAT BIG BULLY, BULL BUSHKA, BY STAYING UNDER WATER AND BREATHING THROUGH THIS REED!

HE MUST BE NEARBY BECAUSE I'M REALLY GETTING NERVOUS!
8-3

I CAN TELL BECAUSE MY PALMS ARE ALL CLAMMY!
BATIUK

FUNKY WINKERBEAN

3001
FLAVORS

I HATE THIS!
FLAVORS

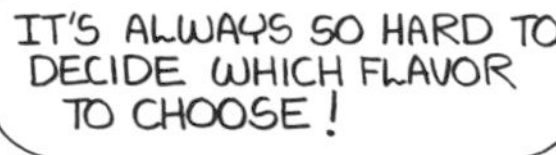
IT'S ALWAYS SO HARD TO DECIDE WHICH FLAVOR TO CHOOSE!

UH, LET'S SEE ··· BANANA-MINT-PUNCH ··· HICKORY-NUT-CHIP ··· BLUEBERRY-BEER-TWIST ···
STRAWBERRY-HAMHOCK
BUTTERFLY-SWIRL
ROCKY-ROAD
TUNA-SPINACH-CARAMEL

WITH ALL OF THESE FLAVORS OF ICE CREAM TO CHOOSE FROM, I JUST CAN'T SEEM TO MAKE UP MY MIND!
8-4

I GUESS THE BEST THING TO DO IS JUST STICK WITH A TRADITIONAL OLD FAVORITE!

ONE FUDGE-MEATBALL-RIPPLE PLEASE!
BUTTERFLY-
ROCKY-ROAD
TUNA-SPINACH

WHEN I'M AT BAND CAMP, I ALWAYS GET UP AT THE CRACK OF DAWN ···
BAND CAMP

··· GO OVER TO THE DINING ROOM ···
BATIUK
© Field Enterprises, Inc., 1974
8-5

··· AND MUNCH ON A FEW DRUM ROLLS!

EACH DAY WHILE WE'RE IN BAND CAMP, I'LL BE GIVING YOU A DIFFERENT LECTURE!
BAND CAMP

THEY'LL COVER THE BASIC FUNDAMENTALS OF WHAT IT TAKES TO BE A GOOD BAND MEMBER!
BATIUK
8-6

WE'LL START WITH HOW TO SELL BAND CANDY!

ONE FINAL THING TO REMEMBER WHEN YOU'RE OUT SELLING BAND CANDY!
CANDY
BAND CAMP

ALWAYS TRAVEL IN TWOS!

THAT'S IN CASE YOU RUN INTO SOME GIRL SCOUTS SELLING COOKIES!
CANDY
BATIUK
8-7

AFTER A HARD DAY AT BAND CAMP ...

WE BAND DIRECTORS LIKE TO RELAX TOO!
8-8
BATIUK

I THINK I'LL JUST MARCH AROUND THE POOL FOR AWHILE!

ONE OF THE JOYS OF BAND CAMP, FOR ME, IS TO GET AWAY TO THIS LITTLE HILL!

IT'S TRULY INSPIRING!
8-9
BATIUK

THE HILLS ARE ALIVE WITH THE SOUND OF MUSIC...

AN IMPORTANT PART OF BAND CAMP IS THE BAND CLINIC...

... WHERE I DIAGNOSE AND CORRECT IMPROPER MUSIC HABITS!
BATIUK
8-10

SOME ARE EASIER TO SPOT THAN OTHERS!

FUNKY WINKERBEAN

WHAT A BUMMER!

LIFE IS JUST PASSING ME BY!

JUST THINK, CRAZY, I'M SWEET SIXTEEN AND I'VE NEVER BEEN KISSED!

OH WELL, AT LEAST WHEN IT HAPPENS, I'LL HAVE AN ESPECIALLY FOND MEMORY TO LOOK BACK ON!
© Field Enterprises, Inc., 1974
BATIUK
8-11

SMOOCH!

SIGH!

THE THROW TO FIRST IS WILD, AND BUNTSKI IS HEADING FOR SECOND --- AND HE'S STOPPING THERE!!

I CAN'T BELIEVE IT! HE'S JUST STANDING THERE!! WHY DO YOU SUPPOSE HE DID THAT, TONY?
BATIUK
8-12

ONLY ONE BASE ON AN OVERTHROW, CURT!

THAT'S INTERESTING, CRAZY?

ARE THOSE POLE BEANS?
BATIUK

I'M NOT SURE WHAT NATIONALITY THEY ARE?
8-13

I THOUGHT THE CORN IN MY GARDEN WOULD GROW BETTER IF I WERE TO SIT AND READ TO IT FOR AWHILE!

WHAT ARE YOU LOOKING FOR?
OH, SOMETHING CORNY!
8-14

HOW ABOUT TODAY'S CARTOON?
BATIUK

TELL ME, JAN ···

··· HAVE YOU GIVEN ANY THOUGHT TO ONE OF THOSE NEW TENNIS CLUBS?
8-15

NO, MARCIA, PERSONALLY I PREFER USING A RACQUET!
BATIUK

ONCE AGAIN IT'S TIME FOR 'TRUTH OR CONSEQUENCES' AND 'LET'S MAKE A DEAL'!

WHAT'S ON, DEREK?
8-16
BATIUK

A FORMER PRESIDENTIAL AIDE IS TESTIFYING BEFORE A CONGRESSIONAL COMMITTEE!

HEY! WAY TO GO, RODNEY!
BATIUK

WHY DID YOU CONGRATULATE HIM, FUNKY? HE STRUCK OUT!

YEAH, BUT HE SWUNG AT ONE! HE BROKE OUT OF HIS SLUMP!
8-17

FUNKY WINKERBEAN
PLAYGROUND

BATIUK

RUMBLE!
8-18

WHUMP!
© Field Enterprises, Inc., 1974

BOY! THAT ECLIPSE SURE CAME UP FAST!

WELL, I DID WHAT YOU SAID, MARY ELLEN!

I WENT STRAIGHT TO THE RECREATION DIRECTOR AND I TOLD HIM I WANTED MORE MONEY...
... AND?
CITY RECREAT
BATIUK

HE DOUBLED MY HOURS!
8-19

THAT PEP TALK YOU GAVE YOUR TEAM DID WONDERS, FUNKY!
CITY RECREAT

I'LL HAVE TO ADMIT THEY'RE REALLY SHOWING A LOT OF HUSTLE!
BATIUK
8-20

THEY JUST CARRIED THAT LAST GUY OFF THE FIELD IN A REAL SNAPPY FASHION!
CITY RECREAT

BRIAN, LET ME TELL YOU SOMETHING!

IF YOU WANT TO BE AN ALL AROUND BALL PLAYER, YOU'D BETTER PRACTICE YOUR SLIDING!
BATIUK
8-21

NOW REMEMBER, GUYS, THE IMPORTANT THING IS TO ENJOY TODAY'S GAME!

JUST GO OUT THERE AND HAVE FUN!
BATIUK
8-22

WE'RE GOING TO GET CREAMED AREN'T WE?
IT LOOKS THAT WAY!

SAYINGS FROM THE
I CHONG
ANCIENT BOOK OF CHINESE PHILOSOPHY

THE MASTER SAYS: WHERE THERE'S A WILL ···
8-23

···THERE'S A BUNDLE TO BE MADE FOR SOME PROBATE LAWYER!
BATIUK

BATIUK
© Field Enterprises, Inc., 1974
8-24

FUNKY WINKERBEAN
POOL RULES
1. NO STREET SHOES IN THE POOL.
2. ALL SWIMMERS MUST HAVE THEIR OWN SUITS.
3. OBSERVE WINTER RULES WHEN POOL IS FROZEN.

OH, OH ... HERE COMES THAT BIG BULLY, BULL BUSHKA!

HE PROBABLY PLANS TO CLOBBER ME, BUT I'VE GOT TO REMEMBER TO KEEP MY COOL!
BATIUK

YOU DON'T SCARE ME, BULL BUSHKA! STICKS AND STONES CAN BREAK MY BONES BUT NAMES CAN NEVER HURT ME!
8-25

PUNK!
© Field Enterprises, Inc., 1974

PUNK!
BATIUK

WHAP!
WHAP!
WHAP!
SCRUNG!
WELL, SO MUCH FOR THAT THEORY!

LIGHT MY FIRE, HUH?
BATIUK

HAS THAT T-SHIRT HELPED YOU MEET ANY GUYS, JENNIFER?

YEAH, IF YOU LIKE BOY SCOUTS!
8-26

HOW'S IT GOING WITH THE GIRLS THIS SUMMER, LES?

BEYOND MY WILDEST DREAMS, FUNKY!
BATIUK
© Field Enterprises, Inc., 1974
8-27

AT THE RATE IT'S GOING, I MIGHT EVEN GET A DATE BEFORE SUMMER'S OVER!

AS I STAND HERE ON THE HIGH DIVE...

... ONE THOUGHT STANDS OUT PROMINENTLY IN MY MIND!
BATIUK
8-28

THIS HAS TO BE THE MOST STUPID WAY OF ALL TO GET INTO THAT POOL!

MR. WINKERBEAN, I SCRAPED MY ELBOW! DO YOU GIVE FIRST AID?

NO! ACTUALLY, I'M ONLY QUALIFIED TO GIVE SECOND AID!
8-29

I'M BLEEDING TO DEATH, AND HE'S MAKING JOKES!
BATIUK

ALL THE PLANETS IN OUR SOLAR SYSTEM ARE DESOLATE, WITH HOSTILE ENVIRONMENTS INCAPABLE OF SUPPORTING HUMAN LIFE...

...WITH THE EXCEPTION OF EARTH...
BATIUK
8-30

...BUT WE'RE WORKING ON IT!

FOR THREE MONTHS THIS SCHOOL HAS BEEN QUIET AS A TOMB!

FOR THREE MONTHS I'VE BEEN ALONE HERE, QUIETLY WORKING AWAY!
PRINCIPAL
8-31

THREE OUT OF TWELVE ISN'T BAD!
BATIUK

FUNKY WINKERBEAN
I NEVER COULD FIGURE OUT WHAT TO DO WITH THIS POOL CUE!

SIGH!

I JUST CAN'T BELIEVE IT!

WELL, HERE IT IS, ANOTHER LABOR DAY WEEKEND...

AND I'VE DONE IT AGAIN!
9-1

I'VE WASTED MY WHOLE SUMMER STANDING IN THIS POOL STARING AT THAT BEAUTIFUL BRUNETTE LIFEGUARD!
© Field Enterprises, Inc., 1974
BATIUK

NOT ONLY THAT, I'VE GOT BARNACLES!

THE KEY TO MAKING A SUCCESSFUL HIGH DIVE IS COMPLETE AND TOTAL CONCENTRATION!

BATIUK

GEE, I NEVER NOTICED I HAD THAT HANGNAIL BEFORE!
9-2

SCHEDULE CHANGES
THIS LINE IS FOR DROPPING OR ADDING COURSES ... NOT FOR CHUCKING THE WHOLE THING!
BATIUK
9-3

I REALLY FEEL EXCITED ABOUT THIS COMING SCHOOL YEAR!

I'VE NEVER FELT SO POSITIVE BEFORE! THIS IS REALLY GOING TO BE MY YEAR!
BATIUK
9-4

ON THE OTHER HAND!

BOY! IS THIS EVER A MESS IN HERE!

I'VE HAD IT!
BATIUK

THAT'S THE LAST TIME I SUBLEASE OVER THE SUMMER!
9-5

I'D LIKE TO WELCOME THE STAFF BACK FOR ANOTHER SCHOOL YEAR!

I HOPE WE'RE ALL RENEWED AND REFRESHED BECAUSE WE HAVE A LOT TO DO THIS YEAR!
BATIUK
9-6

FIRST OFF, WE'LL NEED YOUR RESERVATION FOR THIS YEAR'S CHRISTMAS PARTY!

ONE OF THE FIRST THINGS WE HAVE TO DO AT THE START OF EACH YEAR IS GET THE INITIAL ENROLLMENT!

SO TOMORROW, SEND A SLIP OF PAPER TO THE OFFICE WITH ---
BATIUK
9-7

--- THE NUMBER OF INITIALS ENROLLED IN YOUR ROOM!

FUNKY WINKERBEAN

UH ··· LET'S SEE NOW!

THREE TO THE LEFT ··· FOUR TO THE RIGHT ···

STAND UP ··· SIT DOWN! FIGHT! FIGHT! FIGHT!
BATIUK

9-8

LOOK, YOU REMEMBER YOUR LOCKER COMBINATION YOUR WAY AND I'LL REMEMBER MINE, MY WAY!
© Field Enterprises, Inc., 1974

AS I STAND BEFORE YOU STUDENTS AT THE FIRST ASSEMBLY OF THE YEAR ...

... I'D LIKE TO WELCOME ALL OF YOU BACK TO SCHOOL!
BATIUK

I'D LIKE TO ... BUT WHY BE HYPOCRITICAL ABOUT IT?
9-9

FOOT, QUART, MILE ...

METER, LITER, KILOMETER ...
BATIUK
9-10

I CAN'T SEE CHANGING TO ANOTHER SYSTEM OF MEASUREMENT JUST BECAUSE IT RHYMES!

COACH, IF I RECOVER A FUMBLE SHOULD I RUN WITH IT?

IS THE SKY BLUE?
BATIUK
9-11

WHY DO I ALWAYS GET THE HARD QUESTIONS!

I SURE WOULD LOVE TO BE THE COACH OF A SUPER FOOTBALL TEAM...

...AND TO HAVE MY TEAM SWEEP THE CONFERENCE AND WIN ALL THE MARBLES!
BATIUK

I'VE NEVER HAD ANY MARBLES OF MY OWN BEFORE!
9-12

JOHN DARLING HERE, SPORTS FANS, TALKING WITH AREA COACH JACK STROPP!

TELL ME, COACH, ARE YOU LOOKING FOR AN UPSET FROM YOUR TEAM IN TONIGHT'S GAME ?
BATIUK

OH YEAH! MY TEAM UPSETS ME EVERY TIME WE PLAY!
9-13

NEXT WEEK ON THRILLSEEKERS...

BATIUK
...WE'LL FEATURE DAREDEVIL ERIC FROTT...

...WHO WILL ATTEMPT THE AMAZING FEAT OF WALKING ALONE AND UNARMED BEHIND THE BLEACHERS AT A HIGH SCHOOL FOOTBALL GAME!
9-14

FUNKY WINKERBEAN
TODAY'S CARTOON: "TAKE A LITTLE PIZZA MY HEART!"

BOY, AM I EVER TEMPTED TO BREAK MY PLEDGE TO LAY OFF PIZZAS FOR AWHILE!
MAYBE A LITTLE TV WILL HELP!

I MAY BE STARVED, BUT I'M POSITIVELY **NEVER** GOING TO ORDER ANOTHER PIZZA!
BATIUK

WOW! THEY REALLY MADE **MINCEMEAT** OUT OF THAT RUNNER! THAT MIDDLE LINEBACKER JUST GRINDS HIS OPPOSITION INTO **HAMBURGER**!
9-15

MAN, THE QUARTERBACK SURE **PEPPERED** THAT BALL TO HIS TIGHT-END! YOU KNOW IT'S REALLY AMAZING HOW PRO FOOTBALL HAS **MUSHROOMED** THESE PAST FEW YEARS!

HELLO, MONTONI'S...?
I NEVER SAUSAGE ACTION!
© Field Enterprises, Inc., 1973

FUNKY, THE COMPUTER DIDN'T SEEM TO BE ABLE TO SCHEDULE YOU FOR THE COURSES YOU WANT!

SINCE IT WOULD BE TOO COMPLICATED TO GO BACK AND CHANGE THE SCHEDULES, WE THOUGHT WE'D TRY SOMETHING ELSE!
BATIUK
9-16

WE'RE GOING TO EXPEL YOU!

hi there!

i can place your face...
BATIUK

but i can't seem to remember your number.
9-17

LISTEN! I REFUSE TO BE TREATED AS NOTHING MORE THAN A NUMBER ON A PUNCH CARD!

I'M A HUMAN BEING!
BATIUK

nobody's perfect!
9-18

YOU KNOW, DEREK, WHEN YOU THINK ABOUT IT...

WE SURE LIVE IN A FUNNY WORLD!

SO HOW COME NOBODY'S LAUGHING?
9-19

WE'VE BEEN HAVING A REAL PROBLEM WITH FIGHTS AT OUR FOOTBALL GAMES LATELY, FRED!

I THOUGHT MAYBE YOU'D HAVE SOME IDEAS ON WHAT WE COULD DO ABOUT IT!

MAYBE WE SHOULDN'T PLAY THE FIGHT SONG SO MUCH!
BATIUK
9-20

THIS HAS BEEN ONE HECKUVA GAME!

THEY'VE THROWN EVERYTHING AT US BUT THE KITCHEN SINK!
BATIUK

9-21

THIS HAS BEEN ONE HECKUVA GAME!

FUNKY WINKERBEAN
GO TEAM!

MAN IS CONSTANTLY FINDING NEW USES FOR THE COMPUTER ... INCLUDING PICKING WINNERS FOR THE OFFICE FOOTBALL POOL!

SAY, ARE YOU SURE ABOUT THIS FIRST GAME PREDICTION?
© Field Enterprises, Inc., 1974

of course! we computers are infallible. the bears will beat the packers by three.

OKAY...
BATIUK
9-22

the bears always hit more home runs than the packers!

OKAY, HOLLY, THAT JUST ABOUT COMPLETES YOUR STUDENT ACTIVITIES FILE!

ONE FINAL THING...
© Field Enterprises, Inc., 1974
BATIUK
9-23

...WAS THERE ANYTHING ELSE BESIDES BEING 'MISS PERFECT POSTURE' OF WALNUT COUNTY?

YOU WANTED TO SEE ME, MR. DINKLE?
YES I DID, HOLLY!

© Field Enterprises, Inc., 1974
BATIUK
9-24

AT EASE, HOLLY!

HOLLY, I'M AFRAID I HAVE SOME BAD NEWS FOR YOU!

FIRST, LET ME START BY SAYING THAT YOU'VE BEEN ONE OF THE FINEST HEAD MAJORETTES I'VE EVER KNOWN!
© Field Enterprises, Inc., 1974
BATIUK
9-25

BUT YOU'VE BEEN WITH THE BAND NINE YEARS NOW...

TELL ME SOMETHING, HOLLY, WHAT DO YOU PLAN TO DO WHEN YOU GET OUT OF SCHOOL?
© Field Enterprises, Inc., 1974

I MEAN, AFTER ALL, YOU CAN'T BE A MAJORETTE YOUR WHOLE LIFE!
9-26

YOU CAN'T?
BATIUK

AND NOW PRESENTING HEAD MAJORETTE, HOLLY BUDD, AND THE DANGEROUS FLAMING BATON TRICK!

FAWOOMP!
© Field Enterprises, Inc., 1974
9-27

WE'LL ALWAYS REMEMBER YOU THE WAY YOU WERE, HOLLY!

HOLLY? IS THAT YOU?

BATIUK
TWIRL! TWIRL!
9-28

HEY KID, HOW ARE YA?
© Field Enterprises, Inc., 1974

FUNKY WINKERBEAN
COMPOSITIONS
NAME X
IF YOU ARE RUINING YOUR EYES READING THIS IN HOPES OF COMING ACROSS SOMETHING CUTE AND CLEVER, LET ME SAY RIGHT NOW, YOU'RE WASTING YOUR TIME!

CLACK! CLACKITY!
CLACK! CLACK!

FINISHED!

OUR ENGLISH TEACHER IS GOING TO LOVE THIS FIRST THEME OF MINE! IT'S REALLY IMAGINATIVE!

IT'S ABOUT A GUY WHO LEARNS HOW TO TURN HUMID SUMMER AIR INTO GOLD…
BATIUK

…SO HE TURNS ALL THE SUMMER AIR INTO GOLD, AND THEN GOES ON A BIG SPENDING SPREE!
9-29

IT'S CALLED, 'HOW I SPENT MY SUMMER'!

Twinkle,
twinkle, little
star,

How I wonder
what you are.

In the sky
above our
nation,
© Field Enterprises, Inc., 1974
9-30

Rising high
as our
inflation!
BATIUK

TELL ME, BULL, HAVE YOU EVER GIVEN ANY THOUGHT TO EDUCATION AS A CAREER?

YEAH, BUT I DIDN'T LIKE THE IDEA!
© Field Enterprises, Inc., 1974
BATIUK
10-1

I FIGURE I'D RATHER GRADUATE FROM HIGH SCHOOL AND GO ON TO SOMETHING ELSE!

WELL, ROPE, IT'S A NEW YEAR!

AND THIS IS THE YEAR I'M GOING TO CLIMB YOU!
BATIUK
© Field Enterprises, Inc., 1974

I WONDER IF THIS IS THE YEAR I'M GOING TO CLIMB BACK DOWN!
10-2

YA KNOW, FUNKY, I ALWAYS HAVE THIS FEELING THAT I'M BEING DISCRIMINATED AGAINST!
14

NOTHING OVERT, MIND YOU, BUT JUST SUBTLE LITTLE THINGS THAT REMIND ME I'M BLACK!
BATIUK

PERSONALLY, DEREK, I THINK IT'S JUST A PIGMENT OF YOUR IMAGINATION!
14
10-3

SAYINGS FROM THE
I CHONG
ANCIENT BOOK OF CHINESE PHILOSOPHY

THE MASTER SAYS: IF SOMEONE STRIKES YOU, TURN THE OTHER CHEEK!
BATIUK

I WONDER WHAT YOU DO IF SOMEONE HITS YOU IN THE NOSE?
10-4

IN OTHER SPORTS NEWS, THE NFL'S LEADING RUSHER, BIG BUCK BILLINGSLY, SIGNED A CONTRACT FOR ONE MILLION DOLLARS!

THE CONTRACT ALSO CONTAINS A NO-CUT CLAUSE!
BATIUK

THIS IS BELIEVED TO BE THE HIGHEST CONTRACT EVER AWARDED FOR A SHAVING COMMERCIAL!
10-5

FUNKY WINKERBEAN
REWARD

BEING A GUIDANCE COUNSELOR IS A VERY REWARDING JOB!

WHEN YOU'RE A GUIDANCE COUNSELOR, YOU'RE THE ONE THE STUDENTS COME TO WHEN THEY'RE IN TROUBLE AND NEED HELP!

IT'S VERY SATISFYING TO KNOW THAT YOU GIVE THEM THE ANSWERS AND HELP PROVIDE DIRECTION FOR THEIR LIVES!
BATIUK
© Field Enterprises, Inc., 1974

EXCUSE ME! WHERE'S THE GIRL'S RESTROOM?
10-6

DOWN THE HALL AND TO YOUR LEFT!

YAWN!

I MAY RISE ···
BATIUK

··· BUT I DON'T THINK I'M GOING TO SHINE!
10-7

ZiiiiP

THUNK!
BATIUK

UNLESS I MISS MY GUESS, WE'RE DUE FOR AN INDIAN SUMMER!

AND NOW WE'LL HAVE THIS YEAR'S FIRST REPORT FROM THE CURRICULUM STUDY COMMITTEE!

AS YOU KNOW, WE MET SEVERAL TIMES DURING THE SUMMER AND WE THOUGHT WE WOULD BRING YOU UP TO DATE ON OUR PROGRESS!
BATIUK
10-9

SO OUR FIRST REPORT IS ENTITLED: 'WHAT WE DID LAST SUMMER'!

MISS WRIGHTON, I HAVE SOMETHING TO CONFESS!

YOU KNOW THAT EXCUSE I GAVE YOU YESTERDAY THAT SAID I WAS IN BED ALL DAY WITH A COLD? WELL, IT WASN'T TRUE!
BATIUK
10-10

I GOT OUT OF BED TWICE!

I'M GETTING KIND OF TIRED OF CARRYING THESE TWO MICE AROUND!
SQUEAK!
PIP!

I THINK I'LL KEEP THEM IN THE TOP DRAWER OF MY DRESSER!
BATIUK
10-11

BUT WHEN WE GET BEHIND CLOSED DRAWERS!

AND NOW COMING INTO THE GAME AT FULLBACK FOR STATE IS CLARK KENT!

LET ME TELL YOU ---
BATIUK
10-12

THIS BOY CAN REALLY FLY!

FUNKY WINKERBEAN
I'M NOT SURE BUT I THINK IT'S A FOOTBALL NUT!

WHAT A CATCH! THAT MOVES THE BALL DOWN TO THE TWENTY-TWO!

LET'S GO DOWN TO THE SIDELINES WHERE JIM IS WITH COACH CASSIDY!

TELL ME, COACH, WHAT WAS THAT LAST PLAY DESIGNED TO DO?
BATIUK

WELL, THAT WAS A PASS PLAY! ON A PASS PLAY THE QUARTERBACK THROWS THE BALL THROUGH THE AIR TO THE RECEIVER!

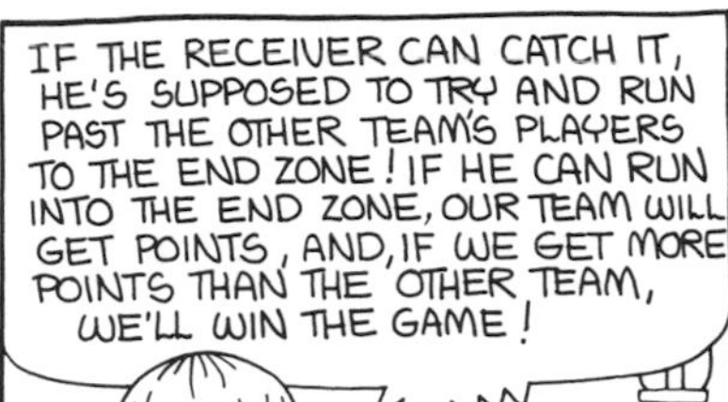
IF THE RECEIVER CAN CATCH IT, HE'S SUPPOSED TO TRY AND RUN PAST THE OTHER TEAM'S PLAYERS TO THE END ZONE! IF HE CAN RUN INTO THE END ZONE, OUR TEAM WILL GET POINTS, AND, IF WE GET MORE POINTS THAN THE OTHER TEAM, WE'LL WIN THE GAME!

© Field Enterprises, Inc., 1974

AND THERE YOU HAVE IT FOLKS, ANOTHER INSIDE LOOK AT THE STRATEGY AND THINKING GOING ON DOWN HERE ON THE FIELD!
10-13

HEY FOG!
HOW MUCH IS
TWO AND TWO?
10-14

UH, FIVE?
BATIUK

BOY, TALK
ABOUT A
DENSE FOG!

TELL ME, CRAZY, DID YOU
EVER ASK YOURSELF THE
OLD ETERNAL QUESTION,
'WHY'?
SURE, FUNKY!

SO WHAT DID YOU
COME UP WITH FOR AN
ANSWER?
BATIUK

WHY NOT?
10-15

YOU SEEM TO HAVE IT
UPSTAIRS, CRAZY! THE
PROBLEM SEEMS TO BE
THAT YOU'RE NOT TRYING
ENOUGH!
BATIUK

THAT'S STRANGE!
10-16

MISS WRIGHTON SAID
I WAS THE MOST TRYING
STUDENT SHE HAD!

I'VE JUST FINISHED AN ARTICLE ON HOW COMPUTERS ARE CAUSING SCHOOLS TO BECOME DEHUMANIZED, FUNKY!

I LIKE THAT, LES! IT'S GOOD TO SEE SOMEONE GET INVOLVED AND TAKE A STAND ON AN ISSUE AFTER CAREFULLY CONSIDERING BOTH SIDES AND COMING TO A REASONABLE, INTELLIGENT AND INFORMED DECISION!
10-17
BATIUK

NO, ACTUALLY I'M JUST PREJUDICED!

THIS NEW MATH COLUMN I'M DOING FOR THE SCHOOL PAPER REALLY SEEMS TO BE CATCHING ON!

Les' Logs! Today's topic:
CLACK!
CLACK!
BATIUK

A new look at counting on your fingers.
10-18

LIVINIA, YOU CAN'T POSSIBLY BE SPORTS EDITOR FOR THE SCHOOL NEWSPAPER! YOU JUST DON'T KNOW ENOUGH ABOUT SPORTS!

OH YEAH? TRY ME!
OKAY, NAME THREE SPORTS TEAMS IN NEW YORK CITY!
BATIUK

THE RANGERS, THE KNICKERBOCKERS, AND THE PHILHARMONICS!

FUNKY WINKERBEAN

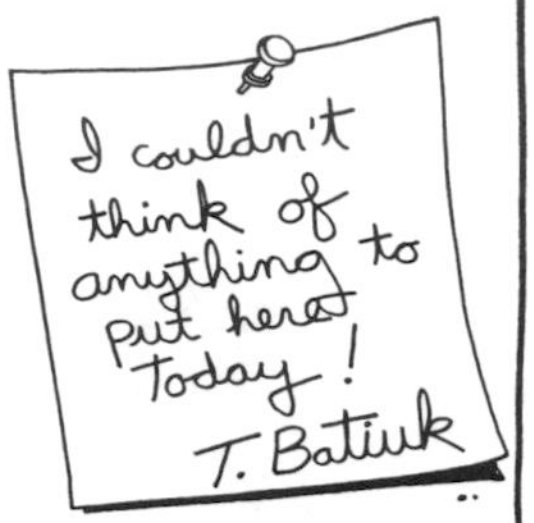
I couldn't think of anything to put here today!
T. Batiuk

GET READY! HERE COMES ANOTHER ONE!

76

BATIUK
8
7
9
8
9
© Field Enterprises, Inc., 1974
10-20

I DON'T KNOW WHY YOU'RE AFRAID TO CLIMB THE ROPE, LES!

LOOK AT BULL HERE! HE'S CLIMBED THAT ROPE A HUNDRED TIMES AND NEVER HAD ANY PROBLEM!

EXCEPT FOR THE TIME HE GOT LOST!
BATIUK

I DON'T KNOW WHY I'M AFRAID TO CLIMB THAT STUPID ROPE!

YOU JUST CLIMB UP AND THEN YOU CLIMB DOWN! WHY, SURE! IT'S THE EASIEST THING IN THE WORLD TO DO!
BATIUK

AND YET---

SAYINGS FROM THE
I CHONG
ANCIENT BOOK OF CHINESE PHILOSOPHY

THE MAN WHO CAN GIVE A POLITICAL SPEECH ---
BATIUK

--- IS A MAN WHO KNOWS HOW TO TAKE THE BULL BY THE HORNS!

HEY, MOM! IS THIS MY REGULAR BOX OF 'ALL-AMERICAN SILO MUNCHIES'?

YES, IT'S JUST THE NEW IMPROVED VERSION!
BATIUK

I WONDER WHAT THEY ADDED?
10-24

ABOUT TWELVE CENTS TO THE PRICE!

HEY, A WOOLY BEAR CATERPILLAR!
BATIUK

IT'S SAID YOU CAN TELL HOW HARD A WINTER IT WILL BE BY THE SIZE OF THE BAND AROUND A WOOLY BEAR CATERPILLAR!
10-25

DO YOU PLAN TO COME OUT THROWING IN THE SECOND HALF, COACH?

NO, JOHN! I PLAN TO LET MY QUARTERBACK DO IT!
BATIUK
10-26

GOTCHA, JOHN!

FUNKY WINKERBEAN
AND NOW, HERE ARE SOME SPORTS BRIEFS!

JOHN DARLING HERE, TALKING TO COACH JACK STROPP ON THE EVE OF THE BIG GAME!

WELL, COACH, HERE YOU ARE PLAYING BIG WALNUT TECH FOR A SHOT AT THE LEAGUE TITLE!

HAVE YOU EVER TAKEN A TEAM THIS FAR BEFORE?
BATIUK

OH YEAH, JOHN! WE ONCE PLAYED A TEAM THAT WAS SIXTY MILES FROM HERE!

IN FACT, BEFORE WE JOINED THE LEAGUE WE USED TO GO AS FAR AS...
© Field Enterprises, Inc., 1974
10-21

OLD MACDONALD
HAD A FARM...

EEEii EEEii
OOOO!
BATIUK
10-28

I JUST LOVE COUNTRY MUSIC!

MR. FAIRGOOD, THE COMPUTER SCHEDULED ME FOR THE SAME ALGEBRA COURSE TWICE!

LET'S SEE, LIVINIA!
BATIUK

WELL, WE CAN'T CHANGE YOUR SCHEDULE, BUT WE CAN GIVE YOU A MAJOR IN IT!
10-29

HERE'S YOUR HOT CHOCOLATE, FUNKY!

IN DEFERENCE TO THE HALLOWEEN SEASON, I ADDED A SPECIAL TOUCH!
WHAT DID YOU DO?

I MADE IT WITH CIDER!
10-30

IT'S HALLOWEEN NIGHT, DAD!

DOZEN OF TRICK-OR-TREATERS ARE GOING TO BE COMING TO OUR DOOR! AREN'T YOU GOING TO DO ANYTHING TO GET READY FOR THEM?
BATIUK
10-31

YOU'RE RIGHT, I ALMOST FORGOT! TURN OFF THE LIGHTS AND WE'LL LIE ON THE FLOOR!

11-1

THERE'S SOMETHING ABOUT A CHEERLEADER UNIFORM THAT TRANSFORMS A GIRL INTO A SENSUOUS SIREN!
BATIUK

BAND UNIFORMS, ON THE OTHER HAND...

LOOK AT THOSE CHEERLEADERS IN THEIR SEXY OUTFITS!

AND HERE I AM IN THIS CLUNKY BAND UNIFORM!

HALF THE PEOPLE IN THE STANDS CAN'T TELL IF I'M A BOY OR A GIRL!
BATIUK

I THINK I'LL GO EMPTY MY SPITVALVE ON SOMEBODY'S POM-

FUNKY WINKERBEAN
JOKER
JO

I JUST DON'T KNOW WHAT TO DO, LES!

THIS GUY I'M GOING WITH JUST DOESN'T SEEM TO CARE FOR ME ANYMORE!

IF YOUR BOYFRIEND IS TAKING YOU FOR GRANTED, BARB, WHY DON'T YOU GO OUT WITH ME AND MAKE HIM JEALOUS?

BATIUK
76

© Field Enterprises, Inc., 1974
GIGGLE! SNICKER! HEE! HEE!

HA! HA! HA! HO!
CHEER UP!
11-3

NO ONE THINKS I'LL EVER AMOUNT TO ANYTHING!

BUT I'LL FOOL 'EM! SOMEDAY I'LL BE AN OXFORD DON ···
BATIUK
11-4

··· INSTEAD OF JUST A HIGH SCHOOL HARRY!
© Field Enterprises, Inc., 1974

YOU TRADED CRAZY HARRY TO ANOTHER SCHOOL?

YEAH, FRED! IT WAS A CASH DEAL ···
11-5

··· WITH TWO HOODS TO BE NAMED AT A LATER DATE!
© Field Enterprises, Inc., 1974

THE PRINCIPAL DIDN'T TRADE YOU AFTER ALL, HUH, CRAZY?

NO, BUT I'VE DECIDED TO PLAY OUT MY OPTION!
11-6

OF COURSE I'LL HAVE TO TAKE A TEN PER CENT CUT IN GRADES!
BATIUK
© Field Enterprises, Inc., 1974

I CAN'T BELIEVE IT, FUNKY! THE PRINCIPAL TRIED TO TRADE ME TO ANOTHER SCHOOL FOR TWO AVERAGE HOODS!

THAT'S THE MOST RIDICULOUS THING I'VE EVER HEARD, CRAZY!
BATIUK
11-7

YOU'RE WORTH AT LEAST FIVE AVERAGE HOODS!

BATIUK
11-8
RUMBLERUMBLERUMBLERUMBLERUMBLERU

IT CERTAINLY IS PEACEFUL WORKING HERE ON A SATURDAY!

IT'S HARD TO BELIEVE THAT ON MONDAY MORNING THE HALLS WILL BE FILLED WITH RETURNING STUDENTS!
BATIUK
11-9

SOB!

FUNKY WINKERBEAN
....BUT THE SIGN FOR THE DANCE SAID TO BRING YOUR OWN FORTY-FIVES!

BOY! MARY SUE SURE LOOKS 'TUFF' TONIGHT!

I'D LIKE TO ASK MARY SUE TO DANCE, BUT I'M AFRAID I'D MAKE A BIG FOOL OF MYSELF!

THAT'S SILLY, LES! WHO'S GOING TO CARE? NOBODY CAME HERE JUST TO WATCH YOU! NO ONE'S EVEN GOING TO NOTICE YOU TALKING TO HER!
BATIUK
11-10

YEAH, I GUESS YOU'RE RIGHT, FUNKY!

NOW I FEEL UNWANTED!
© Field Enterprises, Inc., 1974

LOOK, TRUST ME, LES! IF YOU AREN'T AFRAID OF FALLING YOU WON'T BE TOO CHICKEN TO CLIMB DOWN THAT ROPE!

JUST TIE THIS AROUND YOUR WAIST AND I'LL HOLD SECURELY ONTO THE OTHER END!
BATIUK

SOMETHING TELLS ME I'VE BEEN HAD!
11-11
© Field Enterprises, Inc., 1974

IS LES STUCK UP THERE ON THE ROPE AGAIN, FUNKY?

YEAH, DEREK, IT DOESN'T LOOK LIKE HE'S GOING TO MAKE IT!

OKAY, WE'D BETTER CALL THE FIRE DEPARTMENT!

HOW EMBARRASSING!
BATIUK
11-12
© Field Enterprises, Inc., 1974

LET'S SEE WHAT'S ON GUNSMOKE TONIGHT!

TONIGHT'S EPISODE: MATT DILLON STARTS HIS BALLET LESSONS!
TV
BATIUK
11-13
© Field Enterprises, Inc., 1974

THERE'S REALLY BEEN AN EMPHASIS ON MARSHALL ARTS IN WESTERNS THESE DAYS!

THE TROUBLE YOU ARE EXPERIENCING IS NOT WITH YOUR SET!

PLEASE STAND BY
BATIUK

11-14

YOU KNOW, CRAZY, THE WORD 'NOSE' IS REALLY ODD!

I WONDER IF IT WOULD STILL BE ABLE TO SMELL THINGS THE SAME WAY IF WE CALLED IT SOMETHING LIKE A BANANA?
BATIUK
© Field Enterprises, Inc., 1974
11-15

CERTAINLY, FUNKY! A NOSE BY ANY OTHER NAME WOULD SMELL AS SWEET!

THE AIR POLLUTION INDEX IS CURRENTLY AT SIX HUNDRED!

WHEN YOU GO OUTSIDE TODAY---
0700
BATIUK
11-16

---BE CAREFUL NOT TO BUMP YOUR HEAD ON THE AIR!

FUNKY WINKERBEAN
I'D RATHER PICK UP A GIRL THAN A BOOK
BY BULL BUSHK

MEDIA CENTER

MISS WRIGHTON SAID WE HAVE TO READ SOMETHING OFF OF HER READING LIST!

'MUTINY ON THE BOUNTY'!
© Field Enterprises, Inc., 1974
BATIUK
11-17

THAT WAS PRETTY EASY!

UH, COULD I SEE THAT LIST AGAIN? I'D LIKE TO READ ANOTHER FOR EXTRA CREDIT!

YOU SHOULD'VE SEEN THE FISH I CAUGHT AT BAND CAMP LAST SUMMER, FRED!
11-18

HOW BIG WAS HE?
BATIUK

OH, HE WAS AT LEAST TWO OCTAVES LONG!

THERE ARE TWO KINDS OF STUDENTS TO BE FOUND IN A TYPICAL HIGH SCHOOL!

BAND STUDENTS...
BATIUK
11-19

AND JUVENILE DELINQUENTS!

IF I HURRY, I CAN MAKE IT TO THE END OF THE HALL BEFORE THE BELL RINGS!
BATIUK
11-20
RRRING!

I SHOULD'VE SIGNALLED FOR A FAIR CATCH!
RUMBLERUMBLERUMBLERU

I JUST DON'T BELIEVE IN MARRIAGE IN THE TRADITIONAL SENSE ANYMORE, MARCIA!

I KNOW WHAT YOU MEAN, LIVINIA! OUR HEADS ARE IN THE SAME PLACE ON THAT ISSUE!
BATIUK
11-21

WHY GET MARRIED IN THE TRADITIONAL SENSE WHEN YOU CAN HAVE A GUITAR WEDDING INSTEAD!

LOOK AT THIS AFGHAN I KNITTED, JAN!
11-22

FAR OUT!
BATIUK

OH, JAN!
FAR IN?

I SAW EVELYN THE OTHER DAY...

SHE SAID SHE WAS TAKING MY ADVICE ABOUT GETTING INTERESTED IN SOMETHING SO SHE WOULDN'T BE SO BORED!
BATIUK
11-23

WHAT'S SHE DOING?
DRINKING!

FUNKY WINKERBEAN
MARY SUE
LES

HERE COMES MARY SUE SWEETWATER NOW!

GERONIMO!

SAY, MARY SUE, WOULD YOU LIKE TO GO WITH ME TO A SHOW THIS WEEKEND?
OKAY!

OH, THAT'S TOO BAD! WELL, I'LL TAKE A RAIN CHECK ON THAT AND CATCH YOU SOME OTHER TIME!
BATIUK

© Field Enterprises, Inc., 1974

HE'LL DIE WHEN IT HITS HIM!
11-24

YOU LOOK PRETTY HAPPY TODAY, HOLLY!

I AM, FUNKY! I'M GOING TO A MAJORETTE CLINIC NEXT WEEK!
BATIUK

GOOD LUCK, HOLLY! I KNOW YOU CAN KICK IT!
11-25

CAN'T YOU SEE WHAT YOU'RE DOING, HOLLY?

THE BOYS AROUND THIS SCHOOL JUST REGARD YOU AS A SEX OBJECT!
BATIUK
11-26

THEY DO?

YOU KNOW, THANKSGIVING IS A HOLIDAY THAT EVERYONE CELEBRATES IN HIS OWN SPECIAL WAY!

WHAT ARE YOU DOING FOR THANKSGIVING, LES?
BATIUK
11-27

I THOUGHT I'D GOBBLE MY DINNER!

I'D LIKE A DRUMSTICK, PLEASE!

BATIUK
11-28

GOOD OL' MOM! ANYTHING FOR A YUK!

OKAY, MEN! LISTEN UP!
11-29

THIS SECOND HALF WE'RE GOING TO COME OUT THROWING!
BATIUK

HAS ANYBODY SEEN THE TOWEL?

TELL ME, COACH, WHAT WENT WRONG ON THAT LAST PLAY?

WELL OUR RECEIVER WAS WIDE OPEN ON A FLAG PATTERN AND HE DROPPED THE BALL!

WHAT DO YOU PLAN TO DO TO MAKE THAT PLAY WORK?
BATIUK
11-30

ASK HIM NOT TO DROP THE BALL!

© Field Enterprises, Inc., 1974

THIS IS MY NEW BABY COUSIN, LES!

HIS NAME IS WALLY WINKERBEAN!
BATIUK
12-2

I HOPE HE'S JOKING!

SO THIS IS THE WORLD!

WELL, IT'S GREAT TO BE HERE!
12-3

NOW THAT I'M HERE ...
BATIUK

... LET'S SEE WHAT WE CAN DO TO CUT BACK ON THE POPULATION EXPLOSION!

CRY!
CRY!
CRY!

OH, OH! IT LOOKS LIKE THE BABY IS A LITTLE BIT CHAFED!
BATIUK
12-4

FRANKLY, THAT SOUNDS LIKE A RASH STATEMENT TO ME!

WHERE AM I?
BATIUK
12-5

IT'S ALL DARK! I CAN'T SEE ANYTHING AT ALL!

I WAS AFRAID OF THIS! I'VE BEEN RECALLED!

HMM! THE BABY SEEMS A LITTLE RESTLESS!

HERE! THIS BALLOON SHOULD BE FUN FOR HIM!

BATIUK
12-6

NEATO TORPEDO!

MISS WRIGHTON, IS THIS COURSE PASS-FAIL?

YES IT IS, DEREK!
BATIUK
12-7

IF YOU GET AN A, B, C, OR D, YOU PASS... IF YOU GET AN F, YOU FAIL!

FUNKY WINKERBEAN

WELL, HERE YOU ARE, HOLLY, AS A FINALIST IN THE WALNUT COUNTY PICKLE QUEEN PAGENT!

OH, WOW!

HOLLY, WE REALLY ENJOYED THE WAY YOU HUMMED 'RAINDROPS ARE FALLING ON MY HEAD' IN THE TALENT COMPETITION!
BATIUK

IT SAYS HERE ON YOUR CARD THAT YOU'RE PLANNING ON BECOMING A BRAIN SURGEON, IS THAT RIGHT?

YES IT IS, JOHN!

WOULD YOU LIKE TO SAY SOMETHING TO OUR VIEWING AUDIENCE?
OH WOW!
© Field Enterprises, Inc., 1974

Twinkle, Twinkle little Boeing,

How I wonder where you're going!
BATIUK

I wish I were on you tonight,

'Cause I could use a Champagne flight!
12-9

BEING A HALL MONITOR IS A TREMENDOUS RESPONSIBILITY!

IT'S AWESOME TO EVEN THINK OF THE BURDEN THAT IS PLACED ON MY SHOULDERS!
BATIUK
12-10

WHY, IF IT WASN'T FOR MY BEING HERE, PEOPLE WOULD BE ABLE TO WALK DOWN THE HALL WITHOUT WRITTEN PERMISSION!

THE INDIANS COMPLAINED THAT THE GOVERNMENT HAD TAKEN THEIR LAND!

THEY SAID THIS WITH NO RESERVATIONS AT ALL!
BATIUK

BOO!
HISS!
BOO! BOO!
12-11

THAT'S AN INTERESTING WALL DECORATION, MARCIA!

DID YOU MAKE THAT IN YOUR CRAFTS CLASS?

NO! THAT'S SOME GRANOLA THAT I ACCIDENTALLY FUSED TOGETHER IN MY OVEN!
BATIUK
12-12

RATTLE
RATTLE
RATTLE

RATTLE
RATTLE
RATTLE
BATIUK

IF I HAD MY CHIHUAHUA, I'D DO MY XAVIER CUGAT IMPRESSION FOR YOU FOLKS!
12-13

I JUST FOUND OUT SOMETHING VERY DISTURBING TODAY!

SOMEDAY I'LL GET VERY OLD AND THEN I'LL HAVE TO GO BACK WHERE I CAME FROM!

I HAVEN'T ADMITTED THIS TO ANYONE…
BATIUK
12-14

…BUT I DON'T KNOW HOW I GOT HERE!

FUNKY WINKERBEAN
LES + MARY SUE

I DON'T KNOW WHAT IT IS ABOUT ME, FUNKY!
I JUST CAN'T SEEM TO GET TO FIRST BASE WITH A GIRL!

IF YOU WANT TO STRIKE UP A CONVERSATION WITH A GIRL, LES, JUST USE SOME GOOD OLD STANDARD OPENING LINE!
12-15

SOME OF THOSE OLD CHESTNUTS MAY SEEM TRITE, BUT THEY'RE WELL KNOWN BECAUSE THEY WORK!

I'M CONVINCED, FUNKY! I'LL TRY IT!
BATIUK
© Field Enterprises, Inc., 1974

DOCTOR LIVINGSTON I PRESUME!

JUST LOOK AT MARY SUE OVER THERE!
© Field Enterprises, Inc., 1974

BOY, IF SHE ONLY KNEW WHAT I WAS JUST THINKING!
BATIUK
12-16

OH, OH! I WONDER IF I'VE JUST BLOWN IT FOR MYSELF WITH SANTA CLAUS THIS YEAR!

THIS NEW QUADRAPHONIC SOUND SYSTEM IS REALLY GOING TO BE GREAT!

I CAN'T BELIEVE IT! FOUR DIFFERENT CHANNELS OF SOUND!

TOO BAD I ONLY HAVE A TWO-TRACK HEAD!
12-17

YOU KNOW YOU'VE GOT A GOOD STEREO SYSTEM WHEN YOU GET GOOD SEPARATION!

I THINK I'VE FINALLY REACHED IT!
BATIUK
12-18

MY RETINA IS STARTING TO SEPARATE FROM THE BACK OF MY EYE!
© Field Enterprises, Inc., 1974

I THOUGHT I'D PLAY SOME OF MY FAVORITE OLD FROZEN PIZZAS FROM A FEW YEARS BACK!

HOW ARE THEY?
BATIUK
12-19

WELL, IT'S GIVEN A WHOLE NEW MEANING TO THE TERM 'MOLDY OLDIE'!

DO YOU THINK YOU'LL WIN ANYTHING IN THE CITY'S CHRISTMAS DECORATION CONTEST, CRAZY?

BATIUK
I SHOULD, FUNKY!
12-20

I'M THE ONLY ONE ENTERED IN THE LOCKER COMPETITION!

I'VE GOT SOME NEWS, DAD!

BATIUK
CRAZY HARRY AND I ARE GOING TO TAKE OFF AND VISIT SOME FRIENDS OVER THE CHRISTMAS BREAK!

THERE REALLY IS A SANTA CLAUS!
12-21

FUNKY WINKERBEAN
ARE YOU MRS. CLAUS?
NO! I'M CHRISTMAS CAROL!

JINGLE BELLS, JINGLE BELLS, JINGLE ALL THE WAY! OH WHAT FUN IT IS TO RIDE IN A ONE HORSE OPEN SLEIGH... HEY!

JINGLE BELLS, JINGLE BELLS, JINGLE ALL THE WAY!

OH WHAT FUN IT IS TO RIDE IN A ONE HORSE OPEN SLEIGH!
BATIUK

© Field Enterprises, Inc., 1974
THAT WAS GREAT, GANG! ONE MORE PRACTICE AND WE'LL BE READY TO GO CAROLING ALL OVER THE NEIGHBORHOOD!

COULD WE REHEARSE SOMEPLACE ELSE TOMORROW NIGHT?

BOY, LIVINIA, WE SURE HAVE A GOOD TURN-OUT OF KIDS FOR OUR ENVIRONMENTAL WORKSHOP!

ENVIRONMENTAL WORKSHOP?
BATIUK
12-23

I THOUGHT WE WERE GOING TO SANTA'S WORKSHOP!

MY UNCLE BOB ALWAYS SENDS A PICTURE OF HIS FAMILY AT CHRISTMAS, FUNKY!

HOW ABOUT THAT! THEY EVEN INCLUDE THEIR DOG!

NO, THAT'S MY COUSIN ALICE!
BATIUK
12-24

JUST LOOK AT THAT CHRISTMAS TREE AND ALL OF THOSE PRESENTS!

AND THEY WERE ALL BROUGHT BY A MAN IN A BRIGHTLY COLORED COSTUME WHO FLEW FROM ROOF TO ROOF IN A SLEIGH PULLED BY REINDEER! DO YOU KNOW WHO THAT WAS?
BATIUK
12-25

EVEL KNIEVEL?

WAH!

WAHHA!
BATIUK
12-26

WHY IS IT I ALWAYS HAVE TO GET MAD BEFORE SOMEBODY COMES WITH DINNER!

AND NOW SOME FURTHER CANCELLATIONS DUE TO THE STORM!

THE KAWANGA VALLEY E.S.P. CLUB WANTS US TO LET ITS MEMBERS KNOW THAT TONIGHT'S MEETING HAS BEEN CANCELLED!
BATIUK
12-27

THAT IS, FOR THOSE MEMBERS WHO HADN'T ALREADY SENSED IT!

I REALLY GET A LOT OF JOY FROM MY STEREO!

IT'S PROVIDED ME WITH SOME EXCITING MOMENTS!
BATIUK
12-28

LIKE THE TIME I ACCIDENTALLY PLUGGED MY EARPHONE JACK INTO THE ELECTRICAL SOCKET!

FUNKY WINKERBEAN

THAT'LL BE FIFTY-FIVE CENTS!
STUDENT BOOKSTORE

I'VE JUST GOT MYSELF A BRAND NEW NOTEBOOK AND THIS TIME I'M NOT GOING TO DO ANY DOODLING ON THE COVER AT ALL!

BATIUK
© Field Enterprises, Inc., 1974
12-29

ARRRGH!
SCRIBBLE
SCRIBBLE

YOUR HOROSCOPE
BY CLAIR VOYANT
12-30

CLAIR VOYANT'S PREDICTIONS FOR THE COMING YEAR!
BATIUK

A HOLLYWOOD STAR WILL GET A DIVORCE, THE PRESIDENT WILL HOLD A NEWS CONFERENCE, AND IT WILL RAIN A LOT IN OREGON!

5 4 3 2 1

HAPPY NEW YEAR!
BATIUK

SOMEHOW, 1975 SEEMS AN AWFUL LOT LIKE 1974··· AND 1973 ··· 1972 ··· 1971 ···